[spooks]

First published in Great Britain in 2006
by HEADLINE BOOK PUBLISHING

1

Cataloguing in Publication Data is
available from the British Library

Trade paperback 0 7553 3396 9 (ISBN-10)
Trade paperback 978 0 7553 3396 7 (ISBN-13)

Designed by Ben Cracknell Studios
Printed and bound in Great Britain by Clays Ltd, St Ives plc

HEADLINE BOOK PUBLISHING
A division of Hodder Headline
338 Euston Road
London NW1 3BH

www.headline.co.uk
www.hodderheadline.com

[spooks]

THE PERSONNEL FILES

MEMORANDUM

To: ▮▮▮▮▮▮▮▮▮▮▮▮▮

From: ▮▮▮▮▮▮▮▮▮▮▮

Date: ▮▮▮▮▮▮▮▮

Subject: Spooks: The Personnel Files
Introduction

There are forces at work in this country of which you have no knowledge.

You probably think you live in a free society. You can walk down the street at will. But do you know how many CCTV cameras are tracking your position as you do so? Or satellites, for that matter? You can exercise your right to free speech. But if your conversation includes words such as "Osama" or "CIA", someone will be listening. Send those words by email and someone will be reading them.

You could get away from it all and go abroad, but they will know where you've been and who you've spoken to. Borrow suspicious books from the local library and they will hear about it. Develop a taste for compromising Google searches and you'll be sharing your internet history with them. Most of the time you won't even know this is happening to you.

This is a book about the people who operate in the shadows. These are the files on those people – the full biographical and operational details of the key players in MI5's Counter Terrorism Department, Section D.

On the one hand they are just like us. They have school reports and end-of-year assessments. Their university tutors wrote glowing references. They, themselves, filled out application forms detailing their most team-oriented, pro-active endeavour.

But then they are also much more interesting than us. Adam Carter endured months of torture in the Yemen. Here we learn how he came to terms with that. Harry Pearce underwent an early experience in Northern Ireland which shaped his career afterwards. Here are the transcripts of his debrief. We also learn what happened to Tom Quinn and Zoe Reynolds after they left MI5.

And there is much more besides.

But this is also a book about you. The security services have never been more vital, nor more feared by the general public. Post 9/11 and 7/7 you want to be protected. But post Iraq you also want to be told the truth.

To date, you've been fed a truth.

You deserve the *whole* truth.

[spooks]

THE PERSONNEL FILES

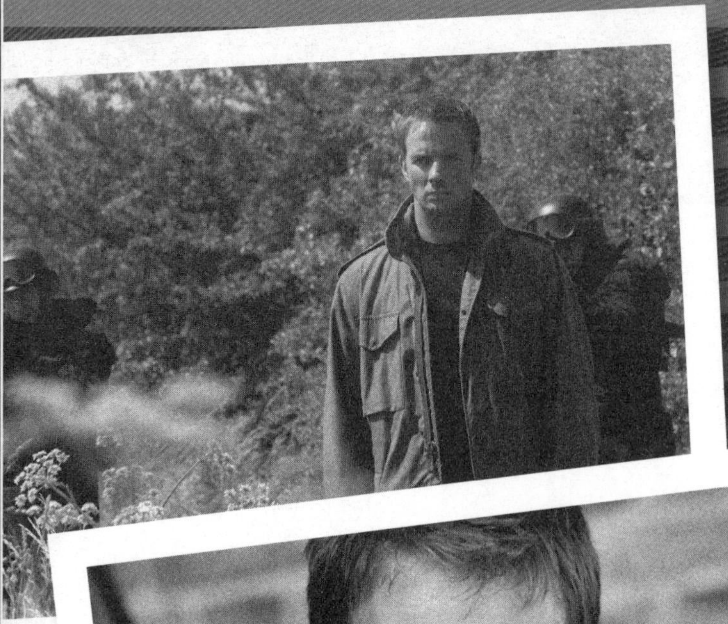

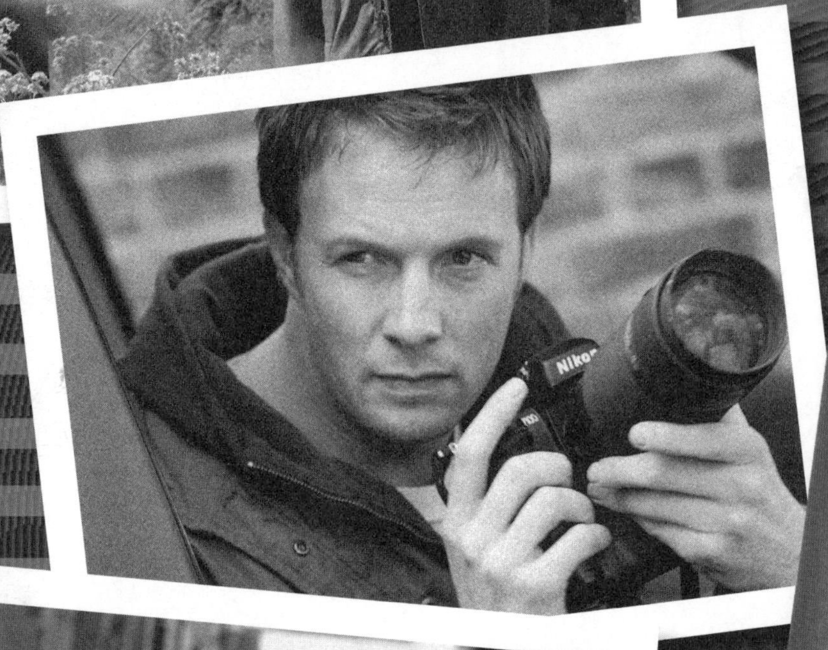

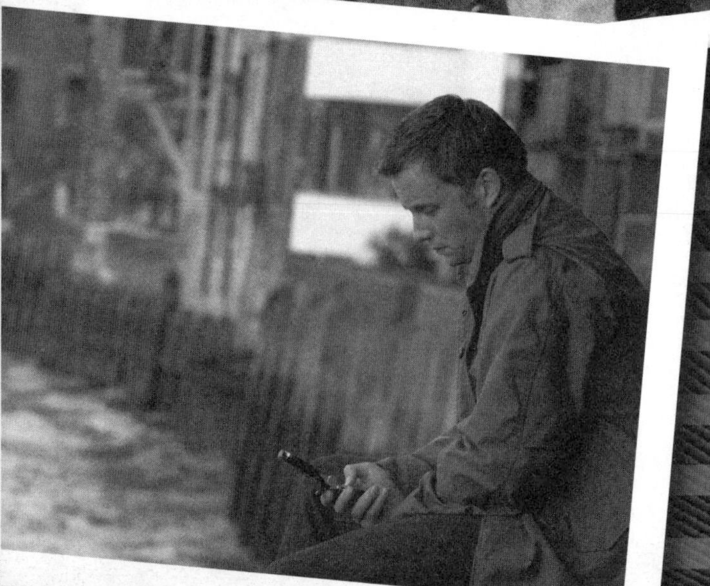

[Adam Carter]

Private and Confidential

Name: Adam Carter
Position: Senior Intelligence Officer
D.O.B: 31.10.1972
Hair: Brown
Eyes: Blue
Height: 6'2
Marital status: widower
Dependants: Wesley; D.O.B: 09.01.1998
Blood type: B, RL positive

Adam Carter came to MI5 on short-term loan during a successful eight-year tenure at MI6. He was subsequently made a full-time employee, leading Section D in operational duties following the retirement of Tom Quinn.

Carter's laid-back, easy-going charm belies a ruthless dedication to the service's aims.

Carter lost his wife – Fiona, who was also an MI5 officer – on operation in 2005.

Major operations include:

- Defused bomb in Pegasus, Royal Protection Bunker, St. James's
- Infiltration and neutralisation of racist political party, The British Way
- Neutralisation of Shining Dawn's London bombing campaign
- Successful interrogation of mercenary arms trafficker
- Investigation of kidnap of son of Sir Riff and Lady Monro
- Framing of pro-Israeli media mogul David Swift
- Framing of Syrian Intelligence officer Farook Sukkarieh

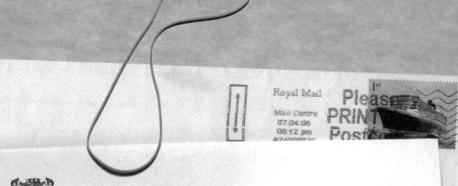

UNIVERSITY OF CAMBRIDGE

Trinity Hall
University of Cambridge
CB2 1TJ

Simon Jacques Esq.

30th October 1994

Dear Simon,

I hope you're well and the crop I sent over to you last year are doing all right.

This year has been a rather barren one for potential recruits. There is, however, one outstanding candidate who I think more than justifies the old adage of quality over quantity.

His name is Adam Carter and I have been his Arabic tutor here for the past three years. He can be rather laid-back at times but he's one of those people for whom things always work out. He is bright, articulate and very well travelled. He is also a natural leader among his peers and he has earned the respect and affection of many in college.

He is in his final year now and has few plans for what to do with his life. We shouldn't let this one die in the City. Shall I have a quiet word with him?

Yours aye,

Dr Nick Lampen
Lecturer in Arabic
University of Cambridge

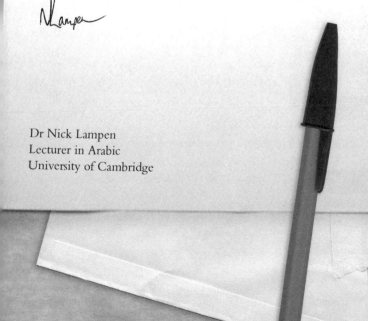

UNIVERSITY OF CAMBRIDGE

Trinity Hall
University of Cambridge
CB2 1TJ

Simon Jacques Esq.

21st November 1994

Dear Simon,

Thank you for your letter of 10th November.

As suggested, I spoke to Adam Carter in a roundabout way about a fast-track career involving foreign affairs. He immediately worked out what I was talking about and was very interested by the prospect.

Thank you also for sending over an application form. It is good to see you giving the appearance, at least, of doing things by the book these days. I'll make sure he fills it in.

Let me know when you're next up here.

Yours aye,

Dr Nick Lampen
Lecturer in Arabic
University of Cambridge

MI6 Application Form

Surname

Carter

Forenames

Adam Henry

Date of birth

31.10.1972

Place of birth

Wimbledon, London

Nationality at birth

British

Permanent Address

Trinity Hall,
Cambridge University,
CB2 1TJ

Current occupation

Student

Date of availability for employment

June -
from graduation

Do you hold a full, clean driving licence?

Yes, but 9 points for speeding

Medical

Do you have any conditions – either physical or psychological – which might affect your employment?

Broken leg - sustained during a
rugby match - which required setting
under general anaesthetic in 1988.
No subsequent problems

Father's name, address and occupation

David Carter, 42 West Kensington
Road, London SW10

Retired diplomat

Mother's name, maiden name, address and occupation

Lucy Carter (nee Johnson), 42 West
Kensington Road, London SW10

Architect

Brothers / Sisters (with names and D.O.B.)

Jack - 12.9.1971

Olivia - 24.5.1975

Secondary Schools / Colleges
Dates : Names : Town

1985-1990 : St. Paul's School :
London

GCSEs or equivalents

3 A* (French, German, English
language), 5As (History, Geography,
Maths, English literature, Biology),
2Bs (Chemistry, Physics)

A levels and AS levels or equivalents

French - A

German - A

English language - B

MAP|06.fa|vii.1

Gap Year

How did you spend any break during your education?

Spent seven months teaching English in a Palestinian school in the West Bank

University or Further Education

Cambridge University - 1991-1995

B.A. (Hons) in Arabic - pending (2:1 - predicted)

Awards

Please give details of any other awards (e.g. music)

Grade 3 guitar

EMPLOYMENT

Dates	Employer	Position
Summer 1994	MRKG	Intern

Have you served in HM Forces (including Reserves)?

Officer Cadet in Cambridge University Officers Training Corps, 1991-1995

Do you have applications pending for other jobs?

This is the one job I want. If I don't get it, I plan to travel and re-apply next year.

PERSONAL QUALITIES AND SKILLS

SUMMARY

Provide a pen-portrait of your life to date

My father was in the Foreign Office so I spent much of my early life either abroad or in English boarding schools. My childhood was idyllic but it was short-lived. I felt as if I had to grow up faster than I would have liked.

I was always happy at school as well as quite hard-working. I'm outgoing and laid-back, and I don't like to plan ahead too much.

I studied Arabic at Cambridge University - mainly so I could use it to travel - and I've spent most of my holidays travelling. I am rarely happier than with a rucksack on my back and meeting new people. However, there is nothing I love more than returning home again at the end.

MAP|06.fa|vii.2

MOTIVATION

Why do you think you would be suited to a public service career?

- My family upbringing instilled a love of public service in me
- I am politically highly aware
- I am well travelled
- I quickly adapt to new environments
- I speak Arabic, as well as French

POLITICAL CURIOSITY

Give three political topics (historical or current) which interest you

- Israel vs. Palestine conflict – time spent teaching there
- Islamic fundamentalism in Egypt – spent 3rd year of university course in Cairo
- Balkans – father stationed in Sarajevo

ADAPTABILITY

Give an example of a time when you had to adapt to unexpected circumstances

I spent seven months after school teaching in the West Bank. I had a bit of time in the holidays to travel and decided to go up to Syria. Unfortunately, I travelled via Jerusalem and so my passport was stamped with an Israeli entry and exit visa.

When the lady in the Syrian embassy in Amman told me that this would prevent me from entering Syria I ignored her. A group of Australians were heading north and offered me a ride to Damascus if I hid in the back of their truck.

Initially, the plan worked fine. I spent two weeks travelling around Syria, but I faced problems getting back into Jordan again. The Australians were heading up into Lebanon but I had to get back to catch a flight from Amman.

In the end, I had no choice but to brazen it out at the border. The confrontation started well, but the guards on the Syrian side started to doubt my story. Then I recognised someone on the Jordanian side who I'd met during my time in Amman. He gave me the nod; I moved round to an unguarded side of the fence; and he let me through unmolested.

A bit of extra tipping persuaded him to leave my passport alone as well.

MAP|06.fa|vii.3

RESPONSIBILITY

What positions of responsibility have you held – at school, university or otherwise?

```
School - Head boy; captain of rugby
University - Captain of rugby
Officer Cadet in Cambridge University Officers Training Corps,
1991-1995
```

FOREIGN LANGUAGES

Please indicate level of competence

```
Arabic - fluent, verging on bi-lingual
French - fluent
German - functional
```

OTHER INTERESTS

```
Rugby - training twice per week; weekends
Socialising
```

TRAVEL

Give details of all foreign travel in the last 10 years, including reason for travel

```
Lived in Sarajevo and Paris (through father's work), and
Egypt (year abroad)
Visited for interest, mainly backpacking - Jordan, Israel,
Syria, UAE, Morocco, Algeria, Spain, France, Peru, Ecuador,
Bolivia, Mexico, India
```

EQUAL OPPORTUNITIES

This information is not used as part of our selection procedures

Gender	Ethnic origin	Disabilities
(Male) Female	White British	None

REFEREES

Please give details of three referees. One of these should be a contemporary who knows you well

```
1. Dr Nick Lampen, Lecturer in Arabic, Cambridge University
2. Michael Wynne, Director of Audit, MRKG
3. Sam Edes, childhood friend
```

SIGNATURE

Adam Carter

DATE

2nd February 1995

MAP|06.fa|vii.4

[APPLICATION FORM]

page 17

NSEA, SA6 7JL

ROYAL MAIL
POSTAGE PAID GB

MRKG

REFERENCE: Adam Carter

To Whom It May Concern:

Adam came to us last summer as an intern in the audit department of MRKG – mainly, I think, because he wanted to spend the summer in London with his friends. He was paid sufficiently well to leave on a backpacking holiday as soon as his eight weeks were finished. I also believe there was an element of parental pressure for him to start earning his way in life.

Adam was not a good accountant – his maths, in particular, was dreadful – but he is clearly very bright on all other levels. He was a very popular member of his team and displayed a natural leadership ability which I have rarely encountered at such a young age.

We have stayed in touch since his internship, and he has proved a loyal and trustworthy confidant. He was a welcome breath of fresh air here.

What is no great loss to the world of finance will be a great gain to foreign affairs. I strongly recommend him to you.

M Wynne

Michael Wynne
Director of Audit, MRKG

RIDLEY PREPARATORY SCHOOL

FROM THE HEADMASTER OF RIDLEY PREPARATORY SCHOOL
COLONEL T.L. REEVE M.A. T.A.
RIDLEY PREP SCHOOL
UPPER BICKMINSTER
NR. HUNGERFORD
BERKS

MR AND MRS DAVID CARTER
42 WEST KENSINGTON ROAD
LONDON SW10

3RD JUNE 1982

Dear Mr and Mrs Carter,

Adam ran away from school this week for the third time this year. Ridley is all for nurturing independent, free-thinking individuals within the supportive environment of a modern boarding school. We would prefer it, however, if this character development took place within school boundaries, especially when it concerns our nine-year-old charges.

I know Adam has been known to slip unnoticed out of French classes before. This time, however, his evasion took place on an altogether grander scale.

Mr Harrison tells me that Adam disappeared during a cricket match he was umpiring last Saturday. A fielder in a neighbouring game says he saw Adam zigzagging into some nearby woods. When Adam did not return, we investigated the woods and found his cricket whites buried beneath a tree. We deduced that he had changed his clothes and run towards Hungerford train station.

Mr Smee, the stationmaster, told me later that Adam bought a return ticket to Bedwyn in cash at the ticket office. Adam also bought a postcard in the station, wrote a message to this effect and sent it to Harry Finlay – one of his good friends at Ridley. The postcard arrived this morning.

It then transpires, however, that Adam bought a second ticket – from the ticket machine this time – to go to London. Fortunately, the Maths master Mr Monro was on his half-day and happened to alight from the same train at Paddington. He recognised Adam and frog-marched him back to school.

I would very much like to speak to you about this duplicitous behaviour. We at Ridley are very happy to act *in loco parentis*. That is, after all, why you sent Adam here. However, I do not believe this remit extends to tracking a pre-pubescent boy across three separate counties when he is meant to be keeping wicket for the Under XI against Crossfields.

Yours sincerely,

TL Reeve

Thomas L. Reeve

SECURITY CLEARANCE & BACKGROUND CHECKS

Adam Carter

I was tasked with carrying out routine background checks into Adam Carter's family and friends, as well as standard fact-checking of his application details.

On this latter point, I found only one discrepancy — Adam actually received a C in Chemistry GCSE, not a B as stated. However, I think we can put this down to administrative oversight, not deliberate falsification.

Adam's father, David, is a career diplomat who has served with distinction in Bosnia, in particular. He was awarded the MBE in the Queen's Birthday honours last year. Despite a youthful flirtation with the righter-wing of the Conservative party at university, his political views are now fairly mainstream.

Adam's mother, Lucy, is the daughter of a diplomat and met David on his first posting in Washington. They married after a brief courtship. There are widespread rumours of ongoing affairs — confirmed by a number of off the record conversations. Otherwise theirs seems a solid marriage. Lucy trained as an architect but now barely practises, opting instead for the supportive role of diplomatic wife.

There is nothing in either their, or their extended families', background to cause alarm.

Adam has an elder brother, Jack, whom he looks up to. Jack works in the city and has a minor cocaine habit, but no other incriminating habits, interests or contacts. Adam is fiercely protective of their younger sister, Olivia, who followed him to Cambridge University. An ex-boyfriend of hers whom Adam felt had treated her badly was roughed up a bit. However, no charges were pressed.

I spoke to Adam's childhood friends — Sam Edes, in particular, whom he has known since the age of three — and a picture emerged of a happy, confident young man. He does, however, share many of the vices of his gender and generation. At Cambridge, he enjoyed something of a playboy party reputation. The police once raided rooms on the same corridor as his after repeated complaints of all-night noise. Adam, however, had a solid alibi at the time, so I think we can overlook this.

There is no reason to suspect any actions in his past that might lead to blackmail opportunities. His political views are practical rather than ideological — if anything, perhaps too much so.

I have no hesitation passing his security clearance.

Amanda Hogan, HR Security
4th April 1995

TRAINING ASSESSMENT
Adam Carter, 3rd June 1995

SCORES

Practical		Other core competencies	
Surveillance	3.8	Calm under pressure	4.9
Counter-surveillance	4.8	Leadership	4.7
Physical endurance	4.6	Team work	3.5
Shooting	1.3	Communication	4.5
Driving	4.3	General attitude	3.4
Technical	2.0	Average	4.2
Average	3.47		

Intellectual		Overall average	3.81
Linguistic	4.2	On a sliding scale of 1 to 5 where	
Decision-making	4.9	1 is poor, 5 is outstanding and 2.5 is	
Research	2.5	average for a new recruit	
Average	3.87		

Adam Carter performed well above average in the training exercises, turning in outstanding performances in many of the core competencies. In particular, he displayed excellent leadership qualities as well as a promising natural talent in counter-surveillance skills.

Areas to improve upon include his shooting which is currently well below average. His attitude, although generally good, is liable to flippancy and insubordination at times.

However, I have no hesitation in recommending him as a field officer – particularly in the Middle East where he has assimilated himself excellently.

Geoff Bowles
Head of recruit training, MI6

Counter-interrogation training for new recruits

Presentation by Adam Carter

Speaking notes

Introduction by AN Other Officer

There used to be an old joke about military recruitment: "Join the army, go to interesting places, meet interesting people, and then shoot them."

Being a spy can, of course, be very similar. One crucial difference is that captured soldiers tend to be treated quite well. Sure, they might be slapped around a bit and paraded on Al Jazeera, but the rules of combat under the Geneva Convention normally apply.

It's altogether different when an intelligence officer is captured. How often have you seen terrorists claim that the 80-year-old aid worker they're holding is a spy? And how often do you see genuine spies paraded in front of the cameras? Answer: never.

The truth is that if you're captured by hostile groups, you're on your own. There will be no international petitions. No tearful vigils outside Downing Street. No mass marches. The British government will know about it, of course. And they'll make every effort behind closed doors to secure your release. But it will still be one of the loneliest and most terrifying things you'll encounter in your career.

To talk to you today is a senior field officer from Section D – Adam Carter – a man who knows more than most about counter-interrogation procedures.

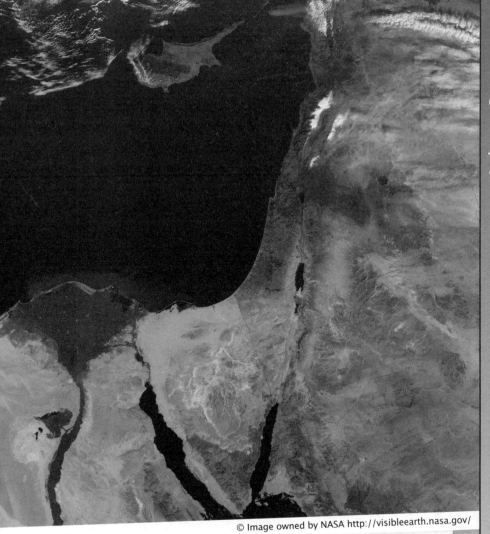

© Image owned by NASA http://visibleearth.nasa.gov/

AC's introduction

1   Although I can't promise you a particularly enjoyable time in the classroom today, I can promise you it's worth it. About ten years ago I sat where you are, listening to someone like me. The advice I heard that day saved my life five years ago when I was captured, interrogated and tortured in the Yemen.

2   It was obviously the lowest time in my life. But it also changed me profoundly and for the good.

3   I want to take you through this in stages. We'll be looking at capture, coping with pain, answering questions, facing death, escape and the aftermath.

Capture

1   The eleventh commandment of undercover espionage is: Don't get caught. You'll develop good instincts in the field; use them. If you suspect a mole, investigate quickly. If you think an operation is about to go wrong, pull the plug. Despite what you might think, there is no place for false bravado and have-a-go heroes in MI5. We spend a lot of money training you. You're more use to us free than captured.

2   If your cover is suddenly blown, the most important advice is: Do not act like a spy. It might seem obvious, but the shock of a suspected discovery has turned some officers into wrecks before questioning has even started. You have to be prepared, and you have to think like your cover story. What would your agency worker, journalist etc. – whatever your alias is – feel like if he was suddenly accused of being a spy? You'd be livid, wouldn't you? Throw the toys out of the pram. Demand to see a lawyer, and so on. At the very least, you'll confuse the hell out of them.

3   The early stages of capture also provide the best time to escape. There will be no established routine at this point. Your captors probably won't know exactly what they're dealing with. They might be as scared of you as you are of them. They might have superiors to answer to.

4   You'll also be moved around a lot in these early stages. Try and get a sense of your bearings – you'll need to know for any later escape attempt. If you're hooded, you can still discern a surprising amount about traffic volume and so on. Use your other senses. Can you smell a market place? Or a farm? Or a sewer? You might be able to hear the sounds of church bells or a Muezzin or schoolchildren at play. All these details need to be stored for later.

5   One technique is to bundle you into the boot of a car, which terrorists copy from scenes they've seen on television. In reality, though, it's not actually that effective. Many old cars have faulty boot latches which can easily be sprung open from the inside. Often they come undone of their own accord on bumps.

6   Being hidden in a boot also gives you time to prepare out of sight. I know of one operative who worked out there was an interlinking compartment between the boot and the back seats, designed originally, I think, to accommodate a set of golf clubs. When the car stopped and his captors got out to open the boot, he simply scrambled from the boot to the seats and out of the unguarded door to freedom.

7   I once put my time in a car boot to good effect by staging my own death. As I was unbound, I deliberately cut myself on the metal rim of the spare tyre and smeared the blood down the side of my mouth. I had a boiled sweet in my pocket which a child had given me in the market place. When my captors opened the boot, I had managed to work up enough saliva to make it look as if I'd had a fit and died. I was able to make my escape while they discussed what to do with my "corpse".

8   But let's assume for the moment that the worst has happened. People you were infiltrating have decided they want to know a little more about you, and they're prepared to hurt you to achieve their goals. How do you react to this?

Coping with pain

1   It has been said that the human mind is conditioned not to remember pain. This is meant to explain why women will give birth to more than one child. The agony might be almost unbearable at the time. A year later and they will have forgotten about it.

2   Think about an episode from your own lives. Can you conjure up real, intensive, excruciating pain? The time you broke your arm, perhaps? Or when you had a wisdom tooth taken out? Probably not, I guess is the answer.

3   And it's the same with torture. I don't want to alarm you, but when I close my eyes I can see electrodes, and baths filled with boiling water. I can recall what they did. I can recall how they did it. And I can certainly recall the fear I lived under. But the pain itself? The searing strips of agony? That I can't remember accurately. It's probably a good thing.

4   Fantastic, I can see you all thinking. But I say this to reassure you that there are worse things than physical pain. Scars heal. Emotional scars – in my experience at least – run much deeper.

5   So, how, practically, can you train to cope with intense physical pain? Well, you might have heard doctors say things to you like, "Pain is all in the mind." They're wrong, of course. Try telling that to them when they've been beaten for a week solid. But they're also right. Pain is merely the body's way of telling the brain that something is wrong. You can teach yourself to ignore those signals.

6   One trick which I used is a form of reverse psychology. Train yourself to look forward to the pain. Take it as a welcome sign that you're still alive.

7   Another is to set yourself challenges. Tell yourself that you'll hold on a little longer this time before you pass out. The key is not to think about what they're doing to you.

Disassociate yourself from it in any way you can. Count to 1,000 in another language. One colleague counted out loud. They thought he'd gone mad and left him alone for a bit.

8   The tricks used by hostages to combat boredom can also be used by a torture victim. Terry Waite used to set himself long mathematical puzzles. Or start writing your autobiography in your head, focusing on all the tiniest details of your life story – the people you've met, the places you've been. You can then view the pain merely as unwelcome interruptions to this routine. Carry on multiplying and dividing even as you're screaming.

9   These are the mental ways of coping with torture. There are, of course, physical considerations as well. Try and exercise as much as you can – even if it's only a few sit-ups every day. It will keep your spirits up, too. Eat when you can, even if it makes you sick. You'll need any strength you can get. Demand water regularly. Drink whenever you're offered.

10 As for the physical processes of torture, remember that the body is incredibly durable. Skin can be burned. Bones can be broken. But they're there to protect what really matters – your internal organs. Scars heal. Nails aren't that important. It might not sound very uplifting, but think of how many PoWs have survived unimaginable conditions in various wars. The average binge-drinker in London is probably damaging his body as much as a torture victim.

11 Ultimately, you have to remember that for most torturers, inflicting pain is a means rather than an end. Of course, there is the raw, sadistic pleasure that appeals to the nastier specimens. But you're no use to them whatsoever if you're dead.

Answering questions – talking without saying anything

1   The first step to effective counter-interrogation is to work out how much the other side knows. Why exactly have you suddenly come under suspicion? Was it a mole within the organisation? Did you slip up at some point in your cover story? Or were you caught red-handed? How compromised are you exactly?

2   All these factors will determine your approach. If you know – or even suspect – they have nothing on you, you have to give nothing in return. Learn to recognise their fishing questions and don't jump to the bait. Stick to what they know already. Trust your cover story. The guys in research are generally excellent at foreseeing every eventuality. Dealing with pain is easier if you know they have no means of getting at what they want. Act as if you have nothing to hide for long enough and they'll start to believe you.

3   But even if your captors know for certain that you are an intelligence officer, the game still isn't up. One tactic is to talk freely and fluently without really saying anything. Study politicians giving interviews for a good example of how to do this. You can't completely ignore the question, but you don't have to answer its central crux. Choose the most random element. Lead your questioners down cul-de-sacs and twisting, narrow alleyways which come to dead-ends. Frustrate them. Tantalise them. And give them nothing.

4   You can also insert deliberate inconsistencies into your story. Play your interrogators off against each other. One colleague tried being friendly to the "nasty cop" and venomous to the "good cop". Confuse them and maintain your own sanity.

5   The final thing to remember is that people say things under duress which aren't true. This is why the British government – in theory, at least – doesn't make use of "evidence" obtained under torture. Some people will say or sign anything to make the pain go away.

Forced confessions are often just that – forced. And entirely fictitious. You can use this to your advantage if you yourself are the subject of vicious questioning. If you unwittingly blurt out the truth, deny it strenuously later. Tell them you were scared into admitting to anything. I know one MI5 officer who told his captors he was a Walter Mitty figure who had always longed to be a spy, whereas he was, in fact, just a slightly lonely journalist. They eventually believed and released him.

6 And remember this: you can confuse your captors as much as you like, but you have to recall exactly what you said, when, and to whom. Like all good liars, you need a mind like a filing cabinet in this job.

Breaking point

1 So far, I've focused on the positives.

2 Ultimately, though, every human being has a breaking point. The only difference with us is that we're trained to cope with interrogation for longer before breaking. When you do break, you'll find that you break in stages, giving snippets of information at a time. The information you give has to be low-grade intelligence that is no longer relevant. As soon as you're captured, your colleagues will immediately change plans to invalidate any information you hold.

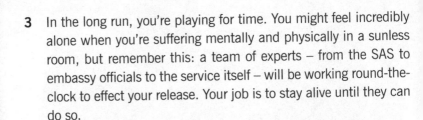

3   In the long run, you're playing for time. You might feel incredibly alone when you're suffering mentally and physically in a sunless room, but remember this: a team of experts – from the SAS to embassy officials to the service itself – will be working round-the-clock to effect your release. Your job is to stay alive until they can do so.

4   To do this, you have to keep your captors interested. Tell them too much and they'll have no more use for you (except as a potential bargaining chip). Remain too taciturn and they might despair of ever getting something out of you. Drip-feed them just enough information to keep them coming back for more. Every minute you stay alive makes your escape or rescue more likely.

Escape

1   As I mentioned earlier, any good intelligence officer will have been thinking about their escape routes from the very first moment they're captured. This process is ongoing. At the very least, it will give you something to keep your spirits up and your mind occupied.

2   No building – however secure – is entirely impregnable. Your interrogators will have to come and go. Food has to be brought from outside. If there's a way in, there's a way out. Get to know your cell intimately – every loose brick and chink of light needs to be explored. Acquaint yourself with the guards' routine. There will be a point in every day or night when they are at their most vulnerable. Maybe they're always sleepy after lunch. Or undermanned first thing in the morning.

3   In any team of captors there will be a weak link. Find it – the person with the conscience, the forced conscript, the cleaner – and exploit it to your advantage. Tell them about fictitious family and friends. See if you have a common interest in football or music. You have to make them see you as a human being.

Then they can be worked on. One MI5 officer implemented the Stockholm Syndrome in reverse: his captor fell in love with him and released him.

4   There is a wealth of literature on great escape stories. Read it, all of it. What has worked in the past can often work again (although you're unlikely to find yourself playing in an eleven-a-side football match with Pelé while Germans guards look on haplessly).

Rescue

1   Rescue is the ultimate fantasy of every hostage. I remember waking up one morning in the Yemen with a massive smile on my face as I'd been dreaming about my cell being stormed by SAS troops. That smile soon turned sour when I realised it was only a dream.

2   You have to retain a sense of perspective, therefore. Longing for release can drive a man insane.

3   That said, there are certain things you can do to make your rescue more likely. Much of this is enshrined within your standard code of practice in the field. Back-up teams will know your routine. Failure to file a report at a standard time should put out an instant alert.

4   But your role isn't over once you're captured. One officer was thrown to the ground during capture and managed to write his captors' car number plate into the dust with his finger. Another succeeded in rigging up an impromptu radio set using the electricity from his torturer's discarded electrodes.

5   In general, though, you'll have to sit tight during any rescue attempt. The SAS is known to use certain codes to indicate that an operation is imminent. This can sometimes be signalled by a staged argument within earshot of your cell.

6   Once the raid itself actually starts, the best thing you can do is stay down and stay out of the way. And always, always thank your rescuers afterwards.

The aftermath

1   Obviously, the first thing you'll feel after release will be an overwhelming sense of relief. This euphoria can last several days as you are reunited with close family and colleagues.

2   In the longer-term, however, you might find yourselves facing more worrying emotions. You'll probably feel angry – angry with others for letting you down; angry with yourself for letting others down. You might feel bitter and resentful. You might question your continuing commitment to the job. You'll almost certainly feel as if no one understands.

3   Maybe you'll want to talk about this; maybe you won't. Everyone reacts differently. The mental healing process can take longer than the physical, but it can also be more complete. There is some truth in the old cliché: "What doesn't kill you makes you stronger."

Postscript – facing up to death

1 I deliberately didn't mention death earlier as I wanted to focus on the cycle of capture to release that is typical of most intelligence officers held hostage. We save a lot more than we lose.

2 It is inevitable though that a period of incarceration, interrogation and torture will raise issues of your own mortality. And it might sound perverse, but the worst thing you can do in this time is fear death. You can't show it too much respect. This is the one thing your captors have over you. Conquer that fear and you've conquered them. You'll also earn their respect – which is sometimes even more useful.

3 Some prisoners try to turn to religion to help them face their tormentors. Research has shown that this is fine for those who already have, or had, a fledgling religious faith. It is less effective, however, for those who attempt to discover religion under these circumstances. It is less likely to provide solace than anger at God's inability to rescue you. Brutally, you're better off focusing on yourself.

4 Sadly, though, there will be some unique hostage circumstances when death will be an inevitable consequence of capture. The kind of fanatical ideologues we're seeing more of these days like to make bold statements. And, tragically, this might involve your execution.

5 What use is advice in this kind of situation, you might ask. But I know colleagues who have died courageously – as well as cowards – and I have seen the value of a good death. Maintain your defiance. Remember why you joined MI5 – to protect the lives of people you care about. Die well, and you're the winner, not your captors.

Counter-surveillance training for new recruits

Presentation by Adam Carter

Speaking notes

Introduction by AN Other Officer

Speaking to you today we have one of our best field officers from Section D. Adam Carter made his name perfecting Category A counter-surveillance techniques in the Middle East.

Today, we'll be looking at how to evade prying eyes. Later this week, Danny Hunter will be telling you how to pry yourself. Surveillance and counter-surveillance: two very different things. Over to you, Adam.

AC's introduction

Thank you. As you will have realised by now on your training, there are many different ways of finding stuff out about a person. Our "bin men" go through rubbish bags in the hope of finding clues to someone's lifestyle – bank statements, drinking habits, dietary requirements, even sexual preferences. Or we can listen into someone's life – their phone calls, their "private" conversations, their emails. We call this SIGINT (or signal intelligence).

Ideally, though, you get close to your subject, befriend them, spend time with them, betray them. We call this HUMINT (or human intelligence). It allows you to add your own subjective analysis – your gut instincts – to more concrete data obtained through other means.

But one of the best ways to discover the basic details about someone's life is simply to follow them without interrupting their daily routine. Where do they go? How do they get there? Who do they talk to?

If we're doing this to other people, other people will be doing this to us. This is where counter-surveillance comes in.

Counter-surveillance

Counter-surveillance is much simpler than you think. Its origins are in everyday life. When you were teenagers, did you ever make up a sleeping dummy in your bed so that your parents didn't realise you'd gone clubbing? Or give out a false mobile phone number in a club to someone you didn't fancy? That's counter-surveillance. It's common sense coupled with a devious imagination.

Here we'll go through some of the basic scenarios and techniques. Later you'll get a chance to put these into practice.

How to detect and avoid surveillance on foot

1   Bank robbers in films always have their getaway vehicles, but they'd probably be better off evading capture on foot. Cars have traceable licence plates, model types and colourings. Almost every mile of the public highway is covered by CCTV. And almost 100 per cent of urban areas. However fast you drive, your options are always limited, especially when you live on an island. On foot, however, you can double-back, change clothing, stop altogether. It's about keeping as many options open as possible.

2   But how can you tell if you're being followed? If you're in your normal environment – for example, travelling from home to the office – it's important to clock other people's routines, as well as varying your own. You *will* recognise the same man at the same bus stop; the same lady who goes to the post office at the same time as you; the man on the tube who's always on the same page of his newspaper as it comes to your stop.

3   It's important, then, not to get paranoid. Your task is to recognise the unusual. Trust your instincts. If something seems commonplace, it probably is. If it's out of place, then try and work out how and why. Don't ignore the hairs on the back of your neck. Your sixth sense is every bit as good as your other five.

4   The first step is to establish for sure – in as far as anything is concrete in our line of work – whether you are, in fact, under surveillance. Break your pattern in some way: stop to tie a shoelace; speed up; slow down; double-back on yourself; take your mobile out and make a call; walk into a shop; sit down on a bench and read a book; go down one escalator and up another.

5   You're looking for glitches in the matrix – someone reading an unexpected type of book in an unexpected area, clothes that don't fit the surroundings, and so on. Eye contact is a particularly good

rule of thumb. Even in an anonymous city the size of London, the average person will make eye contact with more than fifty strangers every day. A good tail will always avoid it for fear of compromising their operation. A lowered, surreptitious glance is a more accurate indication of guilt than a direct stare.

6   You can also look for the type of person who you suspect is tailing you. They're unlikely to be very young or very old. They're unlikely to be walking around in large groups, and they're unlikely to have any obvious distinguishing features. The chances are they are conservatively dressed and of average height. It won't be the girl in the red coat or the boy with a hoodie up. They have to blend in.

7   Once you've established that you're being tailed, your next course of action will be to establish how many people are tailing you. Is this an individual or a team? A team will be much harder to shake.

8   You also have to establish why you're under surveillance. If you're the subject of a low-level operation associated with routine intelligence gathering, it is important to give away as little as possible. Don't lead your tail near anywhere with compromising personal history. Don't meet anyone that could be turned against you. Bore the hell out of your pursuers. Meander around drab bookshops and old art galleries. Tire them out with long walks through the city. Your own tedium will be relieved by the knowledge of how much you're tormenting them. Boring a surveillance team is effective because they'll start to miss details.

Counter-s

9   Of course, there will be other occasions when losing a tail is vital for the successful completion of an ongoing operation. Here, avoidance proceeds logically from detection. Slow down and speed up again, but make it more pronounced this time. Dart suddenly into alleyways. Lose yourself in crowds. Large department stores are particularly effective places to shake off a tail. Several lifts can be called at one time. You can stop halfway to your destination and take the stairs in the opposite direction. You can hold up your pursuer by pressing all the buttons as you exit the lift.

10 Public transport can also be used to great effect. Get in a bus at the driver's end and leave immediately by the other door just as your tail settles down. The same can be done on tube trains. At Charing Cross station, for example, the Northern line platform is too short for the last set of doors to open. Many field officers have used this to evade a slow-witted pursuer.

Working in a counter-surveillance team

1   Finding yourself under surveillance can be an unsettling and unexpected sensation. But there are occasions – especially on large operations involving rival intelligence agencies – when this kind of monitoring is expected long in advance. This can also occur if you suspect your information flow to be subject to leaks. An officer might leave for a rendezvous three hours before the appointed time to give him time to shake off numerous tails. At this point surveillance becomes a team game, and so must counter-surveillance.

2   Traditionally in a counter-surveillance team there is one principal officer and a range of support players – often MI5 personnel posing as members of the public. For example, a "newspaper vendor" might hand a paper to the officer with a particular crossword clue filled in – based on a pre-arranged code. A "café owner" might choose a particular special for the menu board on the pavement.

A "beggar" might use a particular turn of phrase in his request. This allows the officer to maintain real-time communication with base without the awkwardness of wires and ear-pieces. It also has the advantage of being almost completely untraceable.

3   This kind of team work also involves distracting the tails to give the lead officer a clear run. Tactics here are as wide as your imaginations are devious. Sometimes direct confrontation works well. You can bump into a tail and try to start a fight. You can pose as a charity salesman and hold them up. It's worth remembering that the last thing a tail wants is attention drawn to them. One of my successful stalling attempts involved feigning drunkenness and telling everyone on Waterloo Bridge that the man in front of them had been sleeping with my wife. By the time he'd managed to brush me off a small crowd had formed to listen to me, blocking his path and tut-tutting at his moral laxity. Our lead officer got away easily.

4   A warning note to finish the section: you have to be absolutely sure you have the right person. A team I was leading once tried its diversionary tactics on a suspicious-looking young man following one of our officers. It turned out our man had dropped a five-pound note and the guy was altruistically trying to return it to him. You can expect the unexpected as much as you like, but you'll never be prepared for everything that happens in this job.

How to detect and avoid surveillance in a car

1   Cars have distinct markings and are therefore easier to trail than people. It might seem an obvious point, but choose your vehicle very carefully. A soberly-dressed Caucasian man of five feet eleven with brown hair can vanish easily in a busy western crowd. You'll find this harder on a quiet road if you're driving a bright red Ferrari. Normally we use pool cars for work, but on one occasion recently we were so overstretched that we had to take my colleague's instead. It was an ostentatious Nissan Skyline and we stood out like a sore thumb.

2   Ultimately, putting clear road between you and your pursuer is all about your driving skills. This is therefore something that is explored in greater detail in the practical side of your training.

3   Before you do so, though, it's worth thinking a little more about the theoretical aspects of shaking off a tail on the road. How do you get away from someone chasing you in a car?

4   If there's only one car on your tail, then driving erratically – too slow, too fast, wandering from lane to lane – can lose your pursuer. But if, as often happens, you have a team of three in pursuit, you'll have to be a little more inventive.

5   In its simplest form, this might mean deliberately misusing your indicators. An opportune last-minute u-turn can leave your tail with nowhere to go if you time the flow of oncoming traffic correctly. Slowing right down as a traffic light turns orange – before accelerating rapidly away again – can also leave a law-abiding tail stranded.

6 Repeatedly changing your light combinations – fog lights, side lights, headlights etc. – can make you look like a completely different vehicle. Pool cars are also equipped with inflatable outlines which look like people so you can change the internal silhouette of a car. Remember that any pursuer has to concentrate on their own driving as well as keeping tabs on you. Sow confusion in their minds and you'll make it easier to lose them.

7 Service stations represent a maze of hiding opportunities before re-entering a motorway in the other direction. Car washes also offer welcome concealment. One officer was even known to radio the local police force before leading his tail at high speed past the nearest speed trap. His pursuer was flagged down while he drove off out of sight.

8 Espionage has been referred to as "the great game". This job takes it out of you, but it can also be a lot of fun sometimes. I hope, like me, you'll grow to find counter-surveillance one of the most interesting aspects of the job.

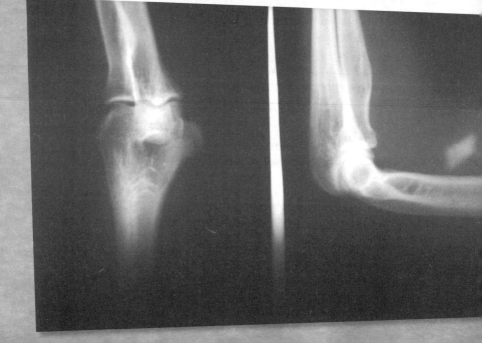

Psychologist's sessions with
Adam Carter

following incarceration and torture in Yemen

Case ID: MI5/379

Date: 3/11/2000

TRANSCRIPTS WITH APPROVED ANNOTATIONS	**AC** – Adam Carter **EL** – Emily Lipscombe

EL Thanks for coming to see me today, Adam.

AC That's okay.

EL Can you tell me in your own words what has happened in the last month?

AC But you're only level 2 cleared, aren't you?

EL I'm cleared for anything you want to tell me.

AC I'm not sure I feel like talking though. It's over now, isn't it? It's happened. I'm fine about it. Really.

EL Still, let's try talking it through together, shall we?

AC Well, the facts are pretty simple, I guess. My cover was blown while on operation in the Yemen. I was pistol-whipped unconscious. When I woke up I was in the boot of a car. My arms were tied behind my back, a bag that smelled of women's perfume was over my head and my kidneys were aching. I was taken to a tiny underground basement in the suburbs somewhere where I was tortured for three weeks. I know it was three weeks because of a tiny shaft of light in the top corner of my basement room. I would watch it wane, vanish and then reappear. It helped me to focus on something.

Anyway, I only saw two people during that time. There was a British guy – a real brute . . . a mercenary who used to be in the SAS. He was hard as nails. I knew him as Soames. And there was his accomplice who I called Ahmed. They tortured me almost non-stop the entire time I was there. And then I escaped. And now I'm here.

There is a brief pause.

ID: M15/379
3/11/2000

ADD PHOTOGRAPH
TO ADAM CARTER
FILE

AC (*cont.*) So, that's pretty much it.

EL And how well are you sleeping at the moment?

AC Not great.

EL Why do you think that is?

AC Why do you think? I get flashbacks sometimes. Sometimes I wake up thinking I'm still there. But I'm coping. I'm getting over it.

EL Have you spoken to Fiona about it?

AC No.

EL Do you think you should speak to Fiona about it?

AC No.

EL Why not?

AC This is difficult to explain, but as far as I'm concerned, she was already part of the experience for me. It was Fiona I was staying alive for. Her and Wes, our baby. As they beat me unconscious I'd hold on to a mental picture of her – laughing, smiling, willing me to come back home to her. I don't want to drag her further into this.

EL And how are you and Fiona at the moment?

AC I don't want to talk about that.

There is a brief pause.

EL Do you blame anyone for what happened?

AC At the time, I blamed myself. Later, I realised that Six's research department bore some responsibility. But we all make mistakes. I don't bear grudges.

EL And do you still blame yourself?

AC No, why would I? That wouldn't get me anywhere.

EL And what were your thoughts when you were first captured?

AC Er, something like, "Oh shit" . . . I knew they knew that I wasn't who I said I was. But I didn't know how much they knew, or what else it was they wanted to know. Does that make any sense?

EL Yes, go on.

AC This made it very hard to collect my thoughts. I didn't know what they wanted from me.

EL What do you mean?

AC I didn't know if they planned just to leave me to rot. I didn't know if they planned on killing me quickly or slowly.

EL And what effect did that have on you?

AC I found the anticipation of what they might do far worse than the reality. The horror of not knowing – that was the worst part. Much worse, in some ways, than all the stuff that followed.

EL And what did follow exactly?

AC leans forward and slowly pulls up his trouser legs to expose his calves. They are wreathed in bandages and blood is seeping slightly. He lets the cloth fall back down again, wincing. He then does the same with his shirt sleeves. His forearms are in a similar condition to his calves.

AC They did everything you can imagine in your darkest nightmares. And more. From the basics to the most advanced techniques. They were professionals. They knew what they were doing. Soames, in particular.

CHECK MEDICAL REPORT

EL How did you manage to get through this?

Case ID: M15/379
Date: 3/11/2000

Case ID: M15/37
Date: 3/11/2000

AC At first I showed outright defiance. It's what we were taught in training. It was supposed to help keep my spirits up.

EL And did it? Did it work for you?

AC In a way. For example, when Ahmed first saw me he spat in my face and yelled, "Kus ukhtak" which is an Arabic insult meaning "Fuck your sister" . . .

There is a brief pause.

EL Believe me, I've heard much worse from my children. Carry on.

AC So I wiped my face on his shirt and said, "Ma fiish aindii ukht – I don't have a sister."

EL And did that work?

AC No. He said, "Kwayyis. Kus umak – Well, fuck your mother then." And beat me unconscious. There was another thing that stood out. Something Soames did . . .

EL Go on.

AC He came in one morning and put down a glass of water, just out of reach. The back of my throat was caked with dry blood. My mouth was too dry to speak properly; it was almost too dry to breathe. I had to drink. So I lurched off the ground, grabbed the water and drank it in one go. It was ice cold, but it had a strange, sweet aftertaste.

He told me that was a silly thing to do. That in fifteen minutes I was going to wish I hadn't done that.

I said "Oh, shit."

He said there would be a lot of that. Vomit too.

And he was right. For the next four hours I puked and shat what remained of my insides. And as I lay there doubled over in agony, part of me couldn't help admiring his little trick.

EL You seem very calm about this. Were you this calm at the time?

AC Oh, I'm far from calm. But I'd seen a lot of what they were doing before. When I was in Beirut. So I knew what they were up to, and

Case ID: M15/379
Date: 3/11/2000

I also knew I was still more value to them alive than dead. Soames wasn't stupid enough to let Ahmed kill me.

EL So, that was a tactic you developed to survive your ordeal? Focus on the positive.

AC Yes, I guess. There were other things I did, too. Other mental tricks.

EL Go on.

AC I suppose I forced myself into a kind of positive reverse psychology, if that makes any sense. When I woke up I'd say to myself, "I wonder what they'll think of to do to me today." I taught myself to embrace the pain, to look forward to it as a welcome sign that I was still alive.

EL And did that work for you?

AC No, pain is where the pain is. Especially when it's 1,000 volts shooting through your balls.

EL But you found a way of coping with the pain?

AC Yes, it was more of a diversionary tactic, if anything.

EL How do you mean?

AC I mean that nothing can prepare you properly for the continual endurance of pain, or the insane longing for it to stop, but I trained myself to incorporate it into my daily routine. As they force-fed me

Case ID: M15/379
2/11/2000

Case ID: M15/.
Date: 3/11/20

glass I'd remember passages of poetry I'd been taught at sch
and try to recite them. As they burned my feet I'd try to recall
name and face of every girl I'd ever kissed. But there, always, at
front of my mind, it was Fiona who kept me going.

There is a long silence.

AC (*cont.*) So, are we done now? Do you have what you need?

EL It's not what I need that matters, Adam. This is about you. There
one more thing that I think we should address. How do you fe
about your captors, now you're free?

AC Well, I escaped. I killed them both. I definitely didn't suffer from
Stockholm Syndrome. What more do you need to know?

EL And did you have to kill them to escape?

AC They're dead now. Why does it matter?

EL Did you have to kill them to escape?

AC Ahmed, yes. Soames, no.

EL And do you want to tell me a little more about that?

Pause.

AC Ahmed was a sadist. I stabbed him as he was . . . as he was trying
to doing something horrible to me with a knife. But at the end of
the day he was following orders. He also believed in something.
He had a cause. He hated what the West had done to his family.
For him, I was the West.

EL But Soames?

There is a long silence.

AC Soames was a traitor and he believed in nothing. He was amoral.
He had sold out to the highest bidder. He wasn't even brave
enough to do anything himself. His existence hurt me more than
Ahmed's blows. God, he was a fucking animal. There wasn't an
ounce of humanity in him. I killed him out of pure, selfish loathing.
I didn't have to, but there was closure in his death. All my anger.
All my love. It all came together the moment he died.

There is the sound of AC weeping – quietly at first, then louder, uncontrollable sobs. This continues for four minutes.

EL It's okay, Adam. It's all over now.

AC Yes. It's all over.

EL You're alive.

AC Yes.

EL Fiona is alive. Wes is alive.

AC Yes. We're all alive. And Soames is dead.

EL It's going to be okay.

E.L

****Transcript ends****

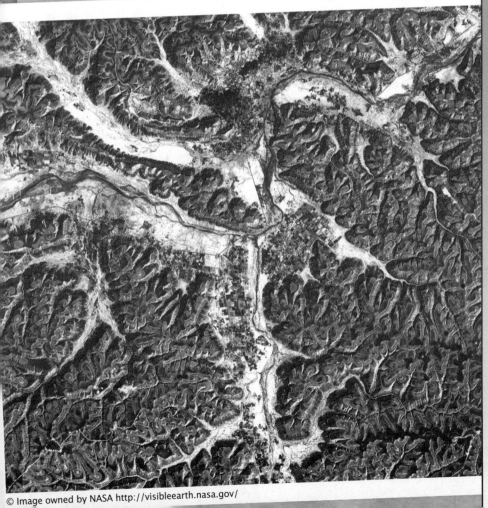

© Image owned by NASA http://visibleearth.nasa.gov/

MEGAMAG!

"Bigger than big" – your celebrity weekly

Spooks hunt Alfie

The story everyone else wanted

By Michelle Molby

It's the story that's gripped the nation for the past fortnight – the kidnap of the son of pop star, Sir Riff Monro, and his beautiful model wife, Bee. Forget football, forget which soap star has slept with which politician this week. There's only one question on all our lips now: where's little Alfie?

Children have been given days off school to look for him. City workers have taken rare annual leave to join in the search. Ports are on full alert. The news bulletins are full of little else. The leader of the opposition has dubbed him the "People's Alfie". Not since the death of Princess Diana has the nation experienced such a collective sense of loss. Such pain. Such outrage. Such anger.

But maybe we won't have to wait that much longer. For Megamag! can today exclusively reveal that MI5 is leading the nationwide search for the small boy. Kidnaps are normally dealt with by the police forces, but the Prime Minister told Megamag! yesterday that he has personally tasked MI5 with this job. "I am a massive fan of Sir Riff's music," the Prime Minister said. "'Nihilistic Realistic' was one of my favourite albums as a student, and I know I must do everything within my powers to help."

MI5 is not used to the media spotlight. Its day-to-day work takes place behind closed doors – defending the country from terrorist attacks and serious organised crime. Insiders are confident, however, that they can rise to this latest challenge. Yesterday I had lunch with the dashing young case officer – known only as Officer C – in charge of the investigation. "We will do everything we can to return Alfie to his loving parents," he told me. "We're not going to let the country down."

Alfie's parents have also expressed their full confidence in MI5's chances of success. "This is far too serious for normal cops," said his beautiful mother, Bee, whose modelling career is again thriving. "We want hard bastards; we want MI5." Sir Riff – the youngest person ever to be knighted for his services to the music industry, and to whales – was unavailable for comment as Megamag! went to press. However, his spokesman confirmed that he was "stricken with grief and pouring out his creative angst into a new album".

MEGAMAG!

"Bigger than big" – your celebrity weekly

Breaking
News
31ST OCTOBER 2004

Celebrities in tragic suicide pact

By Michelle Molby

Everyone knew the story had to have an ending. But no one knew it would be this tragic. Two parents. One kidnapped baby. Three deaths.

After four weeks of twists and turns, false summits and dead-ends, unfulfilled hopes and realised fears, young Alfie Monro's body was finally discovered yesterday. On hearing the news, his parents, Sir Riff and Bee, took their own lives. Police found them in their palatial Camden home late yesterday evening, unconscious from a fatal cocktail of paracetamol and cocaine.

Speaking from the steps of Downing Street this morning, the Prime Minister struggled to disguise the emotion in his quivering voice. "Whoever did this should not sleep easy in their beds tonight," he told the world's media. "For I know the police will not be sleeping until the killers of the People's Alfie are brought to justice."

Security insiders have confirmed that this is now a police investigation, and no longer a matter for MI5. Although the security services were unsuccessful in their job to save young Alfie's life, it is understood that this was due to forces beyond their reasonable control. As Officer C explained exclusively to Megamag!, "There was nothing anyone could do under these circumstances. We extend our heartfelt sympathy to the family."

The nation has watched. The nation has wept. And now the nation must move on.

Daily Tribune
NEWSPAPER OF THE YEAR

55p

15TH MAY 2005 • NEWS 11

FORMER MINISTER IN MURDER COVER-UP

Exclusive by our new editor, Michelle Molby

Former Treasury Minister John Sylvester is involved in a high-level murder cover-up, according to documents obtained today by the Daily Tribune.

In September last year Mr Sylvester – a high-flyer tipped by some as a future Prime Minister – resigned from the government to "spend more time with his family".

However, it has now come to light that there was a more sinister reason behind this resignation.

Sordid

Mr Sylvester – a married man with three children – conducted a sordid two-week affair with a beautiful Polish immigrant, Sophie Szeroki. When Ms Szeroki threatened to take this story of infidelity to the newspapers, Mr Sylvester struck her sharply across the jaw, bringing her crashing to the ground in a remote corner of Kensington Gardens. She subsequently died of a massive brain haemorrhage in St. Thomas's hospital.

When Mr Sylvester discovered this, he tried to do the honourable thing in writing a full explanatory letter of resignation to the Prime Minister. The Daily Tribune can now reveal, however, that this letter was intercepted by none other than the Chairman of the Joint Intelligence Committee – Oliver Mace – and saved until there was a better day to "bury bad news". The more pressing need to bury Ms Szeroki seems to have been overlooked amid this sordid politicking. She languished for ten long days in a West London mortuary.

Burial

The day chosen to "bury" Mr Sylvester's resignation coincided with the dramatic news of the suicide pact between Sir Riff and Lady Monro. By this stage, the former minister's alleged crimes were watered down to little more than the old excuse of wanting to spend more time with his family.

Whether his family will wish to spend much more time with him in the light of these recent revelations remains to be seen. The Daily Tribune has passed the full contents of its dossier to the police. Last night a Scotland Yard spokesman confirmed, "We are taking these allegations very seriously indeed."

Mr Sylvester is detained in police custody and unavailable for comment.

Embattled

This news will be particularly unwelcome for a government struggling in the polls as it enters the third week of a bitter election campaign. It will also raise serious questions over the future of Oliver Mace, the embattled chairman of the JIC. Mr Mace

ASSESSMENT:
Operation Hackette
(Michelle Molby)

FIELD REPORT
TITLE: MI5 AND THE ROLE OF THE MEDIA —
A RECOMMENDATION
FILED BY: ADAM CARTER
DATE: 27 JUNE 2005

MI5 and the media

In the past, the work of the media and the work of the security services have been anathema to one another. We rely on secrecy; they require openness. And while we both cultivate, use and discard confidential sources, our aim is to direct the flow of information through narrow, restrictive channels. Theirs is its widest possible dissemination. Security scoops remain a high prize for investigative journalists.

Five's good news very rarely gets reported. And if it does, it is hidden away in a side-column on page 19. Our failures, on the other hand, are always front-page stories. To journalists, we are secretive and manipulative. The fact that we don't shout about our work suggests – to them, at least – that we have something to hide.

Recently, however, MI5 has got more practised at working with, rather than against, the media. This has involved leaking appropriate stories, sometimes as a warning to rogue elements working against us. And it has also involved cultivating longer-term allies in the media, such as in Operation Hackette.

Michelle Molby

As such, there are some important lessons to be learned from Operation Hackette – the use of Michelle Molby in the staged kidnapping of Alfie Monro and the largely unrelated (yet concurrent) story of John Sylvester MP's alleged crimes.

The first is the way in which Downing Street tried to force the press and MI5 together. To portray MI5 as a cuddly, media-friendly security service in the business of rescuing the kidnapped offspring of fading rock stars inevitably ended disastrously. It was always a job for the police.

This naivety was compounded by the way in which MI5 was manipulated by Sir Riff and Bee. It is not MI5's position to get swept up in the soap opera lives of celebrities – especially those who arrange kidnappings.

On the other hand, our sober, long-term cultivation of Michelle Molby, former editor of *Megamag!*, was more successful. Although Downing Street used her to leak our involvement in the Alfie case, her contact with me kept her more fanciful flights of imagination within check. It also meant she was on message when the news of the parents' "suicide" came to light.

We were able to repay this loyalty later – to our mutual benefit – with documents relating to John Sylvester MP. The result is an editor of a (naturally left-wing) national newspaper with a friendly ear to the security service and its work. We have also succeeded in weakening the bargaining hand of Oliver Mace on the JIC.

Personal conclusions and recommendations

MI5 has modernised in many different ways, yet its approach to the media remains relatively outmoded. I do not propose the creation of a dedicated press office and PR-trained professionals. While secrets remain secrets, I do, however, recommend a thorough overhaul of how we present ourselves to the outside – both to the public, and to our intermediaries in the media. Both channels – as we have seen – have their advantages.

3rd September 2005

How Mr Mad Dog

Natasha Scott is your average young Londoner. She gets up, she goes to work, she has a drink after work. But then in the space of 48 hours she met a handsome MI5 officer at a party, saved another intelligence officer from a kidnap situation, helped the government catch the brutal killers behind Shining Dawn, and ended up kidnapped herself by a rogue CIA agent and strapped to a bomb in a hospital basement.

Here she tells in her own words how she came within two seconds of death.

The exclusive interview they all wanted

Saved My Life

When I went into work on Friday I was expecting a fairly normal day. Sure, there had been bomb warnings but you get used to that as a Londoner, don't you? My grandparents lived through the Blitz. My parents had to put up with the IRA. My generation? Well, it's Al Qaeda, isn't it? Or animal rights protestors. Or whichever other nutcases want to blow us up this week. You just have to get on with life.

"Waitresses are invisible to everyone else."

I work at a coffee stand in a central London train station. Some of the customers can be really rude, but you just learn to ignore it. Waitresses are invisible to everyone else. So when a workman walked past carrying a ladder and knocked into me, I didn't give it a second thought. No one apologises these days, do they? You might get sued like they do in America.

There wasn't much time to think about it anyway. A couple of hours later there was a massive security alert and we were all told we had to evacuate the station. "Don't run," they always say. But try not running when there are 250 people in a station and everyone's shouting "Bomb! bomb!". There was a horrible stampede.

"It really strikes it home when you hear how close they got like that."

It wasn't until later that I realised how serious it could have been. The bomb in the station's rafters was defused with only a few minutes to spare. It really strikes it home when you hear how close they got like that. Bomb alerts happen to other people in other places at other times. Not to you.

A mysterious stranger

My friend Holly was having a party that night. And, to be honest, I wanted to go and get plastered. I find that helps. Stops you thinking about things too much.

So there I was at this party when this guy appears out of the blue. He was really good-looking and well-dressed. And he just said, "I'm a special investigations officer working for the government. You have to come with me." I've had some chat-up lines in the past, but this one really took the biscuit.

Holly was standing next to me and started making silly jokes, but this guy looked serious. It might have seemed a silly thing to get in a car with a stranger, but he had a nice face. And to be honest, I wanted a bit of an adventure. I also thought it would make Holly jealous.

Bacardi Molotov cocktail

This guy took me to pick up his colleague but when we got there he was being held by some seriously nasty-looking blokes. My guy seemed a bit unsure what to do for a bit. He kept on mumbling to himself, "I won't let this happen again; I won't let this happen again." I had no idea what he was talking about.

"It felt like the bravest thing I'd ever done."

Then he had a brainwave. He grabbed my Bacardi Breezer and turned the bottle into a makeshift bomb. I was really scared by this point. I wanted to help but I was worried about freezing on the spot. But I just about managed to hold myself together when I was sent in to distract the nasty-looking blokes. It felt like the bravest thing I'd ever done. My guy set his colleague free.

He then did some really horrible things to the blokes. One of them was dropped over a balcony. The other was dangled over until he started speaking. All my adrenaline disappeared and I was angry. I'd never seen a dead person before. I couldn't understand why "special investigation officers" were letting people die. I started to shout at them. They looked at me as if I'd never understand their world.

On her majesty's secret service

I felt a bit better when I was taken back to their headquarters. There were these two really lovely guys with egg-shaped heads who helped me to describe the man with the ladder who bumped into me at the station earlier. They were much easier to talk to than the original guy who'd picked me up. He scared me. Later, I christened him Mad Dog.

I really wanted to go home by this stage and tell Holly about everything, but there was something strange about the CIA man who came to pick me up. I waited until he was off-guard and then kicked him very hard in the balls. Even intelligence officers hurt down there. He doubled up in pain and I ran off, but then he caught up with me, tied me up, gagged me, stole my pass and ran off. I later found out he worked for Shining Dawn.

Just as I thought my day couldn't get any more horrible I was kidnapped. I had just been driven back to my flat in the East End by another MI5 officer, but as soon as I walked in the door I was grabbed from behind. Mad Dog wouldn't have let that happen to me. The MI5 officer was shot dead only inches away from me. I'd now seen two dead people in 24 hours.

These guys from Shining Dawn bundled me into the back of a car. They'd been masterminding a bombing campaign in London so I knew they were serious, but I had no idea what they planned on doing to me at that stage. They kept on lecturing me. "Human beings are a stain on our planet. We must be dramatically culled" etc. etc. It made no sense to me at all.

But then we pulled up in front of the hospital and one of them turned to me with a horrible leering smile. "You, darling, are going to be our trigger," he said. I told him, if he was so keen on culling the human race, he could do worse than starting with himself. I expected him to blow his top at this, but he just laughed, slightly manically. "My time will come," he said. "My time will come."

"I've never been so terrified in my life."

I was taken down to the basement of the hospital and wired up to a bomb via a laptop. I've never been so terrified in my life. There was a timer on the laptop. I was told that if I freed myself the timer would count down twice as fast. I had absolutely no idea what to do. I wanted to save myself, of course, but what about all the people in the hospital? Someone might find out about the bomb and then they could be evacuated. Then we'd all be saved.

I really needed those egg-heads. Or better still, Mad Dog.

Mad Dog returns

could hear a huge amount of commotion outside. Maybe they were evacuating the building, I thought. Maybe MI5 had traced the bomb to here. I started to allow myself a little hope; hope that turned to despair when still no one arrived to free me.

I started to think about Mad Dog's boss who I'd met at MI5's headquarters. He'd tried to thank me for what I was doing for my country. I told him that I didn't think my country had ever done much for me. My country lectures me on binge-drinking, tells lies about the world, won't fix the tube and treats me like sh*t unless it can get something out of me.

It was hard not to think the same as I lay there in a cold hospital basement, betrayed by the CIA, neglected by MI5 and martyring myself to save as many as possible of my sick countrymen in a hospital upstairs. I started to cry – softly at first, then mad weeps of despair. It was the lowest I'd ever been in my life. You watch this kind of thing on television and think you'd cope fine if it were you, but it's so horribly different when you're actually there.

"He walked away and I broke down, thinking I was going to die alone."

Then, suddenly, Mad Dog appeared and I knew that everything was going to be all right. It didn't seem like that at the time, of course. He tried removing my wires and the clock started counting down twice as fast. We wouldn't have enough time to run for it. He walked away and I broke down, thinking I was going to die alone.

But then he came back. "I'll stay with you, Natasha," he said. "You don't have to be afraid." And he was right. At the last moment he got a call on his mobile. Someone at MI5 had cracked the code to the bomb. Mad Dog keyed in "kronos2". The timer stopped. We were safe.

Hero

The next day I was back in my old routine as if nothing had happened. But of course, it had. I was a changed person.

I went back to my flat after work and sat there thinking about everything. I'm not sure I'd have been that brave if it had been the other way round. I wouldn't have blamed Mad Dog for walking away and never coming back. He could have saved himself even if he didn't save me. But by staying, he saved a lot more than just the two of us. He saved a bit of humanity. He was a hero. My hero.

There was a knock on the door. It was him. He'd come to thank me for what I'd done. And I joked that Mrs Mad Dog was a very lucky woman. He laughed, and I realised I'd never see him again.

"They belong to a world which we rarely see."

But after he'd gone I realised that they were all heroes – from the egg-head boffins in research to the guy with the cool car that Mad Dog had rescued. They belong to a world which we rarely see. A world that operates behind the scenes as we get up, go to work and get drunk at parties with Holly. I feel very lucky to have met these people. And I feel very selfish that they rarely get the recognition they deserve.

I will never take them for granted again, and I will never take my own life for granted again. Coming so close to death makes you understand things. It makes you realise what is important. And it makes you realise who and what matters the most in your life.

I also remembered what Mad Dog's boss had said about what my country had done for me. "It's educated you," he said, "provided you with opportunities to find employment, provided you with financial support if you can't, looked after you when you were sick, protected rather than persecuted you, and allowed you to choose your own government."

And I felt a welling sense of pride inside. He was right. But I reckoned my country and I were pretty much quits by now.

Natasha Scott was speaking to Michelle Molby

FRAMING OF FAROOK SUKKARIEH OPERATION SAUL

FIELD REPORT

TITLE: Framing of Farook Sukkarieh – Operation Saul

FILED BY: Adam Carter

DATE: 10 April 1996

Introduction

In 1995, I took my first posting in Damascus, nominally as FCO cultural attaché. Although I worked under diplomatic immunity my real role was deputy to the MI6 regional chief.

Damascus in the mid-1990s was a hub of overlapping intelligence networks. Beirut was in chaos so the Syrian capital had become a crossroads for spies going to and fro from Lebanon. The CIA used it as their principal base in the Middle East. Mossad teams of kidon assassins came and went. International arms dealers stopped over en route to indiscriminate buyers in Iran and Iraq.

It was therefore a busy time for MI6 in the region. Our liaison work with friendly intelligence agencies was made even more difficult by the Mukhabarat which stepped up its activities at that time.

Farook Sukkarieh

The Syrian internal intelligence service, the Mukhabarat, is feared for its brutality as much as its professional expertise. The MI6 station chief used to describe it as the "KGB on steroids".

After six months in the country, it became my job to shadow one of its senior officers – Farook Sukkarieh – a well-known high-flyer with a particularly brutal reputation. At that time there was a sudden escalation of suicide bombings in Tel Aviv. Sukkarieh came under suspicion of controlling them, and it was my task to see if we could stop, turn or neutralise him.

Although the Mukhabarat is strictly speaking an internal secret police, its remit is wider than the clear demarcations between MI5 and MI6. Many Arab operations within Israel were run from outside due to the effectiveness of Israel's own Shin Bet. Its borders were some of the least porous in the region and, although Arabs within Israel's boundaries could move around relatively freely, it was easier for a controller to operate from outside.

This is where we believed Sukkarieh came in. He was intelligent as well as ruthless, and he had taught himself excellent Hebrew by watching a pirated version of Keshet-TV and reading the smuggled poems of Yehuda Amichai.

We often ran into each other at the drinks parties and cultural events which it was my official job to involve myself in. He used to seek me out deliberately at these events, and we would talk amicably enough in our transparently false roles of cultural attaché and senior civil servant in the department of tourism. He probably knew as much about me as I did about him.

Amal Sukkarieh

I had hit a dead-end, however, when it came to getting something out of Sukkarieh. I could see little prospect of turning him, and, despite early hints, my orders never went further than that.

But then I met "Amal" at an embassy reception. She'd studied Arabic literature at Edinburgh University, worked in a bar in Damascus, changed her name from Amelia to Amal, converted to Islam and married Sukkarieh after a six-month courtship.

By the time I met her, she was very unhappy. She couldn't bear Sukkarieh the child he wanted and he'd started cheating on her. Initially, I approached her thinking I could turn Sukkarieh through her. I thought she would be a way in. But we started seeing each other instead. We began to talk about ways of getting her out of there.

Framing Sukkarieh

When Sukkarieh found out what was going on he beat me severely in front of Amal. The beating was vicious but it was intended to maim not to kill. Thatcher was already poised to expel more Syrian spies from London at that time. The Mukhabarat couldn't run the risk of expelling someone with diplomatic immunity in a body bag.

The sole effect, then, of the episode was to strengthen Six's resolve to do something about Sukkarieh. We couldn't turn him. We could no longer use Amal to get to him. And we couldn't provide sufficient evidence for Mossad to give a kill order for their own kidon agents.

The station chief sanctioned me to come up with a deniable, inventive way of neutralising him. Recruiting Amal under a diplomatic immunity of her own, we worked together to frame Sukkarieh as an Israeli spy.

Sukkarieh's interest in Israel – the poetry, the TV stations – gave us ammunition to work on. We extended this interest beyond anything that could be described as professional. Our embassy in Tel Aviv sent us crates of Israeli trinkets, films, leaflets, tourist maps and books – all under diplomatic cover. A stenographer in the British Council in Jerusalem worked up a backlog of Hebrew correspondence between Sukkarieh and a Mr Benjamin Goldstein of 7 Ben Gurion Road, Eilat.

In Damascus, Amal and I created a secret box of Sukkarieh's supposed fondness for Israel and hid it under a loose floorboard beneath his sink. We also produced faked photographs of our target shaking hands with various Israeli notables, as well as newspaper cuttings from *The Jerusalem Post* and *Ha'aretz* hinting at a significant Israeli double agent at the heart of Syrian intelligence.

When everything was in place, we tipped off Sukkarieh's number two at the Mukhabarat anonymously. The man – Isa el-Dins – suspected his boss of having an affair with his sister. And he wanted his job in any case.

El-Dins's damning indictment – coupled with the mountain of "evidence" that we'd compiled – was enough for Sukkarieh to be hanged as an Israeli spy.

On the day of his execution we discovered the disservice we'd done to Israel. Our fabricated evidence on Sukkarieh was accurate: he was Tel Aviv's best asset in an Arab intelligence agency since Eliahu ben Shaoul Cohen was executed on 18th May 1965.

Amal and I carried out our exit plan and returned to London.

Addendum

For the record, I would like it to be known that Amal and I are very much in love and intending to get married. She has changed her name again – to Fiona. She has also expressed an interest in working for MI6. Her Arabic skills and knowledge of the Middle East would make her a valuable operative.

CASE CLOSED

CASE RE-OPENED

THE SECOND DEATH OF FAROOK SUKKARIEH

FIELD REPORT
TITLE: THE SECOND DEATH
OF FAROOK SUKKARIEH
FILED BY: ADAM CARTER
DATE: 3 FEBRUARY 2005

Farook Sukkarieh – Triple agent

Farook Sukkarieh, believed hanged in April 1996, was a triple agent working for the Syrians from the beginning. He died at an airbase in southern England on 3 January 2005 – stabbed in the neck by Fiona Carter (nee Amelia / Amal), whom he subsequently shot. He was then shot dead.

Sukkarieh's public execution in Martyrs' Square in 1996 was a staged event intended to anger the Israelis further. The Israeli Defence Force decimated a Palestinian refugee camp in Southern Lebanon the following day. Sukkarieh's place at the execution was taken by Ahmed Bukra, a common Lebanese criminal serving a life sentence for murder.

Sukkarieh emerged from ten years' hiding late last year in an attempt to track down Fiona Carter and extradite her to Syria. He was unsuccessful in this attempt.

I hope Sukkarieh burns in hell.

CASE CLOSED

MI5

ANNUAL MEDICAL REPORT

Name:	Adam Carter	
Date:	1st May 2006	

Height:	6'2"	Weight:	12st 7lb	BMI:	22.5

Units of alcohol per week:	19
Cigarettes per week:	none

Blood pressure:	110/60
Resting pulse:	56
Urine:	normal
Chest x-ray:	normal
Exercise ECG:	normal

Adam Carter remains in excellent physical shape and still performs well in all endurance and strength tests. He has cut down on his drinking since requested last year.

His right arm remains slightly weaker than his left after the torture he underwent in Yemen. He has been good at attending physio treatment to correct this, but there is probably not much more we can do about it now. Meanwhile, his left shoulder has made a full recovery from the gunshot wound eight months ago.

S Chapman

Dr Sally Chapman

PASSED

SECTION X

EYES ONLY FOR LEVEL 1 AND ABOVE

LOG FOR ADAM CARTER

Date: 7.07.2006
Subject: Excessive time spent on estate agent websites
Outcome: Referred to Harry Pearce. See note below.

Note from Harry Pearce: He is looking for a new house following his wife's death. Please exercise some sympathy.

Date: 4.05.2005
Subject: Large volumes of cash being moved around between different bank accounts.
Outcome: Leave. AC was transferring money to take the family on holiday.

Date: 7.08.2004
Subject: Cricket. Adam has been spending a large amount of time reading the *Guardian*'s online over-by-over Test Match updates.
Outcome: See note from Harry Pearce below.

Note from Harry Pearce: So what? So have I.

Date: 24.02.2004
Subject: Excessive time spent at work downloading music. Music included Athlete and Stone Roses.
Outcome: Referred to Harry Pearce. See note below.

Note from Harry Pearce: I have issued a mild reprimand — as much for his taste in music as the wasted office time.

Section X exists to keep tabs on members of the security services. We monitor private internet usage, spending habits and extra-mural activities. Our remit is to reduce the risk of blackmail and act as an early-warning system for renegade officers. These notes are retained on file which are "No Eyes" as far as the subject is concerned.

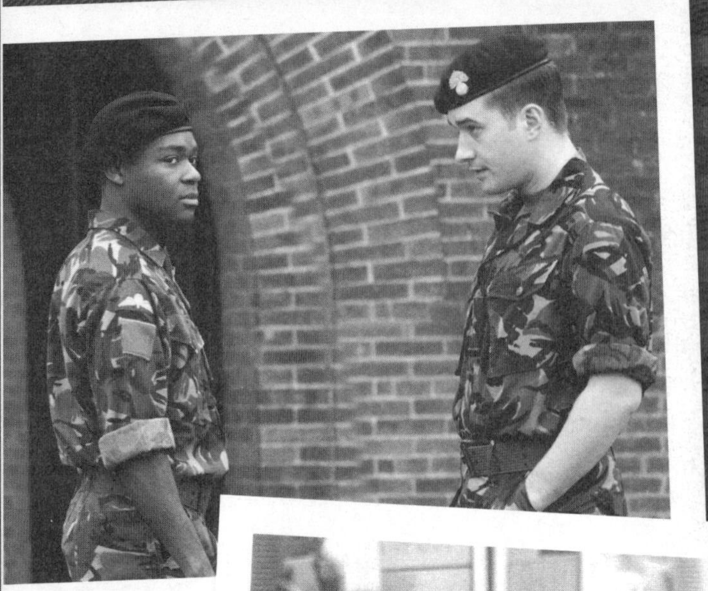

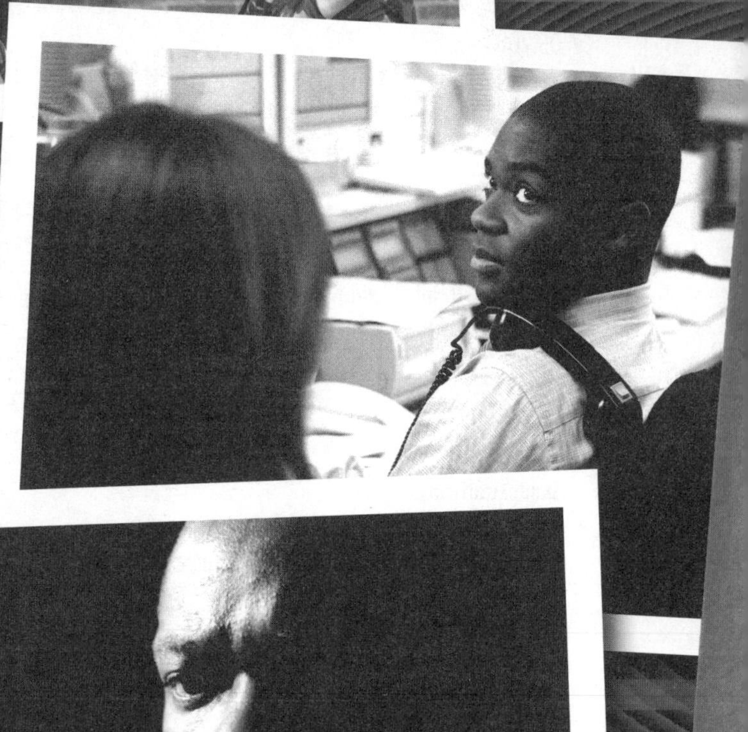

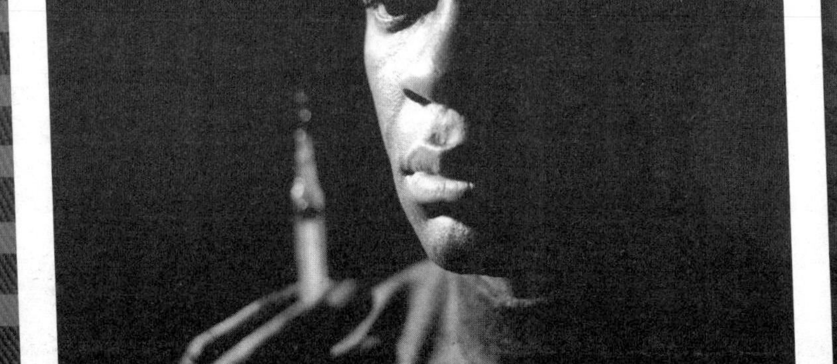

[Danny Hunter]

Private and Confidential

Name: Danny Hunter
Position: Junior Intelligence Officer
D.O.B: 19.07.1976
Hair: Black
Eyes: Brown
Height: 5'10
Marital status: Single
Dependants: None
Blood type: O, Rh negative

Danny Hunter joined MI5 as his first permanent job after dropping out of university. He was a valued member of Section D – working particularly closely alongside Zoe Reynolds and Tom Quinn – before he was shot dead in a hostage situation.

Major operations include:

- Assassination of renegade scientist on North Sea ferry
- Close-quarter protection of Zuli, a writer living under a fatwa
- Undercover trader in Bowman Bank
- Undercover journalist with socialist newspaper, *Red Cry*

MI5
Application Form

Surname

Hunter

Forenames

Daniel (Danny)

Date of Birth

19.07.1976

Place of birth

Kennington, London

Nationality at birth

British

Permanent Address

11c Kernal Street,
London SE11

Current occupation

Temporary work

Date of availability for employment

Sooner, the better

Do you hold a full, clean driving licence?

Yes

Medical:
Do you have any conditions – either physical or psychological – which might affect your employment?

None

Father's name, address and occupation

Unknown

Mother's name, maiden name, address and occupation

Jasmin Hunter
Nurse
11c Kernal Street, London SE11

Brothers / Sisters (with names and D.O.B.)

None

Secondary Schools / Colleges
Dates : Names : Town

1981–1994 : Oval School for Boys : London

GCSEs or equivalents

1 A* (Maths), 3As (Chemistry, Physics, Biology), 3Bs (History, Geography, Religious Education), 1D (English Language), 1E (English Literature)

A levels and AS levels or equivalents

Maths – A
Chemistry – B
Physics – C

Gap Year
How did you spend any break during your education?

N/A

University or Further Education

I took up a place to study Chemistry at University College London in 1994 but dropped out after two years to play cricket for Surrey

Awards
Please give details of any other awards (e.g. music)

None

EMPLOYMENT

Dates	Employer	Position
1998–	Temping / travelling	Temp
1996–1998	Surrey County Cricket Club	Professional Cricketer

Have you served in HM Forces (including Reserves)?

No

Do you have applications pending for other jobs?

No

PERSONAL QUALITIES AND SKILLS

SUMMARY
Provide a pen-portrait of your life to date

I had quite a tough childhood as my father left my mother before I was born so she was left bringing me up alone on a nurse's salary. I had no brothers or sisters.

Cricket was my main form of escapism throughout my teens – I used to read every copy of Wisden from the local library – and I turned out to be a fairly good all-rounder. When Surrey CC offered me a full-time contract in the summer of 1996 I gave up my degree at UCL.

In retrospect, I regret giving up my degree when I only had a year left to go. Surrey didn't turn out to be all it had promised. I was 12th man for most of my first season there. In the second season I barely made the reserves. The money was poor. I left and spent the last year temping and travelling.

MAF|09.fa|vii.2

MOTIVATION

Why do you think you would be suited to a career in MI5?

I've had to struggle hard all my life. I believe my experiences have given me a greater understanding of myself, as well as a heightened appreciation of my abilities.

I also believe I've displayed the courage to follow my convictions, and it's the same with MI5. The last year of temping and travelling has given me time to think seriously about my long-term career goals. I have researched the work thoroughly and I'm under no illusions as to what the day-to-day job entails.

POLITICAL CURIOSITY

Give three political topics (historical or current) which interest you

I wouldn't describe myself as particularly political but I see this as an advantage, not a disadvantage, in a career as a civil servant. I have, however, read and researched a great deal of material about the history of the intelligence services. I am particularly interested in CIA / MI6 cooperation in SIGINT post Second World War.

ADAPTABILITY

Give an example of a time when you had to adapt to unexpected circumstances

I learned a lot about myself when I joined Surrey Cricket Club. It wasn't easy going from student life to the rigours of professional sportsmanship. It was also strange being the only black player in a very conservative team. However, I felt that I quickly made friends and settled in.

Similarly, the decision to leave Surrey was one of the hardest I made in my life. I think many people in my situation would have stayed on longer than was necessary. However, it was clear to me that my career was going nowhere so I had to get out before it was too late.

I was slightly depressed for a bit – I'd stumbled in both my academic and my sporting career. But it gave me the chance to think about what I really wanted to do in life. Once I'd hit rock bottom I pulled myself back up again. I worked hard in the temping jobs. I researched MI5. And I travelled.

RESPONSIBILITY

What positions of responsibility have you held – at school, university or otherwise?

```
School football captain
School cricket captain
```

FOREIGN LANGUAGES

Please indicate level of competence

```
None
```

OTHER INTERESTS

```
Football
```

TRAVEL

Give details of all foreign travel undertaken in the last 10 years, including reason for travel

```
Cambodia, Vietnam, Laos, Kenya, Tanzania, Uganda - tourism
```

EQUAL OPPORTUNITIES

This information is not used as part of our selection procedures

Gender	Ethnic origin	Disabilities
(Male) Female	Black of Caribbean origin	Mild dyslexia

REFEREES

Please give details of three referees. One of these should be a contemporary who knows you well

```
1. Geoffrey Green, Headmaster of Oval School for Boys
2. Dr Miranda Bounds, Chemistry tutor, UCL
3. Tim Brewin, Captain, Surrey Cricket Club
```

Signature

Date

4th December 1999

Surrey Cricket Club

REFERENCE: Danny Hunter

To Whom It May Concern:

I must admit that, when Danny Hunter first joined my team, I was worried about him. He has tremendous natural ability – a fantastic eye for the ball, a useful off-spin action and absolute dedication in the field. He was at heart, however, a decent all-rounder and not much more than that. Good, but not spectacular, in all departments. A bit of a jack of all trades. The kind of guy who might struggle as a jobbing cricketer after a while. It seemed a shame that he had given up his degree for a pipedream.

But I was even more worried about Danny socially. He seemed rather young and naive to be joining a team full of seasoned pros. And there were a lot of edges on his personality that needed to be knocked off.

As it turned out, my first set of fears were fairly grounded – Danny struggled to retain a place in the first team. He became a little sluggish in the field; he lost confidence with his batting; umpires started to call him up for a throwing action with his off-spin.

On the other hand, I couldn't have been more wrong about Danny socially. He really blossomed within a team environment, cheerfully polishing the pads of the more experienced players. He seems to thrive on knowing his place within a structured hierarchy.

Danny also joined in all manner of off-field activities. He was a much-loved member of the dressing room, and a particularly gregarious (and generous) companion in the bar afterwards. Danny soon acquired the nickname "Armani" for his love of sharp clothes. However, this nickname was never meant anything but affectionately. While it was the right thing for him to leave, we were all sorry to see him go. We still miss him.

I'm not, of course, in the best position to comment on Danny's intellectual abilities (although he would regularly turn up for nets with his bag overflowing with books). As for his personal qualities, I cannot recommend him strongly enough. You won't find an abler, funnier, more loyal colleague anywhere.

Tim Brewin
Captain, Surrey Cricket Club

FROM THE HEADMASTER OF OVAL SCHOOL FOR BOYS
147 KENNINGTON GROVE
LONDON SE11

Mrs Hunter
11c Kernal Street
London SE11

4th March 1986

Dear Mrs Hunter,

I know we live in the 1980s, the decade of consumerism where greed is good, time is money and lunch is for wimps, but I fear your son may have been taking the central tenets of Thatcherism to extremes.

Let me explain. While some of the bigger, older boys are continuing to cajole lunch money out of the smaller children, Danny's approach, I've recently discovered, is altogether more sophisticated. He appears to have been acting as a mediator between the youngest boys and the bullies. The six and seven-year-olds have been encouraged to bring their 50p to school in two twenty-pence coins and one ten-pence coin. Danny takes 20p for himself as "protection money" (his words, I'm afraid, not mine), 20p for the older bullies and leaves the original owner with the remaining 10p.

Extraordinarily, everyone seems happy with this arrangement. The younger, weaker boys get to keep more money than they did; the bullies are guaranteed a steady low rate of income for little work. Previously they used to collect on around 30 per cent of their targets. Now their hit rate is well into the nineties.

Danny then keeps everyone happy by spending half of his daily takings on confectionery for everyone at the shop opposite the school (where he appears to have struck some kind of "regular customer" deal with the owner).

Now, some of my colleagues in the common room applaud this kind of entrepreneurial zeal. What is the problem, they ask, if everyone is happy at the end? On the other hand, Danny is only ten years old. My bigger concern is that he does this kind of thing more for the love of money – the love of the thrill, the chase, the danger – than any altruistic love of his fellow students.

I should tell you that we have also had unconfirmed reports – from a number of reliable witnesses – that Danny has been stealing in more direct ways as well. Bags have gone missing from outside classrooms, some of them containing these expensive new "Walkmen". Teachers have complained that their wallets are being rifled if they leave their jackets hanging on a chair. The finger of blame keeps on pointing at Danny.

Theft or entrepreneurial zeal? It's a blurred line, I suppose, these days, but it's one we should clarify sooner rather than later. Perhaps you'd be so good as to arrange a time to come and talk to me about this.

Yours sincerely,

G Green

GEOFFREY GREEN, HEADMASTER OF OVAL SCHOOL FOR BOYS

SECURITY CLEARANCE & BACKGROUND CHECKS

Danny Hunter

I was tasked with carrying out routine background checks into Danny Hunter's family and friends, as well as standard fact-checking of his application details.

The basic facts of Danny's back-story stand up to close scrutiny. This is an honest man whose CV displays none of the self-aggrandisement which typifies many of our applicants.

A major cause for concern, however, is Danny's attitude towards money. I have tracked down a letter which his headmaster sent to his mother when he was only ten years old. It appears that he was running some kind of protection racket with the younger boys' lunch money.

This behaviour has only improved slightly over the ensuing thirteen years. Danny has one of the worst credit ratings of any of our applicants. He has barely made any inroads into the interest on the money borrowed for the drinks he bought all his cricketing team mates. His situation has not been helped by some unadvisable day-trading on the stock exchange during the quiet winter months.

"It's a beautiful thing, money," he was heard to say at interview, when asked how much he expected to be paid as a junior civil servant. I think the interviewer's response may have shocked him slightly.

However, my concerns are mitigated to a large extent by Danny's tough upbringing. He has never known his father (and shows no desire of trying to trace him. It appears that his mother was not sure who he was, either). He is fiercely protective of his mother who is a well-respected A&E nurse. In this light, I think we can forgive some of his excesses as the escapism of a young man trying to break from his past.

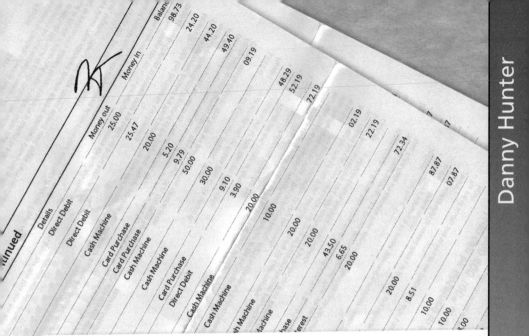

Danny's close friends are the sporting, gregarious type you'd expect. He appears to be as politically unaware as they are. I would say, however, that his worldliness makes up for this.

I also believe that underneath some of his surface excesses, Danny applies a strict moral code to his life (instilled, it would seem, by his mother, who is a regular churchgoer). I'll give you one example: while travelling earlier this year, Danny met, and fell in with, a group of young travellers from Brighton. He smoked some of their cannabis but subsequently discovered that they were also importing it into Britain under a mutual agreement with illegal people smugglers. When they seemed entirely unconcerned by this association, he reported them to the police and disappeared.

I have no hesitation in recommending this excellent young man for employment at MI5.

APPROVED

Rebecca Moore

Rebecca Moore, HR Security
7th March 2000

TRAINING ASSESSMENT
Danny Hunter, 9th June 2000

SCORES

Practical

Surveillance	5
Counter-surveillance	2.3
Physical endurance	2
Shooting	4.1
Driving	3.5
Technical	4
Average	3.48

Intellectual

Linguistic	0.5
Decision-making	3.9
Research	2.2
Average	1.93

Other core competencies

Calm under pressure	3.5
Leadership	2.2
Team work	3.7
Communication	4.1
General attitude	4.8
Average	3.66

Overall average   **3.21**

On a sliding scale of 1 to 5 where
1 is poor, 5 is outstanding and 2.5 is
average for a new recruit

Danny's surveillance scores are the best we've ever seen among new recruits. By the end of the course, the instructors were picking up as many tips from him as he was from them (including one evening when he honed his skills by following them all home). It is very rare for anyone to score a perfect 5. He was less good at counter-surveillance.

Otherwise, Danny put in a solid, above-average performance (incidentally, he clocked exactly the same overall score as Zoe Reynolds, whom I recommend he works alongside – they would complement each other very well).

On the negative side, you will probably have noticed his linguistic score – one of the lowest we've ever had. It's a good thing he's applied for MI5 and not MI6.

R Ferguson

Robin Ferguson, Head of recruit training, MI5

Surveillance training for new recruits

Presentation by Danny Hunter

Speaking notes

Introduction by AN Other Officer

I'd like to introduce you to Danny Hunter, another of our excellent officers from Section D. Earlier this week you listened to counter-surveillance expert, Adam Carter. Danny's going to be coming at this from the other side – surveillance. He notched up the highest ever score in our surveillance training when he was in your shoes, so I suggest you listen to him very carefully. Danny, over to you.

DH's introduction

Thank you. Counter-surveillance and surveillance do, of course, have a lot in common. But the conflict and common ground between the two are more than simple feint and parry. Surveillance is inevitably more complex. In counter-surveillance, your one overriding aim is to get away, to avoid further detection. In surveillance, there are all sorts of things you might be trying to find out. And in this game of cat and mouse, the odds are often with the mouse.

Having said that, surveillance is an absolutely vital tool of an intelligence officer's tradecraft. At its simplest, it is used to gather background data on a target. Where do they go? When do they go there? Who do they meet when they're there? The information obtained here is used as an extra to any given operation, a means to an end.

The stakes increase when surveillance becomes the end in itself. Perhaps you need to lift a target. Or follow him to a place where you can catch him red-handed. Or even neutralise him.

And, of course, surveillance methods are varied – on foot, by public transport, in a vehicle. You might be working alone; you might be in a team. You might be controlling that team from the warmth of Thames House, or a static van parked on a street. Or you might be looking over a technical operative's shoulder waiting to give the command for the SAS to storm a building.

All these methods have their merits and their disadvantages, their secrets and their modi operandi. We're going to be covering some of these today.

Static surveillance

1   Surveillance has a certain glamour to it – shady-looking men whispering into their coat lapels, grainy CCTV images, high-speed car chases and so on. But over 75 per cent of surveillance is static, and I'm afraid a lot of it is highly mundane.

2   By static, I mean the opposite of mobile. You'll find yourselves cooped up in surveillance vans for days on end. You'll go mad as you eat your fifth Nutrigrain bar, trying to stay awake for your 30th hour in a row as Malcolm reads out cryptic crossword clues from the *Daily Telegraph*. And then – just as you're drifting off – there will be a sudden, unexpected development and you'll have to make snap decisions that will affect the outcome of the entire operation.

3   Or you might find yourself sitting in coffee shops for hours monitoring who comes and goes. One officer did this for so long that he couldn't start the day without four espressos. Another went undercover as a pub landlord so he could keep tabs on a group of dangerous ex-soldiers. They bought him so many drinks that he ended up with the DTs.

Surveillance trainin

Surveillance train

4   Or you might end up in the open, observing events from a distance through binoculars. The officers who were sent to monitor subversive elements among the Newbury bypass protestors built their own treehouse in the vicinity. My personal low point was keeping surveillance on an Al Qaeda splinter group who were trying to steal fertiliser to make a bomb. I had to lie low in a stinking farm cesspit for four days to catch them. It rained the entire time.

5   Even if you're in a more convenient spot, there is still the boredom to contend with. One of our favourite tricks is to set up an observation point next door to, or opposite, the suspect's house. We often do this by offering a free holiday to the family so we can move them out for a week. But that's where the fun stops. You might have a roof over your head and someone else's sofa to sit on, but it still comes down to hours and hours of patience. Watching and waiting. That's our game. It's like the parable in the Bible: you never know when the time will come. But if you're in the right place, at the right time, there's almost no end to how much useful information you can glean.

Single surveillance on foot

1   It is unlikely that you'll conduct that much mobile surveillance alone, especially if the target is high risk. It is particularly easy for a professional to shake off a single tail. You only have to be recognised more than once and you're compromised.

2   Admittedly, we do occasionally deploy very obvious, highly visible surveillance on foreign intelligence operatives, simply to make them aware that we know who they are. This scares the more amateur operatives, while luring the professionals into a false sense of security about our own professionalism. Meanwhile, the decoy allows other surveillance teams to carry out their undercover

job undetected. How to follow someone ostentatiously shouldn't require any training.

3 However, circumstances sometimes make single, undetectable surveillance necessary. Perhaps you're alone in the field and there's no time to call back-up. Or maybe the target is a low-level risk with no counter-surveillance training. Or maybe there simply aren't enough resources to go around.

4 So, let's imagine you're out there, in the field, on foot, and you have to follow one person without being detected. How do you do it?

5 The first obvious point is that you must blend in. Wear the right clothes for the area. In general, browns and grey are the best camouflage in any urban setting. Act as naturally as possible. Don't touch your ear-piece. Keep your eyes down but don't look shifty.

6 Surveillance of this sort in a city has its advantages as well as its disadvantages. While it's easier to blend in and remain unnoticed, it's also easier for your target to slip out of sight. On the move you should remain at least 20 yards behind someone. Sometimes you might want to cross the street to give yourself a different perspective. Learn to identify your target by any piece of their clothing – from their shoes up to the shoulder of their jacket. All you should need is a glimpse to keep yourself on track.

7 Surveillance on foot obviously becomes harder when the target stops or alters their stride. The key thing is to act as much like a member of the public as possible. Think like a normal person. How would a normal person kill time? They might look as if they were waiting for a friend. Or pause to answer a text message. Or buy a newspaper. If you don't think of yourself as suspicious, an amateur target won't either.

8 People in large cities, in particular, are prepared to accept all sorts of coincidences. How often do you find yourself seeing someone on the underground or in a bookshop you're sure you've bumped

Surveillance training for new recruits

into before? Ideally, a good surveillance officer will go entirely undetected. If you are clocked by a target, your job is simply to blend into the background and become another coincidence that can be easily shrugged off.

Surveillance in a foot team

1   As I've mentioned, first-rate surveillance often requires team work – especially if you're tracking a dangerous or well-trained target. The best teams train together for years. Each member knows instinctively what the other one will do in any given situation – just like a good football or rugby team.

2   The basic team surveillance – which we'll practise a little later in your training – is the 1,2,3 method. Officer 1 follows directly behind the suspect, as with single surveillance. Officer 2 follows further behind, keeping an overall view on proceedings. And Officer 3 follows between the two but on the opposite side of the street. This means that if the suspect turns unexpectedly, the officers can all swap places without becoming obvious. Similar procedures are followed if the suspect suddenly performs a u-turn.

3   If one officer is compromised, another can easily take his place. In our biggest surveillance operations, we can have up to ten teams of three all operating at the same time. The methods they deploy are similar to zone defence techniques in basketball. As the suspect leaves one area, another team takes over. This can also be coupled with static surveillance – often by innocuous-looking members of the "public" such as "street vendors" and "workmen". I remember one op near Trafalgar Square where MI5 officers and operatives outnumbered members of the public by two to one.

4   If these big operations are carried out against a foreign intelligence service, you might find them using the same kind of anti-surveillance techniques that Adam described earlier in your

training. At this point your surveillance also becomes counter-counter-surveillance. Often we deploy teams purely to identify and sabotage their counter-surveillance efforts. This leaves the surveillance officers free to carry on with their jobs.

5   Finally, team work requires leadership, and it will often be your job as an MI5 officer to direct your surveillance operatives to where you want them to be. Commands need to be clear and simple. There's nothing worse than teams running around like headless chickens. We had one op where the two surveillance teams got so confused that they started trailing each other. The target escaped scot-free.

In a vehicle

1   A lot of static surveillance is carried out from the vantage point of a car and you're least likely to arouse suspicions if you're in a mixed gender couple – ideally doing something innocuous like eating a take-away or reading a newspaper. Be careful about starting your engine, too. Do this in a quiet neighbourhood and half the street will hear you.

2   Once you're on the move, GPS systems have made it much easier to track other vehicles. All MI5 cars now have them fitted as standard. Ideally, you'll have a fellow officer in the car, shouting out instructions like a rally driver's assistant as he plots all alternative routes. Close examination of the map might give clear indications as to where your target is heading. There are generally all sorts of short-cuts you can take to avoid detection.

3   And of course, the old-fashioned rules of vehicle surveillance also apply. Drive an inconspicuous car with good acceleration. Try to

Su

keep at least one car between you and your target. And never think you've been spotted until you're sure. You'd be amazed how many drivers never check their rear-view mirrors.

4   Another skill you'll also have to acquire is the ability to drive fast in the dark using night vision goggles. You'll be glad to hear that this is something we practise in a simulator first before letting you loose on the M4.

Lifting a target

1   As I said in my introduction, surveillance is sometimes used to get officers into a position where they can "lift" a target. This might occur when an MI5 mole within the operation is in danger of being compromised, or if the subject is about to commit a crime and needs to be apprehended immediately.

2   In extreme situations, of course, you can lift a target from the street and bundle him into a car, but we generally prefer to be a little more subtle than that. Members of the public tend to start asking questions. The police get involved. The target's accomplices will notice he's gone missing. At the end of the day, we're a secret service and we like to keep things secretive.

3   So, how do you lift someone without making a scene? The classic scenario is a loud, public nightclub with MI5 officers masquerading as doormen. The target is drugged with a sedative which makes him appear too drunk to remain in the club. He can then be quietly led out of a back entrance and into a waiting car.

4   Lifting someone in broad daylight is altogether more challenging, but not impossible. The service has access to a number of genuine black London cabs which have been used to spirit suspects away to a safehouse. Shopping centres also provide a convenient backdrop. Some large department stores have changing rooms with secret doors that open the other way. Compliant shop

assistants are always happy to show a suspect to the right cubicle so we can lift them from the other side. I once set off the fire alarm in Selfridges and lifted my target in the ensuing chaos.

5   In general, though, the best lifts are carried out in complete secrecy – a dawn raid on a target's home, or a quiet alleyway with only stray cats as witnesses.

A faked accident

1   In extreme circumstances, it may be necessary for MI5 to neutralise a target. The mobile nature of surveillance operations provides plenty of opportunity for this.

2   Over 600 pedestrians are killed on British roads every year. If you choose your location carefully (and plant your witnesses appropriately) it's fairly easy to add to that number. The same is true of a good driver following a target in a car. Your training will teach you how to force someone off the road.

3   Opportunities also exist on foot, especially in large crowds. In 1978 Bulgarian dissident Georgi Markov was killed on Waterloo Bridge by a poison dart filled with ricin, shot from an umbrella. As so often in our line of work, truth is stranger than fiction.

Assessment of Danny Hunter by Miranda Saunders, in-house psychologist

Case ID: MI5/682
Date: 04/04/2004

ANNOTATED TRANSCRIPTS	**DH** – Danny Hunter **MS** – Miranda Saunders

Accompanying note from Tom Quinn

Miranda Saunders was fired the day after producing these psychological assessments. I am particularly disappointed that she played valued team members off against each other in this despicable way. As I've written in Zoe Reynolds' file, Danny Hunter was entirely misrepresented in Zoe's subsequent interview. The feelings Miranda aroused left them both hostile and defensive with each other during an important operation.

I recommend this report be retained in Danny Hunter's file as a warning to any future counsellors.

I was tasked by the DG to conduct a psychological assessment of the key players in Section D. That this had to take place on the same day as the visit of the American President was highly inconvenient to me.

Although I had a clipboard and took occasional notes, the officers were unaware that I was, in fact, recording them as well. These are the transcripts from my session with Danny Hunter.

Long silence.

MS Just be as open and candid as you like.

Silence.

MS (*cont.*) Anything at all. Anything or anyone you feel needs scrutiny. Just let rip. This is your time.

DH It's all good, actually.

MS Good?

DH Everything is great. Fantastic.

Silence.

MS Perhaps if I asked you a few specific questions . . . What do you think of the service's public access line?

DH The weirdo line? The one which members of the public use to complain about their neighbours' hedge?

MS The weirdo line? Very interesting. Why do you put it like that?

DH Oh. No, I didn't mean it like that.

MS You didn't?

DH No.

MS So what did you mean, then?

DH I'm not sure.

MS Interesting.

Silence.

DH Why am I here, exactly?

MS You tell me, Danny. Why are you here?

DH Because Zoe and I tossed a coin to see who would face you first and I lost?

MS No, Danny. These interviews are designed for you. They're to let off steam about your workflow and your office environment.

DH Right. And the small matter of lots of people trying to kill this American bloke we're protecting is by-the-by?

MS Having sessions under live operations facilitates greater honesty.

DH Right.

MS Why haven't I seen you up here on the fifth floor before, Danny?

DH You think we'd voluntarily come up here and talk to you?

MS Should I take that personally?

DH I mean, everyone would think we were mad if we knocked on your door and started pouring out all our internal issues. You know what happened to the last guy who did that.

MS I do.

Another long silence.

MS (*cont.*) But this is different. This is once a year, and this is compulsory. Personnel have asked me to conduct a topography of the department. Find out what everyone thinks. And not just matters of procedure. You can talk to me about people as well.

DH Oh great.

MS So, what do you think of Zoe?

DH What?

MS Zoe. Blonde hair, blue eyes, pretty smile. I'm fairly sure you work with her. What do you think of her?

DH What do you mean, exactly?

MS Do you like her? Is she easy to work with?

DH Now, those are two very different questions. Do I like her? Yes, hugely. Is she easy to work with? No, not at all. Is she easy to live with? No, even less so. Does that make her a bad colleague or a bad flatmate? No, I don't think so.

MS You don't think so.

DH I know so.

MS Go on.

DH Well, she's difficult and a bit bolshy. She's stubborn, and she can be horribly bossy. But I guess that's why I like her.

MS Like her?

DH Yes, I like her.

MS Right.

DH But not like that.

MS Right.

Check date
Z + D started
sharing
house

Long silence.

DH Oh God, what are you trying to make me say?

MS I'm not trying to make you say anything. What are *you* trying to say? That's a different question. And a more important one.

DH I'm not sure.

MS Perhaps I can prompt you. What goes through your mind when you think of Zoe?

DH I think of her smiling. Laughing. Making me smile. Making me laugh . . . Oh shit.

MS Do you see what I mean?

DH That was a mean, nasty trick.

MS I didn't say anything. I just asked the questions.

DH You know what I mean.

MS So, that's settled, then. You're in love with Zoe.

DH No. Yes. I don't know.

MS And do you think that's sensible, trying to form a romantic bond with a colleague?

DH Who said I was trying to do that? You're putting words in my mouth.

MS But, if you were, would it be a sensible thing to do?

DH Dunno. Maybe. Maybe not.

MS Think of what it would actually mean. Think of sharing the same wastepaper bin as your girlfriend at work. Would that be romantic? Think of chatting in bed the same way as you do at the water cooler. Would that be a good thing?

DH I hadn't really thought about it, to be honest. Until now, anyway.

MS And could you really be objective on operations? Could you make life-and-death decisions without bringing personal feelings into it? Would you jeopardise national security for the sake of your hormones?

DH I, I . . .

MS And what would happen if you had a row? Or worse still, broke up? Could you carry on working together? How would you get space if you were still sharing a photocopier? What if she started going out with someone else? Tom, maybe?

DH Oh shut up. Really, shut up.

DH exits, slamming the door.

MS Don't fall in love with anyone else down there, Danny. Malcolm's on the lookout, I've heard.

****Transcript ends****

Psychologist's sessions with Danny Hunter following his neutralisation of Dr Newland on a North Sea ferry

Case ID: M15/71:
Date: 07/01/200

INTERVIEW TRANSCRIPTS WITH APPROVED ANNOTATIONS	**DH** – Danny Hunter **SM** – Sarah Macrory, Deputy Head of Psychology, MI5 rehabilitation centre, Tring

DH So how, er, do you normally do this? Do I talk while you take notes? Do you ask questions? Is it only successful if I break down and cry at the end? That sort of thing?

SM You'd make an excellent psychologist, Danny. No, there are no hard-and-fast rules in this kind of situation. We'll just take it as it comes. You can tell me what you like and withhold what you don't like. And then we'll see how you feel about it all.

DH That sounds good to me.

SM Good. You're in quite a unique situation, you know. Checking yourself into Tring like this. We have to section most of our officers who come here.

DH Thank you . . . I think. So I'm voluntarily mad. Is that what you're saying?

SM laughs.

SM No. I just meant that you're doing the right thing. It was a brave decision for you to ask to see me here.

DH And remind me, Sarah. Why did I make that decision? What am I doing in MI5's psych-tank in the middle of nowhere?

SM I was hoping you'd be able to tell me that.

DH Because I killed a man? Because I assassinated someone in cold blood? Because I'm not coping with being a murderer all that well? Maybe it's got something to do with one of those minor details. What do you reckon?

SM I'm not sure. What do you think?

DH I'm sorry. I know you're trying to help.

Case ID: M15/713
Date: 07/01/2005

SM That's okay. I don't want to turn this into a confrontation.

DH Neither do I. It's just . . . it's just that it's harder than I thought it would be. I thought I'd got closure, you know. Adam Carter told me I'd feel better almost straightaway. And I did. For a bit. But then the nightmares came back, and I can't get any of it out of my mind.

SM That's fine. That's what we're going to try and do today. Get it all out in the open. What I want to do, if it's okay by you, is go through each little detail of the operation. Not the classified stuff, of course, but the personal elements. What you did. How you felt. How others reacted. How does that sound to you?

DH Sounds good.

SM Okay. So, how did you feel when you were first handed this operation?

DH Fine, actually. It seemed like a pretty routine op. Get on a boat, "play scarecrow" to a bad guy and then go home again.

SM And who was this bad guy?

There is a brief pause.

SM (*cont.*) It's all right. I'm level 1 cleared. I wouldn't be able to help people here if I didn't get the full story. Nothing goes beyond these walls.

DH He was a scientist called Newland. A renegade scientist, I suppose. He was researching a plague that could be used in biochemical warfare. We had reason to believe that the Koreans were funding his research . . . with potentially devastating consequences. We were ordered to board this ferry and "explain to him the error of his ways in the strongest possible fashion".

SM We?

DH Yes. Myself and Zoe Reynolds.

SM And what kind of "explanation" were you expected to give?

DH Blackmail. Financial incentives. Threats. The usual. We were also given a briefcase full of paperwork. "Ammunition", Adam called it. It contained photos of his family. That kind of thing. It was meant to be a reminder of what he was putting on the line by continuing his game with the Koreans. Later we discovered that it contained something else as well. We'd only just set sail when we got a phone call from Adam and Harry which changed everything. It had become apparent that Newland was intent on delivering on this trip. All his Swiss accounts had zeroed. The op had suddenly stepped up four gears. We were black-flagged. The whole way from the top.

Essentially, Adam tasked us to kill Newland. "Extreme measures for extreme circumstances", he called it. This was when it became clear what he meant by "ammunition". The briefcase he'd given us had a false bottom. In the base was an array of syringes and insulin. Newland was a diabetic.

SM And you were to give him a lethal injection?

DH Exactly.

SM And how did you feel about this?

DH It was Zoe who took the call. But we were angry. Both of us were angry. This wasn't what we'd been sent to do. I remember Zoe shouting into the phone, "At least have the guts to say it." And Harry did, eventually. We were given a direct assassination order.

SM Was that legal?

DH It was within our rights. Or so Harry said, at least. Newland was a combatant. We were in international waters. But what annoyed me was the fact that we'd been turned into MI5's weapon in this way. Adam started telling us that they'd spoken to Newland lots of times before. They'd tried to dissuade him previously, but all in vain. So why weren't we told this? And why were we sent out into the middle of the North Sea with a mysterious briefcase if this hadn't been their intention all along?

SM You think you were deliberately put into this situation?

DH Perhaps. I don't know. Maybe all that stuff about Swiss bank accounts emptying was rubbish. Maybe it was true. In this job it gets harder every day to distinguish between fact and fiction. It was the duplicity. That's what got me.

SM Was your colleague, Zoe, able to shed any light on this?

DH No. That was the worst thing, really. Zoe had been struck down with this horrible bout of sea-sickness. She just lay on her bunk moaning the whole time. Completely useless.

SM And did you resent her for that?

There is a long pause.

DH Yes, I suppose I did. I remember thinking at the time, I bet she's gone and got herself pregnant by Will. Morning sickness or something stupid like that. I was being all caring, but inside I think I was probably quite pissed off with her.

SM Is there something else here we need to go into?

DH laughs.

DH No, not this time, I think. I've made that mistake with psychologists before. Let's just say I care about her a lot.

SM But on this occasion, she was no help to you at all?

NOTE BOOK

DH No, that's not quite fair. She was supportive and caring given her situation, but the end result was that her illness – whatever the true cause was – meant that I was tasked with the assassination order. I was the junior officer, you see. It should have been her doing this, not me.

SM But you did do it?

DH Yes.

SM How?

DH There was a bar on board the boat. Newland was a heavy drinker. I sat there watching him until most of the bar had cleared, and then I went up and offered him a drink. He was almost completely gone by this stage. I barely needed to slip the sedative into his whisky, but I did it anyway.

DH pauses.

SM Go on, Danny.

DH It sounds so simple when I put it into words like this. Three or four sentences maximum. Newland went back to his room where he passed out. I took a final phone call from Adam to reassure myself. I went to Newland's room and administered a fatal overdose of insulin to his ankle. There you have it. From normal person to murderer in three sentences.

SM But you'd killed before, hadn't you? Surely? This wasn't your first time, was it?

DH It was my first proper time. I had this debate with Zoe. You've killed more than you know, she said, even if I hadn't pulled the

Case ID: M15/713
Date: 07/01/2005

trigger or been in the chain of decisions that led to someone's death.

SM And what do you think she meant by that?

DH I suppose she meant that we have to face up to the consequences of our actions. We run agents. We might not kill people, sure, but we certainly cause deaths. We're in the business of death. It's just this op made me realise what exactly it is I do. I pulled a real trigger. Not a metaphorical one, for once. I became a murderer.

SM But why do you put it like that? Murderer? You were on a state-approved mission to stop a man whose research could have killed millions.

DH But he was still a man, wasn't he? For all that, he was still a human being. He lived, he breathed. He had children. God, I spoke to him in the bar for a good hour before he died. He even made jokes about life insurance . . . that was my cover story: a life insurance salesman. I mean, sure, he was a bad man doing bad things, but if I could talk to him, I could have talked him round. If I could drug him, I could have brought him in. If I could kill him . . .

SM But you could kill him, Danny. You *did* kill him. Isn't that the important thing? You followed orders. You carried out your mission successfully. You completed the op.

DH So I've earned my spurs? Step one in a promising young officer's career: assassination.

SM Maybe.

DH Carry out your first one without blubbing too much and it gets easier every time? Soon you'll be James Bond. Licence to kill, indiscriminately, whenever and wherever the state desires. It's like riding a bike; once you've learned how to do it, you'll never forget . . . Forget, it would be nice to be able to forget.

SM What is it exactly that you can't forget?

Case ID: M15/713
Date: 07/01/200

Case ID: M15/71
Date: 07/01/200

DH Newland's face as he lay there. I suddenly saw myself in his place. I realised the terrifying power we have. The power to create and destroy. To make and break. That's all we do: build up, and knock back down again.

There is a pause. DH laughs.

DH (*cont.*) Shit, listen to me. I've become a third-rate philosopher as well as a third-rate spy.

SM There's nothing third-rate about you, Danny. You did everything you were asked to do. And more.

DH But is that all I am? A means? Or an end in myself? Do they ever justify each other?

SM If the ends are good and the means are legal? Yes.

DH But an eye for an eye? We're going to make the whole world blind.

SM Gandhi?

DH Yes. Sorry. But I remember Tom once saying, "Murder in the name of life must be just about the most stupid thing I've ever heard."

SM He was a combatant, Danny. Newland was a combatant.

DH And I was a soldier?

SM In this instance, yes. Newland was a threat to the country – to the world, even. He didn't care one bit about everyone and everything you stand to protect. His death saved lives – possibly millions of lives. You've saved millions of lives. *You*, Danny. It's really that simple.

DH I suppose it is.

SM So, all that really matters is you, Danny Hunter. How is Danny Hunter going to deal with this?

DH Funny, someone else said that to me as well.

SM Who?

DH Adam. Adam Carter. He's my boss.

Case ID: M15/713
Date: 07/01/2005

SM Yes, of course. I know Adam.

DH Well, he told me how I'd feel afterwards. My legs would go from under me, he said. Then I'd puke. Then I'd cry like a baby. And then, after all that, if I could look at myself in the mirror, I'd be okay.

SM And was he right?

DH Yes. For a bit. But it's never that simple, is it? There's the next day. And then the one after that.

SM And it gets a bit easier over time?

DH Nope, mainly it gets harder, actually. Until today. Today has made things easier. Talking to you like this. No one really makes time for grief, do they? Especially other people's grief. You ask them how they are, how they're coping. You give them a squeeze on the shoulder, a sad, friendly smile over a cup of coffee that implies you understand. But you never really give them time. Time enough, at least. There are always limits on this sort of thing. One week and you're meant to be back at work. One month and it's all forgotten. Forgotten by everyone except you.

SM You don't have to forget, Danny.

DH Don't I?

SM But you do have to move on. You talk as if you've been bereaved. As if you've lost someone.

DH Well, I did. I lost a bit of myself. But there's something else, too. Something I did the morning after.

SM Go on.

DH I told Zoe that her boyfriend had told his brother that she was a spy.

SM And was that true?

DH I thought it was. The brother had tried to sell pictures of her to a national newspaper. But I found out later that Will – the boyfriend – had known nothing about it.

SM So you did nothing wrong, then. You were just trying to protect her.

DH No, it was something else.

SM What?

DH I enjoyed it. I enjoyed seeing her suffer. I enjoyed the fact that she had to split up with Will. It made me feel less bad. Does that make me an awful person?

SM I understand what you're saying.

DH I felt less alone that she was suffering too. Less scared somehow. I cried in the bathroom of our flat. She cried in the living room. One murderer; one dumper. Death and relationships. Together in our self-inflicted grief. Does this make any sense to you? Are these things in any way related?

There is a long pause.

Case ID: M15/713
Date: 07/01/2005

SM "Yet each man kills the thing he loves, by each let this be heard, some do it with a bitter look, some with a flattering word. The coward does it with a kiss, the brave man with a sword."

There is another long pause.

DH I like that. Shakespeare?

SM Oscar Wilde.

DH And what happened to him?

SM He died. Horribly alone and diseased.

DH laughs.

M (*cont.*) But he lived first.

****Transcript ends****

MI5

ANNUAL MEDICAL REPORT

Name:	Danny Hunter		
Date:	1st May 2005	BMI:	23.14

Height:	5'10"	Weight:	11st 7lb

Units of alcohol per week:	25
Cigarettes per week:	none

Blood pressure:	110/60
Resting pulse:	57
Urine:	normal
Chest x-ray:	normal
Exercise ECG:	normal

Danny still drinks too much but he is in excellent shape.

PASSED

Dr Sally Chapman

SECTION X

EYES ONLY FOR LEVEL 1 AND ABOVE

LOG FOR DANNY HUNTER

Date: 8.06.2004
Subject: Flirtatious emails. Danny's email log contains a large number of flirtatious exchanges with Sam.
Outcome: This was referred to Harry Pearce. His note is reproduced below.

Note from Harry Pearce: Don't be ridiculous. As long as they both continue to do their job properly, I see no harm in a little mild diversion.

Date: 4.05.2004
Subject: Alcohol. Danny was required to live a flamboyant lifestyle as an undercover city trader at Bowman Bank. It has come to our attention that he has not entirely given this up. He is drinking far too much.
Outcome: Danny was referred to the in-house doctor who has talked to him about the long-term dangers of alcohol abuse.

Date: 5.03.2004
Subject: Clothes. Danny was loaned an expensive suit by the clothing department to pass as a city trader. This has still not been returned.
Outcome: See Tom Quinn's note below.

Note from Tom Quinn: Leave him alone. It suits him.

(CONTINUED)

SECTION X

EYES ONLY FOR LEVEL 1 AND ABOVE

LOG FOR DANNY HUNTER cont.

Date: 11.12.2002
Subject: Credit ratings. Danny has been using MI5 computers to access and tamper
          with his credit ratings. He has also taken out a large number of credit cards in
          different names — all of which have now reached their limit.
Outcome: This was referred to Harry Pearce. His note is reproduced below.

Note from Harry Pearce: Thank you for passing this on to me. This is just the sort of thing
Section X should be looking out for. Danny's credit cards have been taken away from him
and he has been severely reprimanded. Please return credit ratings to normal after a six-
month grace period. We don't want to leave him open to the threat of blackmail / bribery.

Section X exists
usage, spending
and act as an e

Psychologist session with
Fiona Carter following death of Danny Hunter
while on joint operation

Case ID: MI5/798
Date: 07/07/2005

TRANSCRIPTS WITH APPROVED ANNOTATIONS FROM OBSERVING INDEPENDENT PSYCHOLOGIST	**FC** – Fiona Carter **DJ** – Diane Jewell, Head of Psychology, MI5 rehabilitation centre, Tring

DJ You know why you're here, don't you, Fiona?

FC Of course. The "death chat".

DJ I'm sorry?

FC That's what we call these sessions on the Grid. When we have to talk about a colleague's death with you.

DJ I see.

FC I'm sorry. It's just all so horrible. We all have to come to terms with it in our own way.

DJ That's fine; you don't have to apologise. This is simply standard procedure. When an officer dies on a mission we interview his or her colleagues. And especially the ones who were there with them. It's more about them than it is about you. We like to get the whole picture. How they died, how you felt about it, and so on. Often people find it easier talking to a trained psychologist than their boss. And then we add it to their file before closing it.

FC I understand.

DJ So, tell me, you were with Danny when he was killed?

FC Yes, I was with him the entire day.

DJ And what happened?

FC We'd been assigned to work together. I love working with Danny. He's funny, he's kind and he's very, very good at his job . . . I'm sorry. I just can't get used to talking about him in the past tense.

Case ID: MI5/798
Date: 07/07/2005

DJ That's okay. Carry on.

FC So, we were rooting around in this safehouse when we were suddenly captured. We were tied up, bundled into a van and driven somewhere else. They made me read a statement in front of a video camera. The Prime Minister was giving a speech later that evening. The statement demanded that he use the speech to announce the withdrawal of troops from Iraq. Otherwise Danny and I would be burned alive.

DJ And how did Danny react to this?

FC He was calm. They held a knife to his throat so that I'd read out the statement properly, but he never panicked. I was the senior officer so he was playing second fiddle most of the time, I suppose. But he was so calm the entire time. I know we're trained to be like that, but he really appeared to apply it. On the inside as well as the outside.

DJ How did his calmness affect you?

FC I found it soothing. Later, it was invaluable. The terrorist said that a sniper was targeting my son, Wes, outside his school. He would be shot if I didn't call Adam. I said to the terrorist, "You're offering me a choice between my son and my husband?". I was about to tell him to go to hell when Danny interrupted. "Do it," he said. "Adam would understand." I think Danny saved my life by saying that.

DJ How do you mean?

FC This guy was a psychopath. If I'd said what I was about to say, I think he would have shot me there and then. Out of pure, uncontrollable rage. I owed him my life for that.

DJ But you almost saved Danny's life later, didn't you?

FC Yes, I suppose, but it was a meaningless gesture. I used the brooch that Adam gave me for my birthday to pick our handcuffs. But it was Danny who attacked the guard. Killed the guard, in fact. He punched his ribs into his heart. And then it was me who was caught as we ran outside. I just couldn't run as fast as Danny. I was caught and they held a gun to my head. Danny had to come back. He was that kind of person. He refused to look away; he was never one to look away. I feel so guilty.

DJ You didn't kill him, Fiona.

FC Didn't I? Then who did?

DJ The terrorist. The one who actually shot him.

FC He might have pulled the trigger, but if I hadn't been caught, Danny wouldn't have died. If they hadn't phoned up Adam, Danny wouldn't have died. If Adam hadn't hesitated, Danny might not have died.

DJ I don't understand. What did Adam have to do with this?

FC Our captors were angry that we'd tried to escape. And they were livid that we'd killed a guard.

DJ But who killed the guard?

Case ID: M15/798
Date: 07/07/2005

FC Danny. But that's not the point. Listen, they were angry that we'd tried to escape. That was my fault. We were caught – also my fault. And they wanted to kill one of us in revenge. Adam was told to choose on the phone. It was an impossible situation. He flunked it. How could he say anything? How could he condemn a colleague to death with one word?

DJ So he said nothing?

FC He said nothing. And then Danny started speaking. From nowhere. His voice cut through the air. Fine, noble words of courage and sacrifice. "You will never win," he told them. "If I weren't chained to this chair, I'd be right up in your face saying, 'Fuck you, you death-worshipping fascist'." I remember it so clearly. "Acts of hatred also produce acts of love," he said. He knew one of us was going to die. And he chose to die. He opened his mouth and chose to sacrifice himself.

DJ Did you try and stop him?

FC Of course I did. I begged him not to do it, but his mind was made up. And then they shot him. Just like that. Cold blood. And they spun my chair around to make me look at him. Lying there. Dead, on a cold floor.

FC cries.

FC (*cont.*) There, my dead colleague. My dead friend. It could have been me. It should have been me. He was so young. So bloody young.

DJ He did a beautiful thing, Fiona. You remember the verse in the Bible? "Greater love hath no man than this, that a man lay down his life for his friends." And not just your life. Adam's life. Wes's life. What would they be without you?

FC But what about Danny's life? What about the wife he never met? The children he'll never have?

DJ What's happened has happened, Fiona.

There is a long pause.

DJ (*cont.*) Earn it, Fiona. That's all I ask of you. That's all Danny would have asked of you.

FC I'll try.

****Transcript ends****

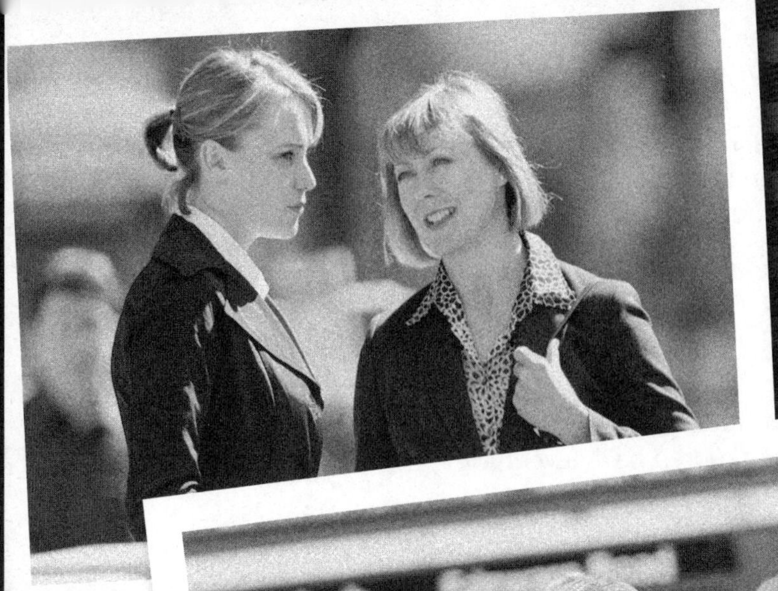

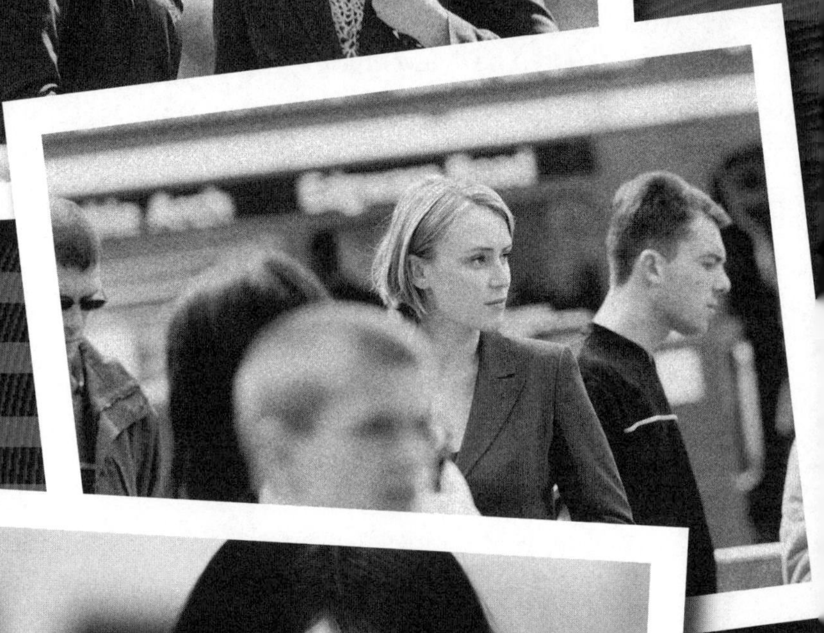

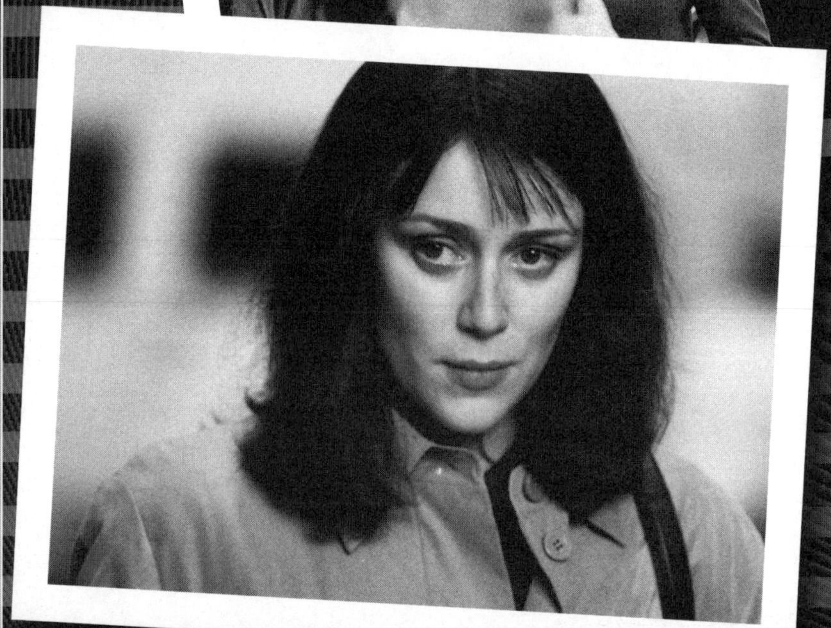

[Zoe Reynolds]

Private and Confidential

Name: Zoe Reynolds
Position: Intelligence Officer
D.O.B: 01.02.1975
Hair: Blonde
Eyes: Blue
Height: 5'7
Marital status: Unknown
Dependants: None
Blood type: O, Rh positive

Zoe came to MI5 straight from university and she was a valuable member of the team – both as a desk officer and in the field.

An error of judgement in an undercover operation cost Zoe her career.

She is no longer employed by MI5. She now lives under an alias abroad, although the public believes she remains in prison in the UK.

Major operations include:

- Infiltration of Turkish mafia. Neutralisation of leader, Emre Celenk
- Befriending the girlfriend of the leader of Colombian Chala Cartel
- Undercover teacher shadowing Gordon Blakeney and pupil Noah Gleeson

FILE CLOSED

MI5
Application Form

Medical
Do you have any conditions – either physical or psychological – which might affect your employment?

```
None
```

Father's name, address and occupation

```
John Reynolds
Professor of History
Keble College, Oxford
14 Church Walk, Oxford
```

Mother's name, maiden name, address and occupation

```
Sarah Reynolds (nee Dalzell)
Newspaper journalist
14 Church Walk, Oxford
```

Brothers / Sisters (with names and D.O.B.)

```
Lucy - 07.5.1971
James - 18.3.1973
```

Secondary Schools / Colleges
Dates : Names : Town

```
1986-1993 : Dibbledon High School :
Newcastle
```

GCSEs or equivalents

```
4 A* (English Language, English
Literature, French, Spanish), 6As
(History, Geography, Latin, Biology,
Art, Drama), 1D (Physics)
```

A levels and AS levels or equivalents

```
English - A
Latin - A
Art - A
General Studies - A
```

Surname

```
Reynolds
```

Forenames

```
Zoe Jane
```

Date of Birth

```
01.02.1975
```

Place of birth

```
Newcastle
```

Nationality at birth

```
British
```

Permanent Address

```
St. Hilda's College,
Oxford University
```

Current occupation

```
Student
```

Date of availability for employment

```
June - from
graduation
```

Do you hold a full, clean driving licence?

```
Yes
```

Gap Year
How did you spend any break during your education?

N/A

University or Further Education

St. Hilda's College, Oxford University - 1993-1996

B.A. (Hons) in English - pending

First - predicted

Awards
Please give details of any other awards (e.g. music)

Grade 7 flute

Junior Gold Medal for Creative Writing

School drama prize

EMPLOYMENT

Dates	Employer	Position
Summer 1993	Oxford school for the disabled	Teacher

Have you served in HM Forces (including Reserves)?

N/A

Do you have applications pending for other jobs?

I've been offered a job on the Home Office Fast Stream but this is my first choice. If I'm unsuccessful, I'll take the Home Office and reapply next year.

PERSONAL QUALITIES AND SKILLS

SUMMARY
Provide a pen-portrait of your life to date

I was born in Newcastle where my father was a university professor. He moved to Oxford at the same time as me.

I enjoy sport and socialising and I have travelled widely. I have a range of friends from different backgrounds. I am quite hard-working and driven but I enjoy a wide range of other pursuits. My drama, in particular, takes up a large amount of my time.

MOTIVATION

Why do you think you would be suited to a career in MI5?

I like the idea of a career that combines public service with excitement. My English degree has taught me to write and research coherently and I am also able to see things from other people's point of view.

I also feel that I'm patriotic in the best sense of the word. I believe our country is worth fighting for; our ideals worth defending; our people worth protecting.

POLITICAL CURIOSITY

Give three political topics (historical or current) which interest you

- Trade Union unrest
- 1917 Soviet revolution
- Cold War

ADAPTABILITY

Give an example of a time when you had to adapt to unexpected circumstances

After A-levels I went inter-railing through Europe. A friend and I travelled down through France and Spain – to Morocco.

However, we enjoyed ourselves so much there that I completely lost track of time. One day I looked at my ticket and saw it expired in three hours' time. I had no money left either.

I managed to give myself an extra 24 hours by forging the last digit of the expiry date. This only got me as far as Cordoba. Thereafter, I bluffed, charmed and flirted my way back to the UK. I spent most of France hidden behind my backpack on a luggage rack. When I got to Calais, I managed to hide in someone's boot as they drove onto the car ferry.

My parents never asked why or how I got home three days late.

RESPONSIBILITY

What positions of responsibility have you held – at school, university or otherwise?

School – House captain; Captain of school hockey team (undefeated)

University – Head of Oxford Amateur Dramatics Association

FOREIGN LANGUAGES

Please indicate level of competence

French – good

Italian – basic

OTHER INTERESTS

```
Drama - most evenings
Socialising - most evenings
Teaching - I used to help out in a local school for the
disabled
```

TRAVEL

Give details of all foreign travel undertaken in the last 10 years, including reason for travel

```
Tourism - France, Spain, Morocco, Estonia, Latvia, Peru,
Ecuador, Bolivia
```

EQUAL OPPORTUNITIES

This information is not used as part of our selection procedures

Gender	Ethnic origin	Disabilities
Male (Female)	White British	None

REFEREES

Please give details of three referees. One of these should be a contemporary who knows you well

```
1. Emma Forbes, Head of English, Dibbledon High School
2. Professor John Stein, Master, St. Hilda's College, Oxford
3. Sarah Gough, university friend
```

Signature

Zoe Reynolds

Date

9th February 1996

PROCEED TO INTERVIEW

.fa|vii.4

Dibbledon High School

REFERENCE: Zoe Reynolds

To Whom It May Concern

I have been asked to provide a reference for Zoe Reynolds' time at school. I do so gladly.

I taught Zoe English for seven years at a girls' school near Newcastle and she has more than exceeded her early promise. She has always shown maturity beyond her years, getting to grips with difficult Chaucer and Anglo-Saxon texts well before the rest of her peer group. She has a natural affinity with the written word, devouring everything from Salman Rushdie to John Le Carré (which, on several occasions, I caught her reading under the desk).

Although she writes concise and elegant literary criticisms, it is her creative writing that really stood out for me. Her ability to imagine herself in someone else's shoes, to assume a persona, to find their true voice – from whatever background – was the most remarkable I ever encountered in ten years as Head of English.

This natural empathy was mirrored outside the classroom where Zoe was a hugely popular pupil – with boys as well as girls, I might add! She also displayed promising leadership qualities as captain of an undefeated hockey team and as house captain. She was also an enthusiastic member of the mixed lacrosse team when we joined up with the local boys' school – perhaps not for purely sporting reasons.

Zoe's sense of fun belies a razor-sharp natural intellect and I believe she would be a valuable asset to any civil service department. Her challenge will be to find something that tests her intellectually while still providing an outlet for her undoubted people skills.

I always wondered whether she might become a teacher. She has a great way with children, and I can imagine few things more enjoyable than working with her myself. I think her time at Oxford reading English might have sapped her enthusiasm for this, however.

E Forbes

EMMA FORBES   Head of English

SECURITY CLEARANCE & BACKGROUND CHECKS

Zoe Reynolds

I was tasked with carrying out routine background checks into Zoe Reynolds' family and friends, as well as standard fact-checking of her application details.

On this latter point, I found no discrepancies at all. I was, however, slightly concerned by Zoe's D in GCSE Physics. I followed this up further and it appears she had a falling-out with her science teacher in 1988 and was stuck with him for the next three years. Otherwise her academic and extracurricular records are outstanding. An Oxford student told me she was a particularly effective Cordelia in *King Lear*.

Zoe's parents are both remarkably strong-minded. I was initially somewhat concerned by some of the work of her father — Professor John Reynolds. He has earned a reputation as a maverick Marxist historian with a specialist interest in the Bolshevik revolutions. He is also a vociferous member of the Senior Common Room and an outspoken critic of the University's admission procedures in the University Senate.

There is, however, nothing subversive as such in his background. In any case, he has shown a significant leaning towards a more revisionist historiography in his approach to Soviet study post *perestroika* and *glasnost*.

Zoe's mother will no doubt be familiar to you through her outspoken national newspaper column. This caused me and my team some alarm. Could we have the daughter of a journalist — in particular, Sarah Reynolds' daughter — working for MI5? However, months of in-depth research have convinced me that Mrs Reynolds' strident journalese is a carefully constructed public persona. She is known to be fiercely loyal to her family and friends, and is as kind in private as she is objectionable in public. I recommend a quiet word in her ear about her daughter's future, but I do not think she represents a blocking factor in her own right.

Zoe's own private life is busy but unremarkable in terms of potential compromise. Friends of both sexes speak warmly of her. Her elder sister, Lucy, is a teacher and a steadying hand on any excesses.

Dirk Muir, HR Security
8th June 1996

TRAINING ASSESSMENT
Zoe Reynolds, 10th September 1996

SCORES

Practical

Surveillance	2.5
Counter-surveillance	2.5
Physical endurance	2.5
Shooting	2
Driving	1.1
Technical	3.1
Average	2.28

Intellectual

Linguistic	4.8
Decision-making	4.8
Research	4.8
Average	4.8

Other core competencies

Calm under pressure	2
Leadership	2.1
Team work	3.2
Communication	4.8
General attitude	4.8
Average	3.38

Overall average   **3.21**

On a sliding scale of 1 to 5 where
1 is poor, 5 is outstanding and 2.5 is
average for a new recruit

Zoe put in a promising – if not spectacular – performance during her
training. I was particularly impressed by her intellect as well as her
emotional intelligence in assuming roles and understanding other people.

She scored slightly below average on the practical tests but I believe these
will improve with time. Her driving, in particular, was appalling. I'm still not
sure how she managed to get her licence in the first place.

Zoe panicked unexpectedly in one of the tests which is why I was forced
to mark her down in her 'calm under pressure'. However, I still think she
would make an excellent operative – perhaps on a desk until she gains a
little confidence before heading out into the field.

Caroline Moyne

Caroline Moyne, Head of recruit training, MI5

Honey-trap training for new recruits

Presentation by Zoe Reynolds

Speaking notes

Introduction by AN Other Officer

One of the worst jokes about spying – which I'm afraid you'll have to get used to – is that, along with prostitution, it's the oldest profession in the world. An even worse joke is that there is little to distinguish between the two. And, on that note, here's Zoe Reynolds to talk to you about honey-traps.

ZR's introduction

Thank you for that introduction. I think the biggest difference between prostitutes and MI5 officers is that they get paid much better than we do. They work better hours, too.

More seriously, I want to talk to you today about how MI5 officers can use their sexuality to good effect in the field. Now, I know this might sound naff and silly to you. You're probably sitting there imagining Pussy Galore tempting James Bond into bed with vast quantities of champagne and oysters, giggling "Oh James" as he produces another atrocious pun. And I admit the term honey-trap doesn't help that much either.

But I can promise you that sexuality forms a vital part of day-to-day intelligence gathering. So I suggest we all have a good snigger about it now and get it out of our systems, because in the field, honey-traps get much closer to their targets than is usual. This puts you at huge risk. It's a very serious business.

Today I'm going to take you through why it works, and how it works. Later, you'll be pleased to hear, we'll be doing a spot of practical role-play with different flirting scenarios.

Human failings

1 Every person has a vice, a human failing, an Achilles heel. It's our job to find out what that is and use it to our advantage. Sometimes, it's as simple as money. Some people I've met would sell their own mothers for money. Other times, it's more complex, like ambition or ego or power or family.

2 Sex, of course, is more powerful than all of these put together. Everyone – from the most vicious gang chief to the lowliest courier – has longings. Almost everyone has a basic human desire to be loved. The advantage of our line of work is that the bigger the ego, the bigger these longings are likely to be. Big egos are also less likely to suspect something is up. Arrogant men – as I'm sure the girls here will know – *expect* to be found attractive, whatever the overwhelming evidence to the contrary.

3 I insert a deliberate note of sexism here as it's more usual for women to be deployed as honey-traps than men – who are more liable to sexual temptations. This is as true of shy men as it is of more arrogant types – sometimes more so. Mordecai Vanunu, a lonely scientist who attempted to expose Israel's nuclear programme, was lured from London by an attractive Mossad agent.

4 That's not to say that male officers can't use their charms in the field. Men can be used as honey-traps along similar lines. And you should also be able to spot similar techniques being used on you – Mata Hari or not.

5 In the field, we use sex – or the promise of sex – in three principal ways. The first is to elicit information; the second is to exert a level of control over our target; the third is to frame and blackmail. I'll now go through each of these in turn.

Elicit information

1 You might have seen those old posters from the Second World War with the chilling warning: "Careless talk costs lives". Yet in our line of work our enemies' careless talk also saves a lot of lives – our lives. Your job is to make someone talk as carelessly as possible. Pillow talk can be extremely informative. You just have to make sure the whispered sweet nothings are really sweet somethings.

2 How do you do this? Clearly, no one is going to talk to you unless they feel you can be trusted. You're playing the long-game with this one, and you also have to show yourself to be interested without being suspiciously over-enthusiastic.

3 I've done this two ways in my career. One is to play the naive bimbo. Powerful men enjoy explaining things, and they especially enjoy showing off if they think you don't really understand what's going on. The other tactic is to play a highly intelligent femme

fatale. Research your subject thoroughly. Pretend you're bored with a humdrum, routine existence. Feign excitement with risk and danger. Your target will believe you are swept up in the glamour and power of his work, and you may well become a trusted confidante as a result.

4   Introductions are everything with either of these approaches. You can't just pop up out of the blue and expect to be taken seriously. Come on too strong at first and you'll come under suspicion as a spy. Or, perhaps worse, a prostitute. Troublesome men might thrive on trouble, but they'll have plenty of acolytes sent to check your back-story.

5   The best – and the most common – method of engineering a meeting is to research the target's interests. Do they like horse-racing? Casinos? Football? Opera? There are few things a man finds more attractive than a woman who shares his passion. He is also less likely to be suspicious if you're talking about a neutral, non-contentious subject such as music. Later – much later – once you've established your credentials, you can move on to take an interest in his work.

6   Another, higher-risk strategy to effect a first meeting is the damsel-in-distress scenario. This can be as simple as a lost coat in a cloakroom or an intentional stumble as you get off a bus. Men love to feel helpful and wanted. A more sophisticated approach might involve

a team of officers – for example, a staged mugging in which the target will chase the "muggers" away, or a public argument with a brutal partner. This will also give your target the chance to offer a further meeting, and it gives you the opportunity to ask to meet them again to thank them. You always have to be thinking of your next step in this game.

7   More than ever you'll also need to know your aliases inside out, especially if you end up spending a lot of time with your target. Keeping up a cover story is much harder 24/7 when you can't return your assumed identity to its box in Thames House at the end of the day.

8   Ultimately, though, it's often worth the trouble. There's a certain type of person who believes their achievements – however dubious these may be – are only vindicated through constant repetition. Earn your target's trust and affection, flatter their ego and you'll find yourself privy to more valuable information than would ever be obtainable through other methods. And then you can betray them.

Exert control

1   Anyone who's been in a relationship will know that a couple is rarely completely balanced. There is normally one person who works harder to gain and retain the affection of the other. And there is normally one person who would cope better if it suddenly ended. The term 'mutual break-up' is rarely accurate.

2   As a honey-trap, your job is to make sure that it's you wearing the trousers. You have to make them do what you want them to do. Ideally, they'll be so smitten that they'll think they're doing this voluntarily.

3   This is where the term "playing hard-to-get" comes in. You've probably read those dating rules that glossy magazines churn out twice a year: wait two days before texting him back; don't sleep with him until the fifth date; flirt with his dad etc. etc.

4   The same is true in the field. Withhold your affections and you'll have your target wound around your little finger. There's nothing a powerful person enjoys more than a challenge. You have to set up an expert chase – thrilling for them, but useful for the service's ends.

5   Let's have a little look now at those ends, as well as the means to get to those ends.

6   One thing MI5 is very good at is using other people to do its dirty work. We are a government department and we need to keep our hands clean. Many of our operations have to be deniable, which means that our operatives have to be as well. Honey-traps can turn their targets into weapons. And there is nothing more deniable than a perceived *crime passionel*.

Honey-

ADD
PHOTOGRAPH
TO FILE

7   As I've already mentioned, this can be done with the promise of future intimacy. You can also harness someone's sexual jealousy to your own ends. A traditional technique is for a honey-trap to befriend a low-ranking and easily accessible member of an opposition cell and then flirt wildly with their boss. In extreme cases this has led to the third-party assassination of a high-ranking target it would have been impossible to approach in any other way. The murder can then be covered-up as internecine criminal politics.

Frame and blackmail

1   The two methods I've just discussed are long-term covert operations. An even more common use of a honey-trap is a short-term, one-off liaison with effective, long-term consequences. To your target, your aim is to be the one-night-stand from hell.

2   With a married target, evidence of sexual infidelity can be used as an effective blackmail technique to make them do what you want them to. Wives don't take kindly to explicit photos of their husband and another woman arriving anonymously on their doorstep one morning. And neither do husbands.

3   This kind of operation depends as much on the technical crew as it does on you. Often they'll bug a hotel suite instead of a house as it's easier to watch from a neighbouring room. All you really have to do is make sure the cameras get a convincing shot of your target's face. There are few things more frustrating than having to go through the whole charade again because the target was facing the wrong way the whole time.

4   In reality, though, MI5 officers are rarely called upon to carry out simple blackmail operations of this kind. The service has a string of prostitutes it can use for what we sometimes call kiss-and-

don't-tell procedures. Your role is more likely to be supervisory than participatory.

5   A more complex operation that does require personal input from a MI5 officer is using sex to frame a target – particularly on rape charges. In a recent example, one of our officers met a well-known target at a public party. Hundreds of witnesses saw them talking, drinking and flirting together. A few also saw them leave the party together. At that point the officer received a bogus important phone call, made her excuses and left.

6   The back-up team's work could then begin in earnest. Taking DNA samples from the target's cocktail glass and discarded crumbs of party food, they were able to put together a rape charge that would have held up in court. The officer was made-up by our cosmetics department to look as if she had been the victim of a vicious sexual assault. A full video "confession" was taped and shown to the target. Had he not complied with our demands we would have had sufficient "evidence" to send him to jail for a number of years.

Conclusions

1   I am aware that some of what I've said today might sound alarming, but sadly we are denied the luxury of moral absolutes in our line of work. I should emphasise that officers are rarely deployed as honey-traps. And, when we are, it is normally possible to maintain the relationship within parameters that are acceptable to everyone involved. Ultimately, it's the officer's personal call how far you take things sexually. It all depends on what it is you're trying to achieve.

2   Targets are more forthcoming when they still have something to gain from a honey-trap. Again, the old cliché, "treat them mean, keep them keen" enjoys a cross-over from the world of glossy magazines to the intelligence community. Often, it is easier to turn an existing lover against the target than to insert an undercover replacement to take her place.

3 Putting officers into vulnerable situations with dangerous, exciting men also carries its own risk. I know of one young agent who "went native" after genuinely falling in love with her target. The glamour of international narcotics was rather more exciting to her than Thames House, it would seem. It took us five years to turn her back.

Role plays

1 And now, onto the fun stuff. In your groups I'd like you to split into pairs of the opposite sex and sit together at the tables dotted around the room. I don't know if you've ever done speed-dating. Well, today, we're going to do speed-honey-trapping. I want the girls to flirt their way into the boys' confidences. And I want the boys to be as stubborn as possible. You have three minutes before moving on to the next table. We'll compare notes afterwards.

2 This evening, we're going to test what we've learned in a more practical situation. Staying in your teams of two, you'll be assigned to various bars around London. I'll give you more details on this later.

MI5 trainer's note

Following the prosecution of Officer X on charges of Conspiracy to Murder, the guidelines given in point two – "Exert control" – of Zoe Reynolds' training are currently under revision. It is believed that stricter parameters are needed to distinguish between implication and demand in an officer's behaviour. This has particular relevance to the use of sexual jealousy to encourage a target to commit an unlawful act.

Case ID: MI5/392

Date: 04/04/2004

Assessment of Zoe Reynolds by Miranda Saunders, in-house psychologist

ANNOTATED TRANSCRIPTS	ZR – Zoe Reynolds MS – Miranda Saunders

I was tasked by the DG to conduct a psychological assessment of the key players in Section D. That this had to take place on the same day as the visit of the American President was highly inconvenient to me.

Although I had a clipboard and took occasional notes, the officers were unaware that I was, in fact, recording them as well. These are the transcripts from my session with Zoe Reynolds.

Accompanying note from Tom Quinn

Miranda Saunders was fired the day after producing these assessments. I am particularly disappointed that she played valued team members off against each other in this way. A glance at Danny Hunter's file reveals the extent to which he was misrepresented during this interview.

I see no need to take any disciplinary action against Zoe in the light of her comments. She made her remarks under a stressful position and on the understanding of confidentiality.

MS Hello Zoe.

ZR Hello.

There is a long silence.

ZR (*cont.*) Is that it? Can I go now?

MS No. Sit down, Zoe. Can I call you Zoe, by the way?

ZR You may.

There is another long silence.

MS Is there anything you want to tell me? Anything at all?

ZR No. Nothing at all. I'm very happy.

MS Absolutely nothing at all?

There is another shorter silence.

MS (*cont.*) Some of your colleagues were very forthcoming . . . oh yes. Some of them were very forthcoming indeed.

ZR Really.

MS Danny Hunter, for example. He had to lot to say for himself. A lot to say for himself about you, in particular.

ZR Well. That's very interesting.

MS It *was* very interesting. Very interesting, indeed.

ZR So, what did he say, then?

MS I'm not sure I should tell you.

ZR Okay, then. Thank you, Miranda. This has all been very instructive.

MS Of course, I could tell you some of what he said.

ZR The edited highlights?

MS If you like. Let's see: where are my notes? Danny Hunter, Danny Hunter. Yes, here we are. Danny's views on the Grid canteen, Danny on his shopping habits, Danny on Tom, Danny on Zoe. Got it. Ready?

Case ID: M
Date: 04/ 0

ZR Yes. For God's sake.

MS "Danny expressed a number of misgivings about workin
alongside Zoe Reynolds. These included the trivial – the wa
she uses her computer monitor as a mirror to apply her make
up at the end of the day, her inability to leave a teabag for more
than a minute to stew, her unpunctuality at the beginning of
the day and her continual confusion between the role of his
desk drawers and the office stationery cupboard."

ZR The trivial little bastard. I bet you didn't ask him the last time
he signed out staples of his own, did you?

MS There's some more serious stuff here, too. He's also accused
you of being moody in the office, prone to bursts of temper
and indiscriminate flirting. Oh yes, and a stickler for the rules,
"over and beyond any usual degree of common sense".

ZR Finished?

MS Not quite. He's also complained about your home life.

ZR Home life? As if this job lets us spend any time there at all.
We're not a bloody married couple, Miranda.

MS "When asked about living together with Zoe, Danny replied
that there were both advantages and disadvantages to
sharing with a fellow intelligence officer. Advantages included
her general cleanliness and her washing-up abilities. He also
mentioned that male friends were impressed that he lived
with 'a fit bird'."

ZR snorts derisively.

MS (cont.) "On the downside, Danny said that living with Zoe
cramped his style with other girls."

Case ID: M15/392
Date: 04/04/2004

ZR snorts again, louder this time.

ZR What, his mum?

MS "There was also a particularly silly game the two of them played which involved gaining undetected access to each other's rooms. This started out as a bit of fun with trip-wires across the doors and so on. Danny, however, felt it went too far when Zoe swapped his vodka for tea one day . . ."

ZR Stop. That's enough. You were only meant to give me the edited highlights.

MS So, now that you've heard that, is there anything you'd like to tell me? Anything at all?

ZR I should bloody well think so.

MS Spill it all out, Zoe.

ZR Where do I start?

MS How about with Danny?

ZR Danny? He's vain and conceited. He thinks he knows everything. And he has serious problems keeping his spending under control. He gets annoyed by me applying my make-up in my monitor reflection? Ha! You should see how long he spends in the bathroom in the morning. What takes him so long in there?

MS That's great, Zoe. Really great. And Tom? What do you think of him?

Case ID: M15|392
Date: 04|04|2004

ZR Hang on. You think I've finished on Danny yet? I haven't even started. The contents of his bathroom cabinet cost more than my entire wardrobe put together. And don't even talk to me about housework. He swings between unbearable anality and complete slobbery. Nightmare.

There is a brief pause.

ZR (*cont.*) Come on, Miranda. I want you to get this all down.

MS Okay, Zoe, okay. You were just about to start on Tom?

ZR Ah yes, our dear emotionally stunted leader. The enigmatic, brooding, mysterious one. He who shall be obeyed.

MS Anything else you'd like to get off your chest?

ZR Oh no, nothing else. The others are all okay, really. Harry: bald fat chauvinist. Sam: giggly Scot who somehow fancies Danny. Ruth: almost certainly in love with Harry from day one. Malcolm and Colin: in love with their gigabytes, and possibly each other. We're a merry little band of loners, misfits and weirdos.

MS What about you, Zoe? Are you in love with anyone?

ZR What?

MS Are you in love with anyone?

ZR No. Well, there was an Italian banker I saw for a while. Anyway, this isn't really any of your business. It all turned out badly. Tom threw a huge strop about it.

MS So, what do you love? What keeps you going?

ZR Honestly? My job. Which is why I'll keep on doing it. Despite all its uncertainties. Despite the fact that I sometimes long for a more normal life. Despite the fact that I have to hide when I see university friends I recognise on the bus. Despite the fact that I've spent twenty minutes sounding off to you about the people I work with. I love them all, really. More than most people in most normal jobs, in fact.

MS Thanks, Zoe.

ZR With the possible exception of you.

There is a brief pause.

ZR (*cont.*) So now, if you'll excuse me, I'll get to it and leave you to your mind-games and your clipboards.

ZR leaves.

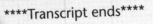

****Transcript ends****

MI5 HUMAN RESOURCES – S24 FORM

Permission for socialisation   21 November 2004

Introduction

MI5 officers are encouraged to form relationships – both platonic and sexual – within the service. No one can understand the job you do in the same way as your colleagues.

However, we do understand that this will not always be the case. In return, we ask you to understand our duty to perform extensive background checks on outsiders with whom you develop close relationships. When you joined MI5 we checked your family, your friends and your relationships. The same must be true of any serious, new liaisons.

Please answer these questions fully and accurately.

1   What is your name and department?

Zoe Reynolds, Counter Terrorism Department, Section D

2   What is the full name of person you wish to socialise with?

William Rhodri North

3   What is his/her profession?

Photographer for Agence France

4   How did you meet?

Danny Hunter and I were performing a routine surveillance operation at a council block in North London. I saw Will taking photos and confiscated his camera. We got on well when I returned it to him later and things developed from there.

5   Does he/she know the nature of your work?

Yes. The first thing he said to me was, "Are you MI5 or MI6?" However, I took this as a sign of his intelligence, not his indiscretion.

6   What is his/her nationality? Do you have any reason to suspect he/she might be involved in terrorist activity?

Welsh. No suspicions.

7   What do you know about his/her family?

I believe his father is a university lecturer in Swansea and his mother is a housewife, but I haven't yet met either parent. He has one brother who is between jobs.

8   What is his/her home address? MI5 may have to perform additional checks at their place of residence. We will, of course, exercise utmost discretion.

9b Bentley Road, Shepherd's Bush, W12

9   What attracts you to this person?

He is charming, funny and very good at his job. And he helps put mine in perspective. I think there's a definite future in this one.

MI5 HR assessment

We have corroborated the details given by Zoe Reynolds with our own checks. William North's mother is actually a primary school teacher, not a housewife. Otherwise, the facts match up.

A residence check was performed at Mr North's London house at 22.00 hours on December 4 when the couple were out celebrating Mr North's birthday. He lives alone and there was no sign of any untoward interests.

Further background checks have revealed nothing more suspicious than 15 parking fines. We can attribute this to the nomadic nature of his job as a photographer. Conversations with Mr North's friends reveal him to be a happy, outgoing character. He has had a string of ex-girlfriends despite his short stature but appears to have been tamed by this one.

Our only cause for concern is Mr North's unemployed brother, Andy. He has an extremely poor credit rating, as well as past history of trouble with the police and debt collectors. Mild caution should be exercised in this area. Otherwise, we have no problems in approving this S24.

APPROVED

National Review

£0.80 • Voted Best Broadsheet Newspaper of 2004

8th April 2005

TEN YEARS FOR OFFICER X

THE trial of the female MI5 officer – known only as Officer X – came to a close at the Old Bailey yesterday after the jury returned a unanimous guilty verdict on two charges of conspiracy to murder and involuntary manslaughter by an unlawful act. Officer X was sentenced to ten years' imprisonment.

During the course of the three-week trial it emerged that the convicted intelligence officer – working under the assumed name of Sophie Newman – infiltrated a Turkish arms-trading cell and befriended one of its junior members, Sevilin Ozal.

Ozal was then used by Officer X to gain access to the mafia group's ringleader, Emre Celenk. Exploiting his sexual jealousy, the attractive young intelligence officer turned Ozal into MI5's weapon, encouraging him into assassinating Celenk. An undercover police officer – Detective Superintendent Mark Loughton – was also killed in the crossfire.

Prosecuting counsel Hillary Watt QC tore shreds out of the MI5 officer in court. "I think your regard for the truth is on a par with your regard for human life," she said in a vicious summing-up. The jury, which took only an hour to reach its unanimous verdict, appears to have agreed with her.

Speaking outside the court the police officer's tearful widow, Sally Loughton, said, "I am happy that justice has been done for Mark. This verdict shows that no one, and no institution, lies outside the law."

The security services declined to comment yesterday.

A POLITICAL SHOW TRIAL?

THE verdict announced in Court 2 of the Old Bailey will be welcome news for many. The family of murdered police officer DS Loughton certainly feels that justice has been done. The Metropolitan Police Service is also pleased that the death of one of its ablest undercover operatives has not been subjected to the kind of whitewash often associated with comparable official inquiries.

In the corridors of Whitehall, too, there has been much self-congratulatory clinking of glasses that the working practices of MI5 have undergone thorough scrutiny. A sense that the security services have been operating out of control – over and beyond their official remits – has finally been reined in. They have been administered a very public slap on the wrist.

In these unique circumstances, however, this newspaper believes we should be asking ourselves more probing questions. What were the true motives of the government in pursuing this prosecution? Did it have anything to do with a forthcoming general election? Was it any way viewed as an opportunity to polish their rusty liberal credentials?

"Brave police officers versus shady spooks – which side do you think we'd be on?" read the leaked memo from the office of the Attorney General last week. But why is the government using language like this? Why are there sides within a side when we are all fighting for the same cause?

The security services have come under a sustained barrage of criticism in the last few years. Some of it has been justified. They have made mistakes. They have omitted to do the things they are supposed to do. And their operations have sometimes spilled over into areas that lie beyond their jurisdiction.

But it is very rare that MI5 and MI6 receive praise for their efforts to protect the country. We only hear about their very public failures; never their private – and numerous – successes.

Soldiers who are sent abroad to fight foreign, unnecessary wars are labelled "brave". Policemen who patrol our streets at home are brave. Doctors are brave. Ambulance men are brave. Yet spooks – is there something in the name itself? – are shady. It should not be forgotten: if they creep around in the dark, it is because they have to. Because their enemies do. We should question their methods. We hope they do so, too. But we should not question their motives.

UNRESOLVED issues also remain in the case of Officer X herself. To what extent was she following orders? How is her case any different from soldiers who have killed in battle? And does she really deserve ten years' imprisonment – more than most rapists – for doing her job? If she overstepped the line – and who's to say that this country isn't a better place without the likes of Emre Celenk? – then she did so in what must have been a terrifying, undercover situation.

The death of DS Loughton, while highly regrettable, cannot, in the view of this newspaper, be blamed directly on Officer X, any more than a fighter pilot dropping a bomb on an Iraqi military target can be court martialled for collateral damage. The fact that the security services were unaware of the police officer's undercover activities speaks volumes about the lack of communication between different government departments. To borrow another military metaphor, this is the fault of the generals, not the foot soldiers.

As ever, more questions remain than there are answers.

[MEDIA]

EMRE CELENK – "THE TURKISH DELIGHT"

Murdered Turkish criminal mastermind Emre Celenk stood at the head of a 400-strong North London organisation which trafficked drugs, weapons and prostitutes into the country.

However, the Turkish mafia was not always this powerful. At the outset few of their activities were strictly speaking of their criminal, simply a small group of ex-pats looking out for one another in an alien country. Turks in positions of authority – police, council, schools – would do their best to favour their own. Traders would offer each other preferential rates.

Over time, this developed along similar lines to the Italian mafia in New York into small-scale protectionism. Local businesses paid small-time crooks not to burn down their shops. The usual groups of disaffected youths became organised gangs. Organised gangs became henchmen. Pitched battles started to erupt between rival factions.

Celenk rose through this loose structure to become the local Godfather, showing extreme loyalty to those he favoured, and equally extreme brutality to those who lied and betrayed him. He was

particularly protective of his teenage daughter, Sophia. Granting permission for one of his henchmen's sons to take her out on a date one evening, he stipulated that she must be returned home by 10pm. When Sophia was dropped off at 10.15, Celenk kept her date hostage for three days, chopping off fifteen fingers and toes – "one digit for each minute you let me down" – and sending them by post to the young man's family. After this episode he became known as "The Turkish Delight" – a nickname that was never voiced within earshot.

Agents who penetrated the Turkish mafia compared Celenk to Hannibal Lecter, the fictional character in *The Silence of the Lambs*. He could certainly be charming. Women found him attractive – calling him "The Turkish Delight" in a less ironic way. And he was known to enjoy the opera and good wines. However, he displayed throughout his career a psychopathic disregard for the sanctity of human life. One of his favourite pastimes was to bundle three or four acolytes into his fortified Discovery Land Rover and go on killing sprees through Greek areas of

London with smuggled Uzi machine guns and crossbows. It is believed that Celenk was orphaned by a Greek Cypriot bomb which killed his parents while they were celebrating their third wedding anniversary in a local restaurant.

In the early 1990s Celenk achieved total control of all Turkish criminal operations in the United Kingdom. He started to turn his attentions to the continent, opening up smuggling routes with young prostitutes from Ankara. These routes were also used to bring arms and drugs into the country.

By the turn of the century, the security services believed Celenk was working as a business liaison for Al Qaeda. This was a relationship born out of necessity and greed, rather than ideology. He quickly realised that there was a lot of money to be made out of an organisation that he viewed as a commercial enterprise as well as a terrorist network.

While he was correct in this assumption, Celenk's sure touch deserted him after the 9/11 attacks in New York. When one of his right-hand men – Mahmud Bihar, a childhood friend – advised him that it

would be prudent to sever all links with a group now viewed as Public Enemy Number One by most of the Western world, Celenk had him killed.

Bihar's blood was made into a lifelike bust and placed on the mantelpiece in Celenk's office. "Emre has no friends; only enemies he has not yet made," ran the silver inscription underneath. "Do you want to end up there talking to Mahmud?" Celenk would ask jovially if one of his subordinates upset him.

Ultimately, yet was this hubris that led to Celenk's downfall. Bribes were left unpaid; informants unpunished; loyal accomplices randomly tortured. Celenk came to believe his own myth. It was only a matter of time until someone killed him. If MI5 hadn't done so, someone else would have.

Celenk's death leaves an obvious gap at the head of an organisation in chaos. It remains to be seen whether the rest of his activities will die with him, or whether a new leader will emerge from the ashes. Like Hydra, has one head been severed, only for nine more to arise?

8th April 2005

HILLARY WATT QC

The successful prosecution of Officer X represents another personal triumph for Hillary Watt QC. Born in 1961 in Huddersfield to working-class parents, Ms Watt won a scholarship to Oxford to read Politics, Philosophy and Economics. She was called to the Bar in 1987 where she made her name defending a string of IRA gunmen on terrorist charges.

She is married – to a foreign office civil servant, Jools Siviter – and they live in Hampstead with two young children.

DAILY TRIBUNE • NEWSPAPER OF THE YEAR

X YEARS FOR OFFICER X

MURDER

The pretty young blonde MI5 officer – known only as Officer X – bit her quivering bottom lip in the dock yesterday as the jury convicted her of conspiracy to **murder** and involuntary manslaughter.

Passing a sentence of ten years, Justice Simon Jones criticised Officer X for her "callous disregard for human life".

Speaking outside the court the brave police officer's weeping widow, Sally Loughton, said, "I still know that woman was hiding something. I felt she was a puppet saying whatever her people had trained her to say." Asked whether she was happy with the verdict, she agreed that justice had been done. "But in ten years Officer X will have her life back," she added, "and mine will never be the same again."

HEAVY BASTARDS

Recent reports have cast doubt on whether Officer X will really serve her full sentence. MI5 moved quickly yesterday to quash rumours that she had already been swapped for a similar-looking prisoner at Belmarsh prison. "This is unsubstantiated nonsense," said a senior intelligence source. "We respect the court's decision and will, of course, abide by its verdict."

Sources within the Metropolitan Police remain unconvinced by these assurances. "This is an unknown sentence for an unknown officer," said one. "I don't trust MI5 further than I can throw them. And they're heavy bastards."

MI5

ANNUAL MEDICAL REPORT

Name:	Zoe Reynolds
Date:	1st May 2004

Height:	5'7"	Weight:	8st 9lb	BMI:	19.14

Units of alcohol per week:	14
Cigarettes per week:	Occasional

Blood pressure:	120/70
Resting pulse:	65
Urine:	normal
Chest x-ray:	normal
Exercise ECG:	normal

Zoe has successfully cut down on her smoking and her blood pressure has returned to normal as a result. I'm not convinced that she's only drinking 14 units of alcohol per week, but she is currently showing no adverse health effects. Physically, she is in excellent shape.

S Chapman

PASSED

Dr Sally Chapman

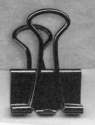

SECTION X

EYES ONLY FOR LEVEL 1 AND ABOVE

LOG FOR ZOE REYNOLDS

Date: 5.01.2004

Subject: Missing S24 form. It came to our attention that Zoe failed to fill out an S24 form for an Italian banker — Carlo Prodi — who she was dating for a while.

Outcome: This was referred to Tom Quinn. His note is reproduced below.

Note from Tom Quinn: This has been dealt with in-house. Carlo Prodi was married. He is no longer seeing Zoe. A disciplinary warning has been issued.

Date: 14.09.2003

Subject: School friends. Zoe met an old school friend — Sarah Barton — on a bus on her way home. Although Ms Barton was given the slip, she has made persistent attempts to contact Zoe through the civil service intranet.

Outcome: An email has been sent to Ms Barton to the effect that Zoe no longer works in the civil service. We have not provided any forwarding details.

Date: 12.11.2002

Subject: Landlord. Zoe's landlord has been making untoward advances and making life miserable for her. This is having an adverse effect on her ability to do her job. We have suggested to Danny (via Harry) that he might like to offer her his spare room.

Outcome: Zoe moved in with Danny on 21.12.2002

FILE CLOSED

Section X exists to keep tabs on members of the security services. We monitor private internet usage, spending habits and extra-mural activities. Our remit is to reduce the risk of blackmail and act as an early-warning system for renegade officers. These notes are retained on file which are "No Eyes" as far as the subject is concerned.

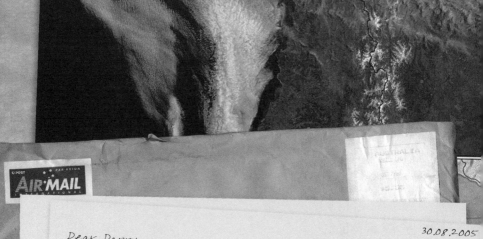

30.08.2005

Dear Danny,

I can picture you now as you read this. You'll have picked the envelope up from the doormat – have you thrown out that horrible old brown thing yet? – examined the clumsily disguised handwriting and wondered how I've managed to write to you from abroad using English stamps. Well, I'm going to leave you to work that out for yourself.

By now, you'll be sitting on the yellow throw on the window sofa having checked that whoever's living in my room now isn't around. You'll probably have poured yourself a whisky – Bell's, from the cupboard above the cutlery drawer. And you'll almost certainly be thinking, Why is Zoe writing me a letter?

The answer is I wanted to say thank you. Not thank you in a two-word postcard – did you ever get that by the way? – but a proper thank you. For everything.

Will told me what you did for him. I thought you might like to know that everything has worked out for the best. We are living in ▮▮▮▮ and I am ▮▮ months pregnant with the girl I always wanted. You did a courageous and noble thing, and we will never forget it.

But I didn't want just to thank you for us – me and Will. I also wanted to thank you for us – Danny and Zoe. Thank you for appealing to my sense of duty and persuading me to take the ▮▮▮▮ passport. But thank you also a million times over for being such a good colleague, flatmate and friend.

I know you might have had it otherwise. And, who knows, perhaps in a different world, things might have been different. But we did some brilliant things together, Danny. Some brilliant, necessary, wonderful things. I'll never forget the ▮▮▮▮▮▮
▮▮▮▮▮▮▮▮▮▮▮▮▮▮▮▮▮▮▮▮
▮▮▮▮▮▮▮▮▮▮▮▮▮▮▮▮▮▮▮▮
▮▮▮▮▮▮▮▮▮▮▮▮▮▮▮▮▮▮▮▮
▮▮▮▮▮▮▮▮▮▮▮▮

Forgive me – I'm getting indiscreet in my old age. Yet I feel entirely liberated out here in ▮▮▮ speaking ▮▮▮▮ and doing what I always really wanted to do – ▮▮▮▮ in a ▮▮▮. I feel like no one can get at me any more. I have rejoined the real world. The world of shadowy dreams, callow betrayals and boxed-up identities is all history to me now.

But I didn't want you to think I'd forgotten you, Danny. There are nights when I wake up screaming from nightmares or days on the ██████ when I find myself smiling at an old memory. I'm very much in love with Will - and we're very happy - but there are times when I feel there's only one person in the world who truly understood all of me. And that person is you.

I must post this before I get second thoughts. I hope you get it in full - if the censors are as useless as they were in my day I think you will.

I've set up a PO Box so you can write back - ██████████████..
I know I'll never see you again, but I can't bear not knowing how you are. In my more foolish moments, I imagine us ending up in the same old people's home one day and I will look at you, and you will look at me, and we'll understand.

All my love,
Zoe

Accompanying note from Harry Pearce for file of Zoe Reynolds

There are a number of saddening elements to this correspondence. It represents a flagrant breach of the Official Secrets Act by three people – two of them MI5 officers. Danny Hunter also disobeyed an explicit order from me not to pass on details of Zoe's new whereabouts to her fiancé. I worried what might happen if they broke up. I feared he might sell the story. I believed I was operating in the best interests of everyone's safety.

Sadder still, is the fact that this letter arrived ten days after Danny Hunter was shot dead. Zoe appears to have used a tourist she befriended abroad to send this letter hidden inside a utility bill to Danny's mother. It was intercepted by Special Branch and passed on to us.

Danny never knew of the depths of Zoe's affections. It shows the horrible price the service exacts from its officers.

I'm happy for this correspondence – with censor black-outs – to be included in Zoe Reynolds' closed file. Her whereabouts and identity must still be protected.

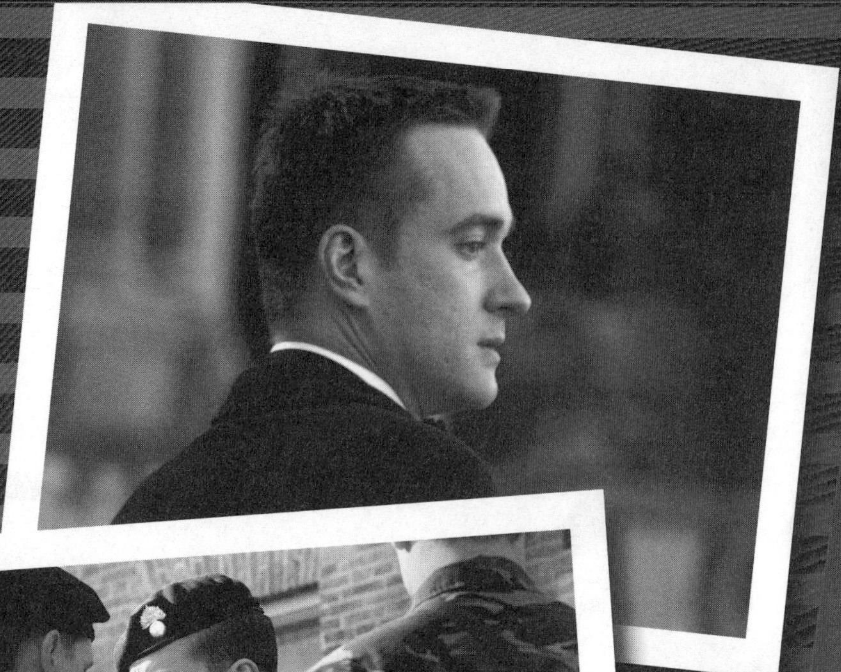

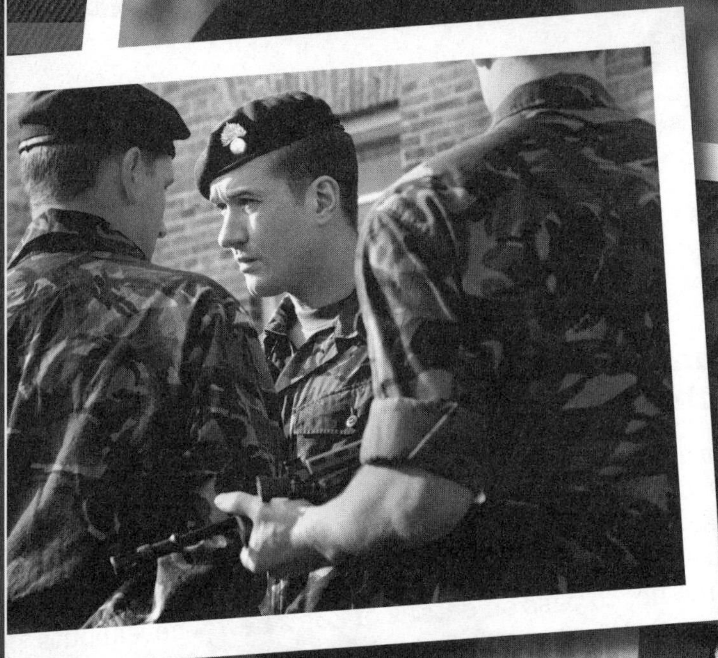

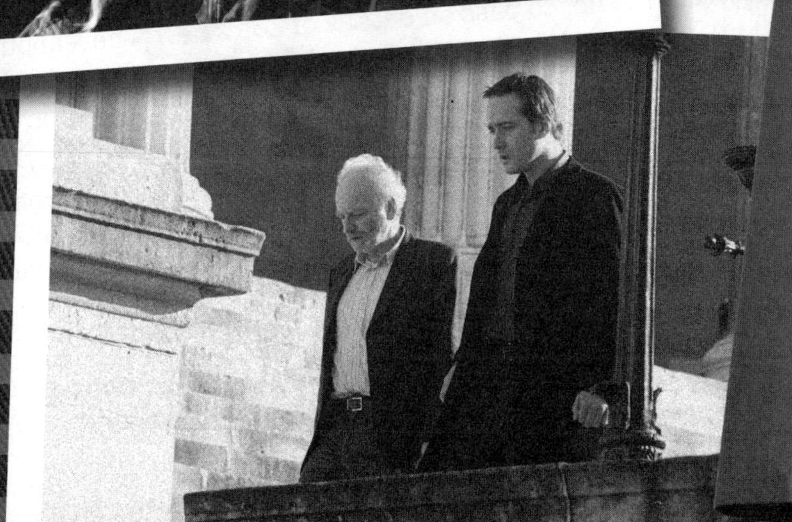

[Tom Quinn]

Private and Confidential

Name: Tom Quinn
Position: Intelligence Officer
D.O.B: 27.08.1971
Hair: Brown
Eyes: Blue
Height: 6'1
Marital status: Single
Dependants: None
Blood type: O, Rh negative

Tom Quinn had a distinguished career in MI5 before his loyalty was questioned in a complicated sting operation. He never really recovered from this and later lost his way on an operation after asking some serious moral questions about the nature of the job. He has now been de-commissioned from the service.

Major operations include:

- Killing of Herman Joyce
- Infiltration of Colombian Chala Cartel
- Turning of Patrick McCann
- Tracking down of American pro-life extremist Mary Kane

FILE CLOSED

University of Cambridge

Churchill College
University of Cambridge
CB3 0DS

Simon Jacques Esq.

30th October 1993

Dear Simon,

I hope you're well. I've got an outstanding candidate for you this year called Tom Quinn. He's doing a masters in International Relations.

Am I okay to go ahead and arrange a discreet chat in my chambers?

Yours sincerely,

Alex

Dr Alex Hollin
Lecturer in Inte
University of C

UNIVERSITY OF CAMBRIDGE

Churchill College
University of Cambridge
CB3 0DS

Simon Jacques Esq.

8th November 1993

Dear Simon,

Thank you for such a quick reply and for sending an application form.

I've had a quiet word with Tom and it appears that it has always been on his mind to apply to MI5. I've passed on the form to him.

I should perhaps warn you that he has a number of other applications pending for various graduate schemes. You might have to ask someone to step in and tamper with these if you want to hook him quickly. I'll leave this in your capable hands.

Hope to see you up here in person some time soon.

Yours sincerely,

Alex

Dr Alex Hollingshead
Lecturer in International Relations
University of Cambridge

MI5
Application Form

Surname

Quinn

Forenames

Thomas (Tom) Matthew

Date of Birth

27.08.1971

Place of birth

Cambridge

Nationality at birth

British

Permanent Address

Churchill College, Cambridge

Current occupation

Student

Date of availability for employment

From June

Do you hold a full, clean driving licence?

Yes

Medical

Do you have any conditions – either physical or psychological – which might affect your employment?

No

Father's name, address and occupation

Matthew Quinn (Headmaster)

17 Grantchester Meadows Road, Cambridge

Mother's name, maiden name, address and occupation

Amy Quinn (nee Robertson)

Died 1971

Brothers / Sisters (with names and D.O.B.)

Only child

Secondary Schools / Colleges

Dates : Names : Town

1982-1989 : Leys School : Cambridge

GCSEs or equivalent

O Levels: 7 As (English Language, English Literature, French, German, Maths, History, Geography) 3 Bs (Chemistry, Physics, Biology)

A levels and AS levels or equivalents

Politics - A

History - A

Economics - A

Gap Year

How did you spend any break during your education?

Worked during gap year to earn money for university

University or Further Education

LSE - 1990-1993

B.A. History - First

Churchill College, Cambridge - 1993-4

MPhil, International Relations

Awards

Please give details of any other awards (e.g. music)

N/A

EMPLOYMENT

Dates	Employer	Position
1989-1990	Office Angels	Temp

Have you served in HM Forces (including Reserves)?

Yes - OTC at university

Do you have applications pending for other jobs?

Yes. I have also applied for a job with the accountancy firm, Andrew Arthurson

---

PERSONAL QUALITIES AND SKILLS

SUMMARY

Provide a pen-portrait of your life to date

My mother died in childbirth and I was brought up by my father as an only child. He was the headmaster at the school I went to which caused a few problems in the early days. However, I found an outlet in various sports teams which made life much easier for me. I have a small group of very close friends from childhood.

I've always worked hard in the classroom. I wasn't a natural academic and I developed late intellectually. International relations was the one subject that really interested me and I enjoyed studying it for a masters at Cambridge after my first degree at the LSE.

While I am able to adapt to different situations, I prefer to be able to plan things in advance. I have a very clear idea of how I want my life to map out.

MOTIVATION

Why do you think you would be suited to a career in MI5?

My university degree sparked an intellectual curiosity about the intelligence world. In my final year I was able to take a paper in the history of espionage which I enjoyed greatly. I therefore think I am approaching a career in MI5 from a more realistic viewpoint than many of your applicants. I am well able to distinguish between fact and fiction.

In addition, my father has obviously been a strong, guiding influence on my life. His dedication to the community – and his love of public service – have also instilled in me a desire for a career where I can enjoy a similar sense of satisfaction about the worth of what I'm doing. He has a strong moral compass which I hope I have inherited.

POLITICAL CURIOSITY

Give three political topics (historical or current) which interest you

* The UN
* Anglo-American relations post WWII
* NATO

ADAPTABILITY

Give an example of a time when you had to adapt to unexpected circumstances

Money was quite tight in the family when I left school and I was unable to spend a gap year travelling like many of my friends. I therefore spent a bleak 14 months working in various temping jobs and living at home. I was able to put up with the tedium by reminding myself of the long-term goal.

Also, every second weekend a friend and I would try to see how far away we could get from Cambridge without paying any money. Sometimes this involved smuggling ourselves onto trains and hiding from the ticket inspectors. By the end of the year we were sufficiently bold to try our luck in airports. I managed to talk an air stewardess into allowing me onto a return Virgin Atlantic flight to Hong Kong – which meant I won the bet.

RESPONSIBILITY

What positions of responsibility have you held – at school, university or otherwise?

```
Head boy
Captain of football
Officer Cadet
```

FOREIGN LANGUAGES

Please indicate level of competence

```
French, German - basic
```

OTHER INTERESTS

```
Sport
```

TRAVEL

Give details of all foreign travel undertaken in the last 10 years, including reason for travel

```
Europe - backpacking in university summers
```

EQUAL OPPORTUNITIES

This information is not used as part of our selection procedures

Gender	Ethnic origin	Disabilities
(Male) Female	White British	None

REFEREES

Please give details of three referees. One of these should be a contemporary who knows you well

```
1. Ed Francis - childhood friend
2. Dr Alex Hollingshead, Lecturer in International
   Relations, Cambridge
3. Sarah Cavendish, Director, Office Angels
```

Signature   Date

REFERENCE: Tom Quinn

To Whom It May Concern:

I have known Tom since we were two years old and I cannot think of a truer, more loyal friend. A lot of people get the wrong idea about Tom when they first meet him. He can come across as aloof, even arrogant. He has a look that implies he is sizing you up and is not all that keen on what he sees.

However, the truth is that Tom is actually quite shy. It can take him a good few years to relax in someone's company. Fortunately, I've known him for twenty! And once you're accepted you won't find a more faithful companion.

Perhaps I can give just one example. When we were fifteen years old we were walking down the street together. I'd started to cross when a car came screaming around the corner from nowhere. Tom was a couple of paces behind me but reacted much quicker. Flinging himself in front of the car, he rugby tackled me out of the way and took the brunt of the impact himself. He was lucky only to suffer a broken leg and a couple of cracked ribs.

What really impressed me about this episode though was Tom's reaction to it. He didn't see it as a heroic thing to do. To him it was simply second nature. And he also made me swear never to tell anyone else how it had happened. For me, that's Tom down to a T: enigmatic, silently heroic and loyal.

I very much hope you can find a job for him.

Ed Francis

SECURITY CLEARANCE & BACKGROUND CHECKS

Tom Quinn

I was tasked with carrying out routine background checks into Tom Quinn's family and friends, as well as standard fact-checking of his application details.

There is nothing factually inaccurate in Tom's application. Indeed, there is little scandalous in his background at all. As he mentions, he had a difficult upbringing with no mother. His father was a gentle character but somewhat cold and Victorian in outlook. This appears to have affected Tom's social abilities in later life. People who don't know him well describe him as a cold fish.

On the other hand, Tom has a fiercely loyal friendship group which he has maintained since the age of seven if not earlier. The enclosed reference from one member of this group — Ed Francis — shows the affection in which he is held.

There is also more to Tom than meets the eye, as shown by his weekend pranks prior to university. When he wants to be, he can be very charming indeed. But his default character remains somewhat aloof and impenetrable.

He has already shown excellent leadership qualities at a young age. His political outlook is very mainstream, and he is physically and intellectually up to the job.

As he mentions, he is someone who likes to plan ahead. This methodical approach to his career appears to have been a motivating factor in his applying for a job in accountancy. He is currently at the final round stage with Andrew Arthurson. I will have a word with someone on their board and ask them to delay making a decision on him. My impression is that we don't want to lose this one. A timely rejection from them will help push him in our direction (a direction I'm sure is his first choice).

It will be interesting to see how he is assessed in training.

Dirk Muir, HR Security
7th March 1994

TRAINING ASSESSMENT
Tom Quinn, 9th June 1994

SCORES		Other core competencies	
Practical		Calm under pressure	4.9
Surveillance	4.6	Leadership	4.9
Counter-surveillance	4.2	Team work	4.2
Physical endurance	4.9	Communication	4.1
Shooting	4.7	General attitude	4.9
Driving	4.4	Average	4.6
Technical	4.4		
Average	4.53		

Intellectual		**Overall average**	**4.34**
Linguistic	1.7		
Decision-making	4.9		
Research	4		
Average	3.53		

Overall average: **4.34**

On a sliding scale of 1 to 5 where 1 is poor, 5 is outstanding and 2.5 is average for a new recruit

Tom put in a near flawless performance during the recruit training. I was particularly impressed by his unflappability under pressure and his ability to make snap decisions when necessary. He is also in excellent physical shape.

My only minor quibble is that, while his leadership abilities are outstanding, he needs to take more notice of the concerns of more junior members of the team.

He will make an excellent MI5 officer nonetheless.

Caroline Moyne

Caroline Moyne
Head of recruit training, MI5

MI5 HUMAN RESOURCES – S24 FORM

Permission for socialisation   28th March 2003

Introduction

MI5 officers are encouraged to form relationships – both platonic and sexual – within the service. No one can understand the job you do in the same way as your colleagues.

However, we do understand that this will not always be the case. In return, we ask you to understand our duty to perform extensive background checks on outsiders with whom you develop close relationships. When you joined MI5 we checked your family, your friends and your relationships. The same must be true of any serious, new liaisons.

Please answer these questions fully and accurately.

1   What is your name and department?

Tom Quinn, Counter Terrorism Department, Section D

2   What is the full name of person you wish to socialise with?

Ellie Lindsay Simm

3   What is his/her profession?

She part owns a restaurant in Brixton where she is also a chef

4   How did you meet?

I was attempting to meet a potential recruit whom I knew went to Ellie's restaurant occasionally. I went there three times a week until he eventually turned up in week six. Ellie and I got to know each other in the meantime.

5   Does he/she know the nature of your work?

Yes, eventually. To start with, she knew me by one of my aliases – Matthew Archer.

6   What is his/her nationality? Do you have any reason to suspect he/she might be involved in terrorist activity?

British. No, none at all.

7   What do you know about his/her family?

Ellie has a young daughter called Maisie and I've formed a close bond with her. Maisie's father is called Mark Hodd. He works in oil in the Gulf and hasn't seen her for two years. Ellie's father is dead. Her mother lives just outside London.

8   What is his/her home address? MI5 may have to perform additional checks at their place of residence. We will, of course, exercise utmost discretion.

Both Maisie and Ellie have recently moved in with me.

9   What attracts you to this person?

She is a good mother to Maisie and an excellent chef. She has an inner toughness which I find attractive. Despite going through a lot in her life, she is still fun to be with.

MI5 HR assessment

We're not particularly happy about this one. Ms Simm (who has reverted to her maiden name) was on a Women Reclaimers' street march in 1992. We are also worried about an officer dating a woman with a young child. What about the risk to the child? Not to mention the possibility that the child might inadvertently talk about Tom's job to her schoolmates.

The father, Mark Hodd, is also a cause for concern. He is a jealous vindictive type and has one or two immoral friends in London who owe him favours.

According to one of her friends, Ellie appears to have thought Tom was "just another lonely guy". She has subsequently fallen for him very fast. We are worried that she might be more involved than is healthy.

Having said this, there is nothing sufficiently worrying in its own right to turn down this S24. Proceed with caution is our advice.

Note
9th October 2003

Tom Quinn is no longer dating Ellie Simm.

FILE
CLOSED

EXTREME EMERGENCY RESPONSE INITIATIVE EXERCISE (EERIE)

FIELD REPORT
TITLE: EERIE
FILED BY: Tom Quinn
DATE: 20th December 2003

Executive Overview

On 13th December 2003 Section D participated in an Extreme Emergency Response Initiative Exercise (EERIE). The chosen scenario was that a dirty bomb had detonated in Parliament Square. Senior members of the government and the Royal Family were incapacitated, leaving MI5 in charge of running the country. As the designated EM-Ex officer, these are my conclusions on the exercise.

Positives

It is difficult to get these training exercises right. Make them too easy and no one takes them seriously. Make them too difficult and people will give up halfway through. I think this one struck the right balance – a believable Doomsday scenario which had the entire team treating it as real from halfway through.

I thought Ruth Evershed kept her cool well throughout the operation, as did Zoe Reynolds. Malcolm and Colin were both inventive where they needed to be. Harry Pearce has clearly missed his vocation as an actor, as have our two visiting friends, Bridget and Mark. Only Danny Hunter disappointed with his snappy attitude.

Lessons to learn

In retrospect, I made a number of mistakes. My biggest was allowing Danny to enter the pods even after the lockdown had been called. I am also disappointed that I wasn't able to establish a more emphatic lead over the team from the start.

As a team, our familiarity with the exact security protocols was shaky. I suggest a thorough revision of the Major Incident Procedure Manual kept in the contingency file.

The EPCUs (Emergency Protective Clothing Units) are also in urgent need of repair. It is very damaging for morale to have such useless, clumsy protection.

In all, though, the operation was successful, if a little draining on staff energy levels. In future, it would be good to know that our existing work is still being covered while we undergo such training exercises.

Note from Harry Pearce:

TOM IS TO BE COMMENDED FOR A SUPERB DISPLAY OF LEADERSHIP UNDER DIFFICULT CIRCUMSTANCES.

LISA JOYCE
HERMAN JOYCE

FIELD REPORT
TITLE: *Lisa Joyce,*
Herman Joyce
FILED BY: *Tom Quinn*
DATE: *30th September 2004*

Introduction & Overview

Ten years ago, one of my first jobs as a MI5 officer was undercover in the London School of Economics. While I was there, I recruited Lisa Joyce, a bright young American student. Her parents were both successful CIA officers – Herman and Carmen Joyce.

Lisa was employed by MI5 to infiltrate a European hardcore anarchist cell. We thought she was up to the job at the time. Our assessment turned out to be wrong. After appalling torture and abuse, Lisa was eventually released and returned to the States. For the last decade she has experienced appalling mental trauma which treatment at a mental health hospital in Maine has done little to alleviate.

Lisa's parents embarked on a personal vendetta of revenge. Five years ago Herman Joyce staged his own death in a car accident so that he could organise an operation that would set me up. Over the course of the last two months he very nearly achieved his goal.

In this field report I explain exactly what happened to Lisa Joyce, as well as my struggle to clear my name after her parents' attempted revenge.

London School of Economics

In September 1994 I was sent undercover as a postgraduate student at the LSE. I had been there as an undergraduate myself so it was an easy early posting. I knew where the common rooms were, and I knew which coffee shops were full of the most seditious conversations.

My main role at the LSE was to monitor the large number of foreign postgraduate students at the college. The radicalisation of muslim student groups is now fairly common. At that time, however, it was a relatively new phenomenon and I was sent in to monitor just how bad the situation might get. With the benefit of hindsight, I can see that I badly underestimated future trends.

My subsidiary role was as a talent scout. As MI5 started to modernise in the early 1990s concerns were expressed about the range of backgrounds among the new officers. Oxbridge was still the primary recruiting tool. The complete exposure of the Cambridge spy ring showed what could go wrong when you relied too heavily on the old boy network.

We were looking for a new type of "right sort". Of course, they had to be intelligent. They had to be socially adept, bright, alert and capable of adjusting to all sorts of situations and personalities. But most of all, they had to be capable of adjusting to the modern world. Our enemies were no longer Communist "gentlemen". They were ruthless terrorists. Home-grown anarchists on northern council estates. Amoral computer whizzkids. We thought we were more likely to find this new "right sort" in one of the capital's best colleges.

And this is where I met Lisa Joyce.

Lisa Joyce

Ironically, Lisa first came across my radar as a potential subversive. I was in the main campus coffee shop – supposedly leafing through my doctoral thesis – while actually listening in to the conversations around me. Lisa was in a group of Lebanese exiles conversing in fluent Arabic. She was so convincing that I thought for a while that she might be a blonde Circassian Arab. But then her mobile rang and she answered it in an undisguisable American accent.

I was intrigued and managed to engineer a chance encounter with Lisa soon afterwards. She was studying international relations – the same, ostensibly, as me – and I was able to bump clumsily into her outside a lecture hall. By the time we'd picked ourselves and our notes off the ground, we'd arranged to go to the cinema together, followed by drink, dinner and a coffee.

It was over dinner that I noticed what a remarkable young woman she was. She spoke a lot about her parents – describing them as diplomats – and detailed the various embassies she had stayed in abroad. She also had a capacity to absorb languages like a sponge. She was pretty much fluent in every place her parents had visited – from Peru to Vietnam.

But it was our discussion of the film which really stuck in my mind. It was the latest spy drama. She was wondering what it would be like to really live like that. I suggested it would be pretty terrifying. You'd live in constant fear, I ventured. Constant loneliness. Your nerves would be shattered. Your friendships ruined.

She disagreed. She couldn't imagine anything more exciting than feeling alive the entire time. I remember exactly how she put it. "You'd just know that there was no one else in the entire world doing what you were doing, right then," she said. "No one else would be thinking what you were thinking. You'd be unique. For that moment, you'd be entirely unique." She was 19 at the time.

The next morning I offered her what she appeared to want. I told her my real job and recruited her as an MI5 agent. She claimed to have known all along who I worked for.

European anarchists

We had something very specific in mind for Lisa.

At the beginning of the 1990s anarchist groups were again springing up all over Europe. They used to be fairly harmless organisations – laughable even – whose main activities consisted of painting graffiti on suburban tube lines and playing loud music.

Recently, however, they had become much more militant, attacking all the fundamentals which keep society ticking over, merely for the sake of it. In Frankfurt, post boxes were ripped up and their contents thrown into the river. In Madrid, bus stops were uprooted and thrown in the road. Telephone lines were attacked in Brussels. In London, anarchists dug into the roads until they could burst a water main or a gas pipe. Electricity pylons in rural areas were sabotaged. And it was all being done for the pure, simple joy of causing trouble.

Annoying though these disturbances were, they were all, ultimately, controllable. It's fairly difficult to dig up a water pipe in a road without someone noticing. All most police forces had to do was round up as many ringleaders as they could until the trouble subsided.

Paris, however, was different. A group of young American anarchists had settled in the 11th arrondissement. Most of them were in their late teens and early twenties. Their recruiting criteria were simple: you had to be a middle-class American who had entirely rejected your background. Many of them were backpackers who had come to Europe to find themselves and ended up embracing nihilism instead. They called themselves the 51st Anarchists – an allusion to the fifty states of America.

They took a lot of drugs. They smashed up a lot of shops. And they generally made a nuisance of themselves. By the summer, the situation had got completely out of hand. Young Americans were travelling thousands of miles to Paris specifically to join them. Hardcore elements joined the group as their activities escalated from mindless pranks to intense criminal activity. High on drugs, and flush with parental funds, they raped, pillaged and terrorised an entire area of the capital.

The crux of the problem was that the French authorities found themselves unable – or unwilling – to do too much about it. Firstly, these were the offspring of rich and influential Americans. The last thing the French wanted at this stage was a diplomatic crisis. Secondly, the 51st Anarchists confined their activities to a poor, multicultural arrondissement which the Parisian police were often too scared to visit themselves. Thirdly, it was impossible for them to infiltrate the group in any way. The selection policy of the 51st Anarchists remained as tight as it was in the early days.

This is where we thought Lisa could come in. Influential voices in America had begun to hear about the damage their young people were doing to their reputation abroad. They had appealed in vain to the French authorities to do something. Now they appealed to us.

Operation Zeus – preparation

When we explained the background to Lisa she jumped at the opportunity. The beneficiary of a privileged upbringing herself, there were few things she despised more than self-indulgent anarchism. Especially from people who "should have known better", as she put it.

We prepared a complete back-story for her which was relatively easy given her existing acceptability to the 51st Anarchists. We made her a little older than she actually was – not too difficult as she could have passed for 30 – and gave her an undergraduate degree in Law from Yale. She had been sacked from a leading law firm after sleeping with one of the directors and harboured a grudge against corporate capitalism ever since. Her father was a high-flying Wall Street banker; her mother a Stepford wife.

Running away from New York, she had decided to fly to Europe and buy an inter-rail ticket. We gave her a new passport, new clothes and a new record collection. For two weeks she stayed in a MI5 safehouse in London, researching the anarchists, memorising her new legend and role-playing scenarios with me in the evening.

This was intended to be a low-grade, intelligence-gathering operation. Lisa was equipped with a tiny camera, but she wasn't armed. All we wanted were names, faces and as much information on the organisation as possible. We expected her to spend no more than three to four days with the group. Then she could quietly slip out and the French authorities would take it from there.

Lisa prepared meticulously. We could have sent her after only three days in the safehouse. By the end of the designated fortnight she could barely sit still any more.

Infiltration

We'd game-played all sorts of scenarios for Lisa's introduction to the group. In the end, however, we settled for the most obvious – she should follow the example of everyone else, approach them and ask to join. Anything more elaborate would have been more likely to arouse suspicions, we reasoned.

We were right. Lisa made her way to Paris with a faked inter-rail ticket and a well-worn Lonely Planet guide to Europe. Within a couple of hours of wandering purposefully around the 11th arrondissement she had been approached. That night she stayed in their makeshift bunker in a disused warehouse. There were almost 100 members of the group by then – much more than we expected.

The next morning Lisa was able to slip away and communicate with us. We thought it too unsafe to give her anything too technical, so she was simply provided with a hotmail address (unsuspicious for a backpacker) where she could compose and then save her messages in the draft folders without sending them. On that first day she was able to provide us with vital first impressions on the group's whereabouts, size and outlook. Everything appeared to be going smoothly.

Compromise

However, it later transpired that the first evening had passed smoothly only because the main ringleaders had been out gathering more supplies for the group. Most of the others were so stoned that they took no notice of the new arrival. People had been coming and going for months in any case.

On the second evening there was some form of initiation ritual which appeared to stretch Lisa to breaking point. She was coerced into a sex act and had to join in a destructive tour through the neighbourhood. On returning to their warehouse she drew attention to herself while trying to refuse the heroin on offer.

During this fuss one of the more established girls suddenly claimed to recognise Lisa as the younger sister of one of her friends. Lisa initially stuck to her legend. When threatened with a heroin needle in the eyeball she owned up to being who she really was but claimed she had invented a new identity for herself as a way of escaping her past. This defence collapsed as well when they searched her bag fully and found recording equipment in a hidden compartment.

Torture

For 36 hours Lisa was tortured horrendously by almost 100 angry anarchists. When we'd heard no news from her on the second day, we red-flashed the embassy in Paris. After much horse-trading, French special forces finally stormed the building. Although unarmed, fifteen American citizens were shot dead. A further twenty were badly injured.

Lisa's physical injuries were serious enough – she spent four weeks in an intensive therapy unit in London. Ten years later, however, and she has never recovered from the mental trauma she underwent. She was flown home to her parents in Maine where MI5 paid for treatment in one of the best mental institutions in the world. To date, however, she remains in a catatonic state of withdrawal.

Revenge

The British government did everything it could to make life easier for the Joyces. Although it was thought sensible for me not to meet the parents, a small delegation of FCO officials paid them a courtesy visit. They were turned away at the door.

The Joyces' hatred of me and MI5 became so intense that they spent ten years plotting their revenge. Five years ago Herman Joyce staged his own death in a car accident so that he would have the perfect cover with which to carry out their operation. We are still not sure whether other senior members of the CIA were involved in this cover-up. What we do know is that he was buried with full service honours before continuing to plot with his wife for the next five years. He succeeded in creating a new identity as Herb Ziegler.

Set up

Earlier this year Ziegler / Joyce found an ideal partner when he met rich Iraqi Baathists during an undercover visit to Baghdad. Joyce had worked in the region before – he had been instrumental in some of the arms sales during the Iran–Iraq war – and he was quick to renew his old contacts.

These Baathists were out of power, but they weren't yet out of money. The one thing they wanted was a British humiliation – ideally an assassination – on British soil. The one thing Joyce wanted was my destruction. They agreed to work together.

On 7th July 2004, Joyce shot dead Sir John Stone, the Chief of the Defence Staff, in Ipswich. I was kidnapped and tricked into putting my finger prints on the murder weapon. My superiors at MI5 initially refused

to believe my side of the story and I was forced to go into hiding under suspicion of treason. Meanwhile, political forces within the intelligence community used this as an excuse to launch an investigation into MI5's "rotten" culture.

Reconciliation

At this stage the world still thought Joyce had died five years earlier. I was able to track him down to a church – he liked to think of himself as a devout Catholic – where I attempted to extract a confession from him. Joyce, however, had spent a year under KGB arrest in the Lubyanka. I had no choice but to shoot him and deliver his body to Thames House as "proof".

It wasn't enough, though. In the end, our only escape route was for someone to talk Herman's widow Carmen into a taped confession of what they'd done. Adam Carter succeeded in doing this before Mrs Joyce took her own life.

Personal Conclusions

I have lived with Lisa Joyce on my conscience for ten years. I expect I will have to endure that guilt for the rest of my life. We took a bright, enthusiastic young woman and threw her to the wolves. In retrospect, we should have envisaged that this would end in disaster. She wanted to feel alive, to be unique. We failed her badly.

We also chose our enemies badly. I can only think of one husband and wife team to match the Joyces in terms of skill and talent and that's Adam and Fiona Carter. We should have monitored their movements much more closely.

In the end, though, MI5 fought back valiantly. Political interference from Downing Street was rejected, and two dangerous loose cannons were neutralised. But the price for this was a dead Chief of the Defence Staff. Was it all worth it in the final analysis, we might well ask. And what exactly are we going to do about Lisa Joyce who we've now betrayed three times over?

MI5 HUMAN RESOURCES – S24 FORM

Permission for socialisation   11th December 2003

Introduction

MI5 officers are encouraged to form relationships – both platonic and sexual – within the service. No one can understand the job you do in the same way as your colleagues.

However, we do understand that this will not always be the case. In return, we ask you to understand our duty to perform extensive background checks on outsiders with whom you develop close relationships. When you joined MI5 we checked your family, your friends and your relationships. The same must be true of any serious, new liaisons.

Please answer these questions fully and accurately.

1   What is your name and department?

Tom Quinn, Counter Terrorism Department, Section D

2   What is the full name of person you wish to socialise with?

Dr Victoria Samantha Westbrook

3   What is his/her profession?

She is a hospital doctor.

4   How did you meet?

I met her when she was treating Danny Hunter in hospital. Danny encouraged the two of us to see each other again.

5   Does he/she know the nature of your work?

Yes. I told her in a bar recently.

6   What is his/her nationality? Do you have any reason to suspect he/she might be involved in terrorist activity?

British. No, none at all.

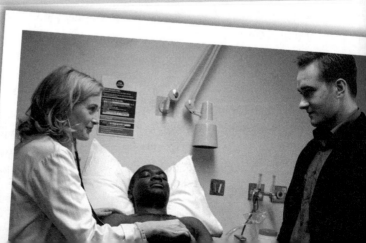

7   What do you know about his/her family?

Nothing yet. I haven't asked her.

8   What is his/her home address? MI5 may have to perform additional checks at their place of residence. We will, of course, exercise utmost discretion.

19 Whitefriar Road, London SE1 7HK

9   What attracts you to this person?

She is attractive.

MI5 HR assessment

This file came across our desk just as Tom Quinn broke up with Vicki Westbrook. Her disturbing behaviour at the end of their relationship – including putting his details on male escort cards all over Soho – means that we are obliged to keep this record in his file for future reference. The way in which she compromised national security during a visit of the American President was particularly embarrassing for the service.

If any officers doubted why we bother with these forms, this scenario provides excellent evidence. We are disappointed that the form didn't make it to us earlier. Otherwise, we would probably have found incriminating evidence in Dr Westbrook's past to reject the application.

She is not to be allowed to date any of our other officers. We will also investigate whether to change our preferred choice of hospital ward.

REJECTED

MI5 HUMAN RESOURCES – S24 FORM

Permission for socialisation   3rd March 2004

Introduction

MI5 officers are encouraged to form relationships – both platonic and sexual – within the service. No one can understand the job you do in the same way as your colleagues.

However, we do understand that this will not always be the case. In return, we ask you to understand our duty to perform extensive background checks on outsiders with whom you develop close relationships. When you joined MI5 we checked your family, your friends and your relationships. The same must be true of any serious, new liaisons.

Please answer these questions fully and accurately.

1   What is your name and department?

Tom Quinn, Counter Terrorism Department, Section D

2   What is the full name of person you wish to socialise with?

Christine Dale

3   What is his/her profession?

CIA Liaison officer, London

4   How did you meet?

Work

5   Does he/she know the nature of your work?

Yes. Obviously.

6   What is his/her nationality? Do you have any reason to suspect he/she might be involved in terrorist activity?

American. No.

7   What do you know about his/her family?

Her father was also in the CIA. Her mother is a former model.

8   What is his/her home address? MI5 may have to perform
    additional checks at their place of residence. We will, of course,
    exercise utmost discretion.

Classified.

9   What attracts you to this person?

Obviously we share a similar lifestyle, the same work interest, but
there is much more to it than that. She's one of the few people whose
company I find relaxing. And we have a deeper understanding of each
other because of the lives we lead.

MI5 HR assessment

REJECTED

Note from Harry Pearce

I have instructed Tom Quinn to stop seeing this woman. We do not want
another Mata Hari on our doorstep. I am to be informed if anyone suspects
that he has not done as ordered.

Exit interview: Tom Quinn   21st November 2004

ANNOTATED TRANSCRIPTS	TQ – Tom Quinn AN – Andrew Nixon, HR

AN You look tired, Tom.

TQ I can never sleep after an op.

AN You don't have to worry about that any more. You can sleep as long as you like now.

TQ shrugs.

AN (cont.) You understand why we have to do this, don't you?

TQ For the files, right?

AN Yes, for the files. It helps us do our job better if we know why people are leaving the service. We like to get a finger on what's happened.

TQ Okay.

AN So thank you for agreeing to this interview.

TQ That's all right.

AN You have to justify the huge pension we're giving you somehow.

TQ snorts.

TQ Oh, I think I've justified that all right.

AN How do you mean?

TQ Ten years of service in which I've been shot at twice a year. Constant pitched battles with fools such as Jools Siviter. Non-stop patronising from Americans who think we're about as important as Oregon. I think that pretty much deserves a pension, doesn't it?

AN Okay, Tom, okay. I was just trying to lighten the mood.

TQ I've seen a colleague's face burned in a deep fat fryer. I've seen scores of innocent people die because we weren't quick enough or sharp enough. Pretty, silly girls caught up in Colombian drug cartels. Radicalised young boys in mosques. I've spied on our own armed forces. So, let's not try too hard to lighten the mood, shall we?

AN What happened to you, Tom? You used to be one of the best.

TQ Did I? What does that mean anyway? The best at what? Lying? Manipulating? Setting people up?

AN You were one of our best intelligence officers. That's what you were, Tom. And you were a fine leader, too. Everyone respected you. Danny practically hero-worshipped you.

TQ Well, he shouldn't have done. Look at me now. What kind of hero is this? Spy, tramp, traitor, hero? None of it meant anything, did it?

AN What are you now?

TQ Dunno. Free, I guess.

AN Free?

TQ Have you ever had everything you've ever believed in turned on you? That's what happened to me when I was set up by Herman Joyce. My own colleagues doubted me. Colleagues I'd taken bullets for. Harry, Zoe, even Danny to some extent. You know what Joyce said to me. He said, "I've destroyed your soul." It was my own personal hell, as he put it. And he was right.

AN But that's over now. You cleared your name.

TQ Yes, but it's never really over, is it? You never forget what it's like to be betrayed. Even Christine betrayed me. You never look at anyone in the same way again. You don't even look at yourself in the same way. Their doubts become your self-doubts.

AN You don't need to leave the service on a crisis of confidence, Tom. We have counsellors at Tring who can talk these things through with you.

TQ I don't have much choice, do I? Anyway, it's not a crisis of confidence. It's more a triumph of confidence. A triumph of conscience, if you like. The crisis I've had is one of morality. Morality about the job I was doing. About the lives we picked up and trashed again.

AN You're referring to Operation Flytrap?

TQ Yes.

AN Tell me about that.

TQ Professor Fred Roberts. He'd agreed to be a sleeper for MI5 over 20 years ago. Last month Harry woke him up.

AN Woke him up?

TQ Yes, Harry reminded him of his obligations to the service. MI5 had given him a helping hand on the career ladder. Now it was time for him to repay the debt.

AN Which meant what, specifically?

TQ Roberts was a renowned chemical engineer who'd won the Nobel Prize. We used him as a bait to lure potential terrorist purchasers of red mercury. To do this, we had to separate him from his family and give the impression that he had huge gambling debts. We needed something to explain why he needed the money so badly.

AN And how did you feel about doing this?

TQ At first I worried the rest of the team by how brutally I dealt with Roberts. I gave the impression that I was enjoying watching him fight with his wife; that I was enjoying playing God – making and destroying a man. I think I scared Danny, in particular, with how detached I was becoming from reality. But in truth, I can see now that this was a cover for what I was really feeling. Subconsciously, I think I'd made my mind up long before I flipped.

AN Flipped?

TQ Yes. I felt we were crucifying the poor man. I lied and promised him that his family were in a safehouse. They weren't. They were in great danger in Leeds. One morning I put the professor in my car and started driving him there.

AN Against specific orders?

TQ Against specific orders. Adam Carter and Harry cut me off in a helicopter. I was decommissioned there and then by the roadside.

AN Why did you disobey orders?

TQ Because I thought it was the right thing to do.

AN Morally or operationally?

TQ Morally. Operationally, it was probably the wrong thing to do. Flytrap was working quite well. And as it turns out, the professor went back to London and we caught our man. But moral considerations and operational considerations are often mutually exclusive. The family remained in great danger. They were almost killed, in fact. That day, I suppose I made a final choice between the two – career and morality.

AN And was it the right choice?

TQ Yes, it was. Not that anyone else saw it, of course. I remember asking Adam by the roadside if he could understand. He just looked at me. This piercing, incomprehensible stare that was more scorn than pity. And he just said, "No, sorry." And then turned away. At that moment, I knew I no longer belonged.

AN I think I understand.

TQ Do you, Andrew? Well, that's great, but to be honest, I'm not asking to be understood. Harry didn't really get it, either. He said he envied me becoming a member of the public. Maybe he meant it. I don't know. But I'm just tired of it all. Tired by the mundane routines – the meddling spin doctors, the counsellors, the paperwork. Exhausted with the stress. Shattered by the emotional uncertainty of being someone else the whole time.

AN The boxes?

TQ Yes, the boxes. After a while in this job, you have to put your real self in a box. And then only when you come home can you open the box and say, "Hello, real me".

AN Hello, Tom Quinn.

TQ laughs.

TQ Yes, I can have a lot of time at home now with the real me.

AN laughs.

TQ *(cont.)* And that thing that Joyce said about destroying my soul . . . he was right in a way. But not in the way he'd imagined. My job was destroying my soul. If I'd carried on, I would have destroyed it myself.

AN Good luck on the outside, Tom. I think you'll be fine.

TQ Thank you.

****Interview ends****

MI5

ANNUAL MEDICAL REPORT

Name:	Tom Quinn
Date:	1st May 2004

Height:	6'1	Weight:	12st	BMI:	22.20

Units of alcohol per week:	15
Cigarettes per week:	none

Blood pressure:	110/60
Resting pulse:	58
Urine:	normal
Chest x-ray:	normal
Exercise ECG:	normal

Tom is in good physical shape but displaying signs of long-term mental stress. I have advised him to take a short holiday to recuperate.

S Chapman

Dr Sally Chapman

PASSED

SECTION X

EYES ONLY FOR LEVEL 1 AND ABOVE

LOG FOR TOM QUINN

There is no log for Tom Quinn.

Section X exists to keep tabs on members of the security services. We monitor private internet usage, spending habits and extra-mural activities. Our remit is to reduce the risk of blackmail and act as an early-warning system for renegade officers. These notes are retained on file which are "No Eyes" as far as the subject is concerned.

PEEPING TOMS

Private security firms used to have a fairly laughable reputation in this country. Most were cheap and amateur, used by paranoid housewives and cuckolded husbands to dig up dirt on their other halves.

In the last five years, however, the sector has broadened and professionalised. Although the lower end of the market still exists, couples have found they can find out more about each other by checking email and mobile phone records themselves. Meanwhile, a rash of serious contenders have sprung up at the top end of the market.

"The demand is there," explains Tessa Phillips, the founder of Phillips Security, whose clients include high income individuals and blue-chip firms. "We advise on infrastructure as well as personal safety."

Many of these security agencies are staffed by former intelligence officers attracted by the financial perks and the operational freedom of the private sector. "We can charge pretty much what we like," says Phillips who used to be at MI5. "We give a tailored service which no government agency can match."

However, Phillips is facing competition from another ex-MI5 officer, Tom Quinn. Quinn works alongside his wife, Christine, a former CIA officer, at Trans Atlantic Security which they co-founded earlier this year.

Note from Harry Pearce

Delighted to see it. And good for Tessa to have a little competition. Please add to TQ's file.

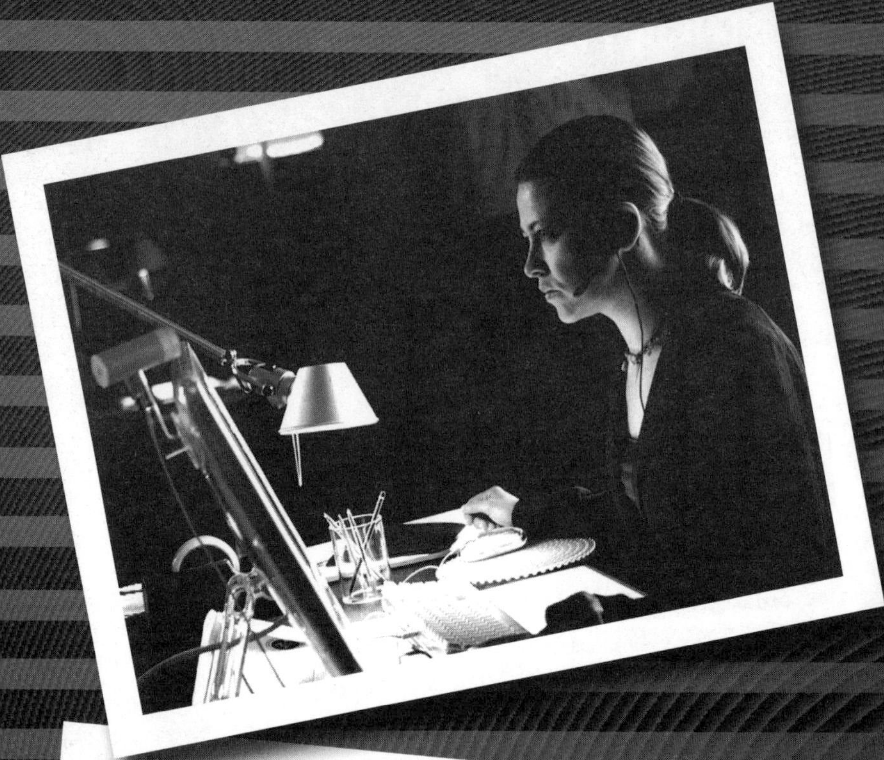

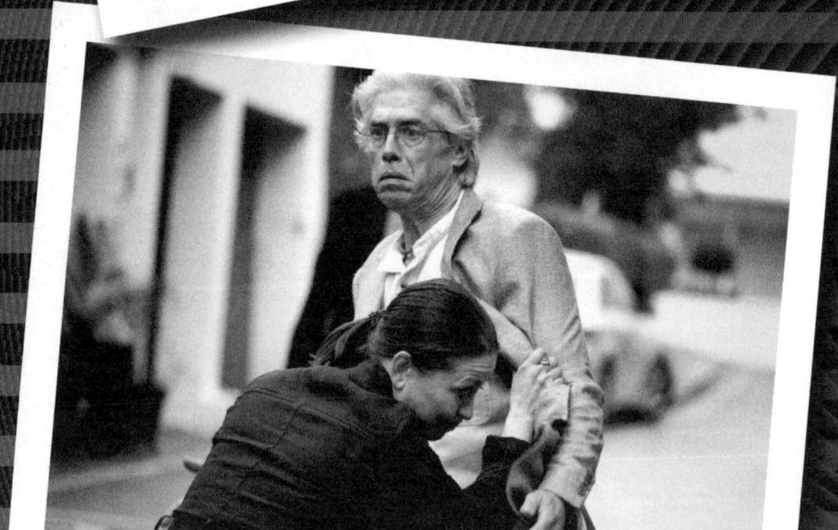

Private and Confidential

Name: Ruth Evershed
Position: Research Officer
D.O.B: 29.04.1970
Hair: Brown
Eyes: Blue
Height: 5'4
Marital status: Single
Dependants: None
Blood type: B, Rh negative

Ruth Evershed was seconded to MI5 from GCHQ before her contract was made permanent. She provides excellent back-up research for the team in Section D. She has also made occasional forays into the field as her confidence grows.

Her enthusiasm and loyalty are particularly commendable although her commitment to the job leaves her with little time for a social life.

Major operations include:

- Using relationship with step-brother to talk round Angela Wells
- Exploitation of Professor Curtis from Shining Dawn
- Kidnapped by GCHQ hacker, Andrew Forrestal
- Recruitment of taxi drivers as MI5 workers

MI5
Application Form

Surname

Evershed

Forenames

Ruth

Date of Birth

29.04.1970

Place of birth

Exeter

Nationality at birth

British

Permanent Address

18 Mulberry Hill, Cheltenham

Current occupation

GCHQ researcher

Date of availability for employment

Immediately

Do you hold a full, clean driving licence?

Yes

Medical:
Do you have any conditions – either physical or psychological – which might affect your employment?

No

Father's name, address and occupation

Dr James Evershed (died 1981)
GP

Mother's name, maiden name, address and occupation

Elizabeth Bickley

Remarried to David Shaw after my father's death but has reverted to maiden name

Housewife

18 New Road, Cheltenham

Brothers / Sisters (with names and D.O.B.)

No siblings

One step-brother, Peter

Secondary Schools / Colleges (Dates : Names : Town)

1981-1988 : Bedales School : Petersfield

GCSEs or equivalent

O Levels: 12 As (English Language, English Literature, French, Latin, Greek, Spanish, Maths, History, Geography, Religious Education, Combined Science)

A levels and AS levels or equivalents

English – A (Cert. of excellence)

Latin – A (Cert. of excellence)

Greek – A (Cert. of excellence)

Arabic – A

Philosophy – A

Persian – A (self-taught)

Gap Year

How did you spend any break during your education?

N/A

University or Further Education

Corpus Christi College Oxford - 1988-1993
MA (Hons) Classics - First
MPhil - Classics
I started a research doctorate but grew bored with it

Awards

Please give details of any other awards (e.g. music)

Grade 8 piano
Grade 8 violin
National schools Classics medal - 1987/1988
National schools Philosophy medal - 1988
M.L.T. Combes prize for classics (Oxford)

EMPLOYMENT

Dates	Employer	Position
1994-	GCHQ	Researcher

Have you served in HM Forces (including Reserves)?

No

Do you have applications pending for other jobs?

No

PERSONAL QUALITIES AND SKILLS

SUMMARY

Provide a pen-portrait of your life to date

I was frustrated by many of the other people at Oxford.
It annoyed me that we were in one of the best centres of
learning in the world and all they wanted to do was get
drunk. It saddened me that they didn't care about ideas,
that they didn't care about books, in particular. I couldn't
understand why they didn't share my excitement every time
they walked into the library.

But then, something changed after I took my finals and
started doing postgraduate research. I didn't lose my love
of learning, but I lost my love of learning for learning's
sake. It seemed self-indulgent, somehow. Wrong, even. I
wanted to apply it. I wanted to see some tangible results
beyond the sad smile of a lonely professor. I suppose what
I'm saying is that I wanted to be useful. That is why I
applied to GCHQ almost ten years ago.

I initially enjoyed my work at GCHQ but I have begun to find
a lot of the tasks very tedious. Since then, I have been
looking for a way out while continuing to work for the

government. This is why I am now seeking to formalise my secondment at MI5 into a full-time role.

MOTIVATION

Why do you think you would be suited to a career in MI5?

I've partly addressed this in my last answer, but I think there is something very satisfying about applying an expert base of knowledge and intensive research skills to a complex problem. This was one of the things that appealed to me most about academia, and it was what appealed to me about working at GCHQ. I would like to put this knowledge to use in real situations that affect real people. And, if possible, I would like to work in the field a little more. My secondment here at MI5 exceeded my own high expectations, and I would very much like to stay on.

Moreover, I have the necessary temperament to work as part of a team on sensitive political issues. I also speak a number of languages.

POLITICAL CURIOSITY

Give three political topics (historical or current) which interest you

- Athenian democracy
- Monetarism
- T.E. Lawrence
- Corn law reform
- Israeli Arab conflict
- The Early Christian Church
- Locke's natural theory
- Machiavelli
- Armenian Holocaust

ADAPTABILITY

Give an example of a time when you had to adapt to unexpected circumstances

I had a happy childhood until the age of eleven when my father's death coincided with my being sent away to a boarding school I detested. I was an only child and close to my father.

These events triggered an emotional reaction from which I'm not sure I've ever entirely recovered. I wouldn't go as far as to say that I've ever been clinically depressed, but something in my chemical make-up changed at around that time.

One day - I remember it very clearly as it was my 13th birthday - I made a decision which has stood me in good stead ever since. I realised that this was something I was going to have to live with. I could let it ruin my life. Or I could accept it. So, I started throwing myself into everything at school - both intra- and extra-curricular. I forced myself to make friends, even when I didn't feel like it. And I slowly learned to come to terms with my father's death.

Churchill used to call his low moments his "black dogs". When I feel a bit sad, I tell myself that it's only temporary, and that makes me feel much better. I couldn't fight it, so I adapted to it.

This attitude helped me accept my step-father when my mother remarried a few years later. It has also helped me through some low moments in Cheltenham. I have thrown myself into all aspects of GHCQ's work – even the ones which were not initially appealing.

RESPONSIBILITY
What positions of responsibility have you held – at school, university or otherwise?

Head Girl

FOREIGN LANGUAGES
Please indicate level of competence

French – fluent	Persian – fluent
Spanish – fluent	Greek (ancient) – fluent
Arabic – fluent	Latin – fluent

OTHER INTERESTS

Theatre (I played Lady Macbeth in the sixth form play)

TRAVEL
Give details of all foreign travel undertaken in the last 10 years, including reason for travel

None

EQUAL OPPORTUNITIES
This information is not used as part of our selection procedures

Gender	Ethnic origin	Disabilities
Male Female ✓	White British	None

REFEREES
Please give details of three referees. One of these should be a contemporary who knows you well

1. Professor D.G.A Finkelstein, Professor of Greek Literature, Corpus Christi College, Oxford University
2. James Davies, Head of R Section, GCHQ
3. Charlotte Price, roommate, Corpus Christi College, Oxford

Signature

Ruth Evershed

Date

9th January 2004

MAF|08.fa|vii.4

CORPUS CHRISTI COLLEGE, OXFORD UNIVERSITY

REFERENCE: Ruth Evershed

To Whom It May Concern:

I have been an academic at this university since 1960. For over thirty years, therefore, I have been writing references to further the careers of snivelling, morally defunct undergraduates.

"I want to work in an investment bank," they say to me. "Will you tell them that I always deliver my essays on Greek poetry on time?"

These are the politer ones. Most of them merely put my name down on the form. The first I hear about my duties as a referee is when some ghastly female in Human Resources phones up asking me about their "character". "Character," I say. "You'd find more rounded human beings in Euripedes." And then they hang up, baffled.

And do they ever show the slightest bit of gratitude? No, never. Thirty years and just one library donated in all that time. That's what we get for providing these poor, delusional souls with a springboard to Mammon.

Why do I digress like this, you ask? The answer, dear whomsoever it may concern, is that young Ms. Evershed is different. Very different, indeed. I have rarely – no, never – encountered such a talented student. Some of my pupils are clever; she has wisdom. Some of them learn facts; she devours arguments. Some of them have brains; she has intellect.

Perhaps I should warn you: she's absolutely bonkers, of course. But aren't we all? She's brilliant, too. Bonkers and brilliant.

So, give her a job in this beastly little wing of your civil service, or whatever you call it these days. She'll turn up late to work with her socks on inside out and smelling faintly of cat vomit, but nowhere, I repeat nowhere, will you find an abler employee.

A final word of warning: behind that bumbling exterior beats a heart of tragic passion. She might look like a librarian; believe me, she's not. I hope you'll be able to provide her with more adventure than I did.

Perhaps I have said too much. I am a foolish old man in love with a muse. A muse, I should probably have said, who was awarded the top first in classics every year of her exams. I hope that, in these dreary egalitarian times, you won't hold that too much against her.

Professor D.G.A.Finkelstein M.A. DPhil (Oxon)
PROFESSOR OF GREEK LITERATURE   CORPUS CHRISTI COLLE[C]

SECURITY CLEARANCE & BACKGROUND CHECKS

Ruth Evershed

I was tasked with carrying out routine background checks into Ruth Evershed's family and friends, as well as standard fact-checking of her application details.

I am happy to report that Ruth's academic record is every bit as impressive as it seems. We've had a few applicants in the past with 6 A-levels, but none who've come in the top three in the country in three of them (including one they taught themselves). Initially, I thought Ruth's nine political interests (she was asked to produce three) were rather showy. On further research, however, I discovered that she had published academic articles on most of them. Her desire not to be viewed purely as an academic is commendable (if a little easy to dismiss). And I rather enjoyed her joke about being fluent in ancient Greek (or at least I hope this was a joke).

I was also impressed by Ruth's honesty. Her candid account of adapting to unexpected circumstances is particularly moving. Her university professor (in an extraordinary reference written ten years ago for her first posting at GCHQ) describes her as "bonkers but brilliant". A decade later, I agree with the latter half. There is a certain underlying sadness in her demeanour, but she is no more troubled (and a great deal more composed) than most young women I come across.

Ruth's family background raises no alarms. She remains close to her mother despite the remarriage. Her step-brother, Peter, was a special branch protection officer for Princess Diana so that side of the family has already undergone all necessary security clearance. Ruth herself cleared all checks when she started work at GCHQ in 1994.

Ruth was a hard worker at Cheltenham who brought a moral dimension to her approach. You'll see from one letter in particular in her file that she likes to follow procedure.

I have no hesitation in passing this stage of her application process. Providing she passes her probation period, I think she will make an excellent MI5 researcher.

Rebecca Moore

APPROVED

Rebecca Moore, HR Security
7th February 2004

TRAINING ASSESSMENT
Ruth Evershed, 9th May 2004

SCORES

Practical

Surveillance	0.1
Counter-surveillance	0.2
Physical endurance	0.1
Shooting	0.3
Driving	2
Technical	4
Average	1.12

Other core competencies

Calm under pressure	1.3
Leadership	1.2
Team work	4.9
Communication	4.4
General attitude	4.8
Average	3.32

Intellectual

Linguistic	5
Decision-making	4.4
Research	5
Average	4.8

Overall average — **2.69**

On a sliding scale of 1 to 5 where 1 is poor, 5 is outstanding and 2.5 is average for a new recruit

Ruth's attitude and intellectual capabilities are first rate. And while her practical skills are currently too low to be considered in any meaningful field role, she clearly took a great deal of pleasure from trying her hand in this area. Perhaps this is something she could return to in the future.

She will be an excellent addition to the team here. I hope you can rescue her from Cheltenham.

Robin Ferguson
Head of recruit training, MI5

Ruth Evershed
Re: UN eavesdropping

9th January 2002

Dear James,

As you well know, I am not one to cause undue trouble in the office. I turn up on time, I often leave late and I do everything that is asked of me and more. I really enjoy this job and I'd do nothing to compromise my future career here.

However, I have recently become very concerned by the way we continue to eavesdrop on the United Nations – both at their headquarters in New York and their various subsidiary offices around the world. I don't want to sound naïve. I am aware that we are a multi-billion-pound eavesdropping organisation, after all. And I know we shamelessly listen in to people's lives all around the globe. Most of the time, I know that we are doing this for a higher end.

With the UN, however, I feel it is rather different. This is not spying on an enemy (which we all do) or spying on our allies (which most of us do). This is spying on an organisation to which we belong. At the moment I believe it is only the British and the Americans indulging in this kind of activity. This strikes me as foolish at a time when we need more allies on the world stage.

My concerns are practical as well as moral. What if this were ever to leak to the press? These things always come out sooner or later. And how can you stop someone with a conscience – in this department or elsewhere – from doing so?

I am not the sort of person to go public with concerns of this sort. I believe these things should always be sorted out in-house, with the proper procedures, by people who understand the intelligence community and are familiar with its unwritten rules. My fear is that not everyone will feel the same.

I hope you don't mind me recording my concerns in this way.

Yours sincerely,

Ruth Evershed

Note from James Davies, Head of R Section, GCHQ

Ruth's moral and practical concerns in bringing this to light are commendable. It is a relief to see someone using the proper complaint procedures for once.

There is little I can do, of course. Eavesdropping on UN delegates will continue so long as it gives us a competitive advantage in international politics. And even if we were to follow through these objections, the pressure from the Americans to desist would be overwhelming. I'm sorry I cannot do more.

Please retain this in Ms. Evershed's file.

OPERATION BARCODE

I have been asked to write up an account of my secondment from GCHQ, my motives for agreeing to act as a mole within MI5 and the operation which ensued when I was turned by Tom Quinn.

Introduction

I was posted on secondment to MI5 from GCHQ in the autumn of 2003. The condition of the transfer was that I occasionally relayed back to GCHQ what I was doing.

Initially, I was uneasy with this situation. Should one department be spying on another in this way? I was also suspicious that most of my communications had to pass through unelected Downing Street adviser, Amanda Roke.

However, my fears were calmed by my superiors, and I also sought to reassure myself. Surely government departments all worked happily alongside one another, I thought. Surely all our intelligence agencies were fighting the War on Terror under one umbrella. Surely the government couldn't betray itself to itself? And wasn't it only in America that the intelligence community had descended into internecine warfare and unseemly budgetary squabbles?

But if I'm honest, my main reason for taking up the offer was that it sounded exciting. I'd always wanted to join MI5. This seemed like the perfect opening, and if the price I had to pay was passing a few harmless bits of information back to my old employer, so be it.

Also, I would have done almost anything to get out of Cheltenham.

Russian mafia operation

In December 2003, a mole in the treasury suggested that the £13 billion earmarked for improvements in the health service had actually come from the Russian mafia. It was suspected that the money was being laundered through Bowman Bank.

Unknown to the treasury, Danny Hunter was sent undercover in Bowman Bank as a trader. This was exactly the kind of event within my remit to report back to GCHQ, and I had no moral or professional problem with doing so at the time. Why were treasury officials, spin doctors and the intelligence services all pulling in different directions? It didn't make any sense. And if my job was to keep everyone together in a more obvious loop of "joined-up government", then it was a job I was happy to do.

However, Amanda Roke was angry that her orders not to infiltrate Bowman Bank had been ignored by MI5. And MI5 was angry that their infiltration had been leaked to Roke. Tom Quinn tasked Colin Wells to find the mole within the Grid.

Caught and turned

Although I had coded my communications back to Downing Street and Cheltenham pretty well, few encryptions are sufficiently robust to stand up to Colin Wells. He found incriminating traces on my hard drive and Tom Quinn confronted me with the evidence. I owned up, explaining my reasoning.

Tom accepted my motives and kept me at MI5 on probation. He also had another proposition – Operation Barcode.

Operation Barcode

As a turned GCHQ mole with loyalties to MI5, I was a valuable asset in inter-departmental rivalries. It was therefore decided that I would maintain my cover and continue to feed regular, false information back to Cheltenham. I had little choice – I was compromised twice over. And, in any case, I wanted to stay at MI5.

This "information" initially focused on the obvious areas in which MI5 could hope to gain an advantage over GCHQ. An ongoing dispute between the two departments is the extent to which our competencies overlap in areas such as translators and technical expertise. I therefore made every effort to play down our abilities in these areas. Our translation team was reduced to a couple of superannuated Russian experts. I told them our eavesdropping equipment consisted of little more than a few Cold War bugs.

All this stood us in excellent stead when the next round of budgetary talks came up.

There have also been recent concerns within the intelligence community about GCHQ's recruitment policy. It was felt that some of their graduate applicants were being poorly vetted – including a number of oversights concerning undetected radical sympathies, as well as tendencies to sudden and indiscriminate flurries of conscience. The service's whistleblowers have been leaking their stories to the Sunday newspapers with an embarrassing regularity.

It was therefore felt that Operation Barcode could be used to exert extra pressure on GCHQ. Through my normal channels, I "leaked" information that MI5 was carrying out a thorough background check on all GCHQ employees and applicants. In truth, we had neither the time nor the resources to do this. We did, however, hope that this news might encourage GCHQ to up their game.

As it turned out, it had the opposite effect. MI5's own mole within GCHQ was turned in late February (in much the same way as I was by MI5). The first thing he told his new employers about was Operation Barcode. The head of GCHQ became involved. Resignations were threatened. It almost got as far as press disclosure at one stage until Harry stepped in and the whole operation was quietly wound up. Relationships between the two services remain frosty.

Personal Conclusions

I was put in an impossible position last autumn. I had sworn loyalty to the crown but my employer was GCHQ. GCHQ then put me on secondment within MI5 on condition that I reported back to them. I was following orders from three sides at once whose stated aims were all the same. It was as ridiculous as an RAF spy in the Navy passing on secrets to the Army.

Operation Barcode might have made sense at the time. It might have seemed like a sensible way of making capital out of a bad situation. In retrospect, however, it achieved little. Next time there's a terrorist atrocity on these shores, or a network based here remains undetected, or another drug cartel diversifies into people-trafficking, we might want to ask ourselves exactly what it is we are doing with the nation's security and the taxpayer's money. There is a time for spy games, and there is a time for sensible, open communication. This was the latter.

We worked on the principle that two wrongs might make a right. And we were very wrong, indeed.

Added note from Harry Pearce

I am satisfied with Ruth Evershed's probation period and approve her full-time, continuous employment on Section D at MI5. For procedure's sake, I asked her to fill out an application form. I am glad to see that she has passed the security and training hurdles.

Her loyalty and intellect are outstanding and she is a very welcome member of the team.

23rd June 2004

Assessment of Ruth Evershed by Miranda Saunders, in-house psychologist

ANNOTATED TRANSCRIPTS	**RE** – Ruth Evershed **MS** – Miranda Saunders

Accompanying note from Tom Quinn

Miranda Saunders was fired the day after producing these psychological assessments.

I was tasked by the DG to conduct a psychological assessment of the key players in Section D. That this had to take place on the same day as the visit of the American President was highly inconvenient to me.

Although I had a clipboard and took occasional notes, the officers were unaware that I was, in fact, recording them as well. These are the transcripts from my session with Ruth Evershed.

MS I hear you've been avoiding me, Ruth, by reading GCHQ reports. That's interesting.

RE They weren't, actually. They were pretty boring.

MS I didn't mean the contents of the reports. I don't find that interesting at all. But I do find it interesting that you were reading reports from GCHQ.

RE Right. I'm not sure I follow.

MS Well, let's see if you can lead, then. Why do you think that I think that that's interesting?

RE This is ridiculous. The US President almost died today. I've had one of the longest days of my life. And you've brought me up here to play mind-games.

MS Ridiculous? You call this ridiculous? I tell you what I call ridiculous: you being sent here by GCHQ as a mole to spy on us. Isn't that pretty ridiculous?

RE Ah, so that's what this is about. Ruth the treacherous mole.

MS Are you a traitor, Ruth?

RE Oh for God's sake, Miranda! No, I am not. Yes, I was sent by GCHQ to keep tabs on MI5. Yes, I felt uncomfortable about doing this. Yes, I didn't have any choice. But I've been over this in my field report for Tom Quinn. These are operational details. Structural details. Bureaucratic details. They've got nothing to do with you. You're a psychologist.

MS Okay, Ruth. No need to get upset. Let's talk about the psychological details, then.

RE Yes. Let's.

MS How are you fitting in here at Section D?

RE It's great. I love it. It's so much better than my old job. I loathed GCHQ, to be honest. Too many bloody mathematicians. I so much wanted to join MI5; to be a real spy.

MS But you weren't more suited to GHCQ?

Case ID: MI5/421
Date: 04|04|2004

RE I suppose, in a way. I was useless at all the field operative stuff in training. I'm much more suited to the research side.

MS But that wasn't enough?

RE No. The thing is, I find MI5's work all rather exciting. I might not look like the most interesting person in the world, but I get bored easily. Really, I do. And I'm bloody good at this job.

MS And modest, too.

RE Sorry. I just really want to stay at MI5, that's all. I can't think of anything worse than being sent back to GCHQ.

MS We'll let others be the judge of that.

There is a brief pause.

MS (*cont.*) Actually, you're one of the few people that no one else has criticised. You seem to have gone down very well here.

RE Really? That's fantastic.

MS Zoe called you "bonkers but brilliant". Harry said you were a "fantastic addition to the team" . . .

RE Harry said that?

MS You like Harry, don't you?

RE He is a fantastic boss, yes.

MS And the others?

RE They're all great, yes.

MS You seem like a very happy person.

RE I am. I have a job I love, colleagues I respect and a cat at home called Fidget. There's really nothing missing in my life.

****Transcript ends****

OPERATION METER

FIELD REPORT
TITLE: *London Taxi Drivers Recruitment*
FILED BY: *Ruth Evershed*
DATE: *3rd November 2004*

For the last three months I have been recruiting black cab drivers to work for MI5. Despite initial successes, the operation (codename Meter) turned out disastrously. Here is the report into its rationale, execution and outcome.

Introduction & rationale

Government departments spend large sums every year on transportation. These are not just the high-end perks which make newspaper headlines such as reinforced Jaguars for cabinet ministers. There is also a culture of waste in most Whitehall departments. Officials from the DTI are sent on expensive fact-finding expeditions, many of which end up on the beach somewhere. Diplomats at the FCO above grade four fly first class everywhere. And the treasury enjoys spending money on itself as much as it enjoys withholding funds from others.

The intelligence services are not immune from such profligacy. Our culture of secrecy has traditionally extended to the most mundane areas of our budgetary requirements. One Section Head refused to disclose how much he had spent on looking after members of the French Secret Service (DGSE). It later turned out that he had spent over £5,000 entertaining them in a central London strip club.

Cost, therefore, was a considerable factor in recruiting taxi drivers to work for MI5. While we have access to a range of expensive pool cars, our needs are often mundane – as simple as couriering a harmless package across to the Home Office or picking up low-level intelligence personnel from the airport.

Another major – more pressing – factor was convenience. London taxis can linger without being noticed; most Londoners don't give them a second thought. We could easily install bugging equipment in the vehicles without arousing suspicions. And if we worked with a large firm, we would be able to summon any of their drivers to any given location in London at short notice.

There was an altruistic element, too. We could take up slack in the economy by finding well-paid employment for under-worked drivers. On a small scale, we planned to run Operation Meter as a mini PFI project.

Recruitment

We started running this operation at ground level, approaching drivers individually who were already known to us through other sources (e.g. former servicemen). When this proved successful, it was decided to roll it out on a larger scale.

We commissioned a series of discreet advertisements in the trade press as well as some of the righter-wing tabloids which taxi drivers traditionally read. Although no direct allusion was made to the nature of the work or the employer, it was hoped that the more intelligent applicants might guess at their real meaning (thereby treating it with the seriousness it deserved).

The recruitment process turned into something of a farce after a freelance journalist spotted one of the adverts and guessed its true meaning. This was then reported in a full-page news article which was subsequently followed-up by most major broadcasters. Many unsuitable applicants applied, some of them under the illusion that they'd be involved in high-speed car chases in modified black cabs.

Here is a sample extract from one of the covering letters: "I know the streets of London like the back of my hand. Years of cheating customers have taught me the most elaborate detours across the capital. I am a fast and aggressive driver. Might MI5 consider upgrading my vehicle – can you make it invisible like in the last James Bond? Or, at the very least, some lasers? I'd also be very grateful if you were able to wipe the nine points which are currently on my licence. They were all unfairly given."

This was by no means the worst of the applications.

By this stage, however, we'd spent so much money on advertising and planning that it was decided to press ahead regardless with the roll-out. We started rumours that the programme had been decommissioned. And then we carried on as before.

Successes

Operation Meter recorded a number of undeniable successes. One cabbie had such a long conversation with an inebriated CIA operative that we "shared" almost as much intelligence in five minutes as in 50 years of a special relationship. On another occasion a hidden camera recorded intimate footage of a married diplomat taking his secretary back to his hotel. We were then able to blackmail him.

Less dramatic were numerous low-level successes, particularly in picking up targets outside hotels and other venues without arousing suspicion. In the best circumstances, this allowed us to discover exactly where they lived without the need for expensive surveillance operations. It also saved a great deal of money.

At its lowest level, the taxis also worked well for couriering services until our disgruntled old couriers leaked the move to the press.

Failures

However, the abiding verdict of Operation Meter must be that it was a failure. In retrospect, our mistake was to attempt to roll out a small-scale successful enterprise onto the larger stage. A number of unscrupulous cabbies slipped through the vetting procedures. Parcels went missing. Expensive recording equipment disappeared. Video footage was leaked to the press first and shared with us second. Garrulous drivers shared secret information indiscriminately.

These were only the minor hiccoughs. Our biggest failure was a misguided attempt to train up taxi drivers as mobile surveillance teams. On the surface it seemed like a very sensible idea. Cabbies could go almost entirely undetected while tracking suspect cars across London. It would take an unusually good anti-surveillance team (or an unnatural level of paranoia) to suspect and identify identical black cabs.

Perhaps we should have foreseen that this would end badly. Numerous drivers were caught speeding by the police whereupon they told them exactly what they were doing in order to avoid a fine. One driver ignored the fact that he had a fare in the back of his cab as he drove him at high speed in the opposite direction to his destination. That fare was a senior backbench MP. MI5 was questioned in front of a scrutiny committee and Operation Meter was wound down.

Personal Conclusions

The unavoidable conclusion to be drawn from Operation Meter was that it was a good idea, badly implemented. Had we kept the operation within its original, narrow remit, it could have enjoyed continued success for a number of years. Our early successes instilled a false sense of security.

There are, I believe, two lessons to be learned from this operation. The first is that small can often be beautiful. Just because something works doesn't mean that it has to be expanded. The second is that MI5 should resist the current trends in Whitehall to outsource at will. We spend a lot of money training our officers. Perhaps it's time we started putting a bit of faith in them.

ADD TO FILE

Recorded disciplinary hearing with Ruth Evershed

2nd March 2005

TRANSCRIPTS WITH APPROVED ANNOTATIONS FROM OBSERVING INDEPENDENT PSYCHOLOGIST	**HP** – Harry Pearce **RE** – Ruth Evershed

HP You know why we have to do this, Ruth, don't you?

RE Of course. I have erred and now I must repent.

HP What you did was a big breach of protocol. Possibly even illegal.

RE I know, and I'm sorry. It won't happen again.

HP Listening into phone taps is all very well – but engineering chance lunches on the table next to the person you're listening to? Going to Requiems so you can sing alongside them? Taking Malcolm along to pretend to be your brother? It's madness, Ruth. That's what it is.

RE I know, and like I said, I am really sorry.

HP You do understand why we can't let things like this happen, don't you?

RE Of course, I do. "Our job is to protect. To serve. To maintain the status quo." Isn't that what you always say?

HP Yes, that is our job.

RE And I was doing none of those things.

HP You have to think about the moral implications of this. What would this man think if he knew you'd been eavesdropping on him in this way?

RE I don't know. I never saw him again.

HP Well, I'll tell you what he'd think. He'd think it was downright creepy; that's what. Just how were you going to break the news to him? "What do I do for a living? Well, funny you ask, but actually I'm a spy and I listen into people's conversations. People like you, for example. And I liked the sound of your voice." Pifff, whiz, Mr Random Man vanishes into the ether, calling the *News of the World* as he goes.

RE It wasn't like that, Harry.

HP Maybe it wasn't, but I don't really care what it was like. Actions have consequences, Ruth. I want *you* to think through the consequences of *your* actions. What if you had seen this man again? What if you'd let slip how you'd actually come across him? What if he had told the press?

RE It doesn't bear thinking about.

HP It doesn't. But let's think about it for a moment. The press would have crucified you. They would have crucified all of us. "Lonely, single MI5 officer uses job as dating agency." I can see the headlines now.

RE That's not a very good headline. They would have come up with something much better than that.

HP laughs.

HP That's not the point, Ruth. What I'm saying is that you would have been hung out to dry.

RE It was a mistake. I'm sorry. A silly mistake. It hasn't happened before, and it definitely won't happen again.

HP But can you explain why? You seem so level-headed, normally.

RE I am. I am level-headed. I was lonely, I suppose, as you say. And there was something different about this man. He was kind; he was fatherly. He was successful . . .

HP That's okay, Ruth. There are worse crimes than being lonely, you know. All I ask is that you separate your life from work life; your time from office time; your goals from our goals. Whatever you do in your time is your business, but you can't let it get in the way of work.

RE My work is my life. They're inextricably entwined.

HP Well, un-entwine them, then.

RE Oh, it's that simple, is it?

HP It's never simple. But we can make it simple. We have to make it simple.

RE Well, I think you're pretty damn simple, Harry. To put it like that. To reduce it to black and white lines. Why did you have to make such a game out of it? Why did you go through the elaborate charade of putting Sam onto me? Why did she keep track of our emails? Why have Malcolm play along too? Dammit, Harry, you can be a coward.

HP Finished?

RE Yes.

There is the sound of RE moving towards the door.

RE (*cont.*) And this disciplinary process is a shambles. Slapped wrist, Harry. That's all it needed. Not this recording nonsense. Have you lost all sense of proportion? What's real for you any more? What turned your heart to stone?

A door slams shut.

HP Not stone, Ruth. Far from it.

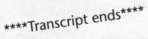

****Transcript ends****

Note from Sam Buxton

In January 2005, Harry Pearce became concerned that Ruth Evershed was taking too much time listening to static surveillance tapes. She appeared to be staying at work later and later. It eventually came to light that she was listening to John Fortescue, a man we'd been tasked to protect. Harry asked me to find out more about what was going on. Here are the transcripts of my internal email exchanges with Ruth on the matter.

-----Internal mail [personal]-----
-----Secure intranet-----

From: Sam Buxton
   To: Ruth Evershed
 Date: 3 January 2005 20.34

Hey Ruth. Still here? Why are you working late?

-----Internal mail [personal]-----
-----Secure intranet-----

From: Ruth Evershed
   To: Sam Buxton
 Date: 3 January 2005 20.34

Hello Sam. I didn't know you were still here, too. What are you up to? It's these bloody transcripts. They take hours to listen to. And there's never any point to them.

-----Internal mail [personal]-----
-----Secure intranet-----

From: Sam Buxton
   To: Ruth Evershed
 Date: 3 January 2005 20.35

You look as if you're quite enjoying listening to them, actually. Or are you smiling about something else?! I'm meant to be on a first date tonight but he was awful. So I'm standing him up by pretending to work.

-----Internal mail [personal]-----
-----Secure intranet-----

From: Ruth Evershed
   To: Sam Buxton
 Date: 3 January 2005 20.36

You're dreadful!

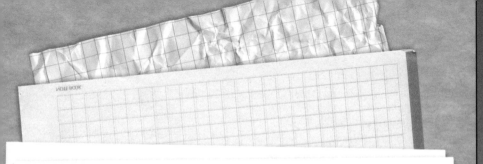

```
-----Internal mail [personal]-----
-----Secure intranet-----
```
 From: Sam Buxton
   To: Ruth Evershed
 Date: 3 January 2005 20.36

I know! But aren't we all? So, what time are you leaving?

```
-----Internal mail [personal]-----
-----Secure intranet-----
```
 From: Ruth Evershed
   To: Sam Buxton
 Date: 3 January 2005 20.37

Not sure. Listen, Sam, if I tell you something can you keep it a secret?

```
-----Internal mail [personal]-----
-----Secure intranet-----
```
 From: Sam Buxton
   To: Ruth Evershed
 Date: 3 January 2005 20.37

That's our job, isn't it?!

-----Internal mail [personal]-----
-----Secure intranet-----
From: Ruth Evershed
  To: Sam Buxton
Date: 3 January 2005 20.38

Ha, yes. No, it's not that kind of secret. Not a state, level 1 secret. Eyes only. It's these tapes. You're right: they are making me smile. I think I'm kind of falling in love with this man. That's silly, isn't it?

-----Internal mail [personal]-----
-----Secure intranet-----
From: Sam Buxton
  To: Ruth Evershed
Date: 3 January 2005 20.39

Silly, yes. But kind of sweet. In a stalker-romantic type of way. Tell me about him.

-----Internal mail [personal]-----
-----Secure intranet-----
From: Ruth Evershed
  To: Sam Buxton
Date: 3 January 2005 20.39

Well, he's called John Fortescue. He loves music and he's got a sore knee from playing too much tennis in Spain. He's working far too hard at the moment and he's got a good friend called Eric. Divorced, no children. Oh yes, and from the sound of his voice I would say he's 5'11", well-built, blue eyes and unfeasibly handsome. Ah, one can dream...

-----Internal mail [personal]-----
-----Secure intranet-----
From: Sam Buxton
  To: Ruth Evershed
Date: 3 January 2005 20.41

I am jealous! Right, I'm off home now. I think I've made it obvious enough to my date that I'm not interested. I'll leave you to your lurrver. Sweet dreams . . . x

****

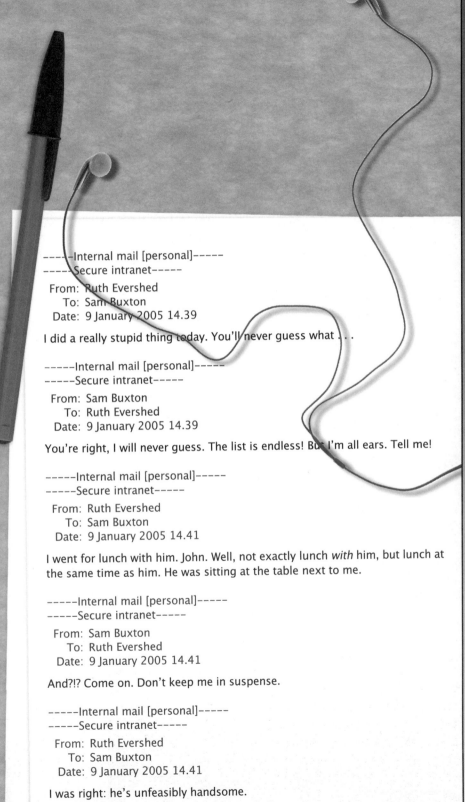

-----Internal mail [personal]-----
-----Secure intranet-----
From: Ruth Evershed
  To: Sam Buxton
Date: 9 January 2005 14.39

I did a really stupid thing today. You'll never guess what . . .

-----Internal mail [personal]-----
-----Secure intranet-----
From: Sam Buxton
  To: Ruth Evershed
Date: 9 January 2005 14.39

You're right, I will never guess. The list is endless! But I'm all ears. Tell me!

-----Internal mail [personal]-----
-----Secure intranet-----
From: Ruth Evershed
  To: Sam Buxton
Date: 9 January 2005 14.41

I went for lunch with him. John. Well, not exactly lunch *with* him, but lunch at the same time as him. He was sitting at the table next to me.

-----Internal mail [personal]-----
-----Secure intranet-----
From: Sam Buxton
  To: Ruth Evershed
Date: 9 January 2005 14.41

And?!? Come on. Don't keep me in suspense.

-----Internal mail [personal]-----
-----Secure intranet-----
From: Ruth Evershed
  To: Sam Buxton
Date: 9 January 2005 14.41

I was right: he's unfeasibly handsome.

-----Internal mail [personal]-----
-----Secure intranet-----

From: Sam Buxton
  To: Ruth Evershed
Date: 9 January 2005 14.42

I'm so glad! Let me guess: this meeting didn't happen entirely by accident?

-----Internal mail [personal]-----
-----Secure intranet-----

From: Ruth Evershed
  To: Sam Buxton
Date: 9 January 2005 14.42

Hmmm, no. It's just possible that I might perhaps have overheard where he was having lunch today.

-----Internal mail [personal]-----
-----Secure intranet-----

From: Sam Buxton
  To: Ruth Evershed
Date: 9 January 2005 14.43

Go Tiger! When are you "bumping" into him next?

-----Internal mail [personal]-----
-----Secure intranet-----

From: Sam Buxton
  To: Ruth Evershed
Date: 9 January 2005 15.20

Ruth? Did you get my last message?

-----Internal mail [personal]-----
-----Secure intranet-----

From: Sam Buxton
  To: Ruth Evershed
Date: 9 January 2005 15.20

Ruth?!

-----Internal mail [personal]-----
-----Secure intranet-----

From: Ruth Evershed
  To: Sam Buxton
Date: 9 January 2005 15.57

Hi Sam. Sorry. Harry just stormed out of his office and I had to minimise all my non-work-related windows. Water cooler in 7 minutes and I'll tell you everything?

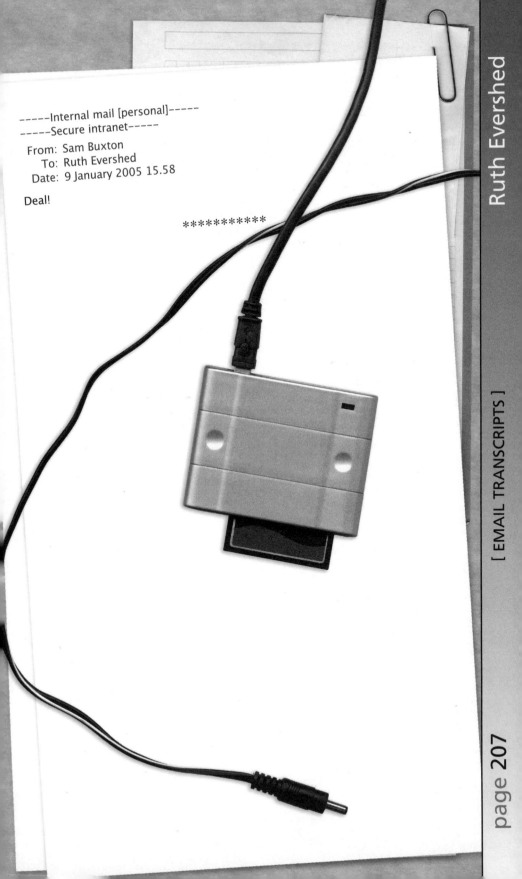

-----Internal mail [personal]-----
-----Secure intranet-----

From: Sam Buxton
  To: Ruth Evershed
Date: 9 January 2005 15.58

Deal!

****

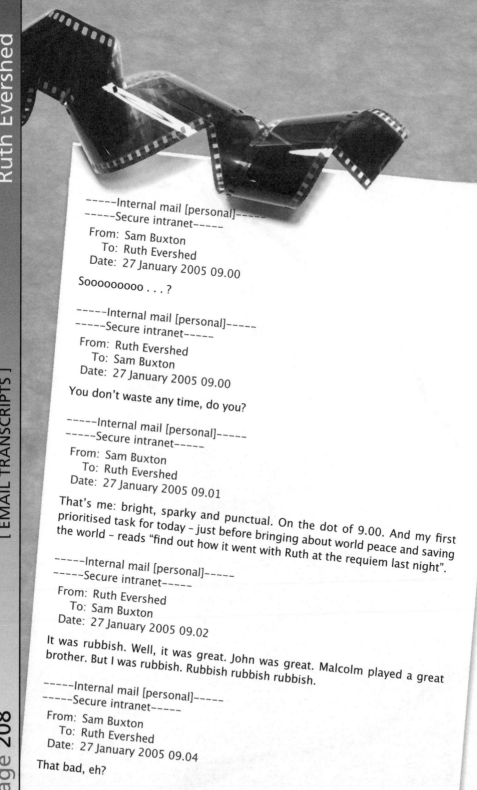

-----Internal mail [personal]-----
-----Secure intranet-----
From: Sam Buxton
To: Ruth Evershed
Date: 27 January 2005 09.00

Soooooooo . . . ?

-----Internal mail [personal]-----
-----Secure intranet-----
From: Ruth Evershed
To: Sam Buxton
Date: 27 January 2005 09.00

You don't waste any time, do you?

-----Internal mail [personal]-----
-----Secure intranet-----
From: Sam Buxton
To: Ruth Evershed
Date: 27 January 2005 09.01

That's me: bright, sparky and punctual. On the dot of 9.00. And my first prioritised task for today – just before bringing about world peace and saving the world – reads "find out how it went with Ruth at the requiem last night".

-----Internal mail [personal]-----
-----Secure intranet-----
From: Ruth Evershed
To: Sam Buxton
Date: 27 January 2005 09.02

It was rubbish. Well, it was great. John was great. Malcolm played a great brother. But I was rubbish. Rubbish rubbish rubbish.

-----Internal mail [personal]-----
-----Secure intranet-----
From: Sam Buxton
To: Ruth Evershed
Date: 27 January 2005 09.04

That bad, eh?

-----Internal mail [personal]-----
-----Secure intranet-----

From: Ruth Evershed
  To: Sam Buxton
Date: 27 January 2005 09.05

Worse. It went so well at the beginning. We sang, drank some wine and we talked afterwards. My word, we talked so well. And then he walked me outside at the end. And it was as if he was about to kiss me and then I said something stupid and the moment was broken. Then he turned away and said goodbye. Never mind. It probably wasn't meant to be, was it? And it would probably all have gone wrong anyway.

-----Internal mail [personal]-----
-----Secure intranet-----

From: Sam Buxton
  To: Ruth Evershed
Date: 27 January 2005 09.10

Ruth, there's something I have to tell you. And I'd rather you heard it from me than from Harry. Meeting room, five minutes?

MI5

ANNUAL MEDICAL REPORT

Name:	Ruth Evershed
Date:	1st May 2006

Height:	5'4	Weight:	10st	BMI:	24.07

Units of alcohol per week:	14
Cigarettes per week:	none

Blood pressure:	140/80
Resting pulse:	75
Urine:	normal
Chest x-ray:	normal
Exercise ECG:	normal

Ruth looks after herself well but she is not currently fit enough to work regularly in the field.

Dr Sally Chapman

SECTION X

EYES ONLY FOR LEVEL 1 AND ABOVE

LOG FOR RUTH EVERSHED

Date: 7.09.2005
Subject: Library books. Ruth's pattern of library book requests has flagged up on our monitors as suspicious.
Outcome: Leave. Operational research purposes only.

Date: 12.10.2004
Subject: CND membership. It has come to our attention that Ruth is still a member of the Campaign for Nuclear Disarmament. An annual subscription leaves her bank account.
Outcome: See Tom Quinn's note below
Note from Tom Quinn: I have asked Ruth to rescind her membership.

Date: 22.08.2004
Subject: *University Challenge*. The BBC quiz show is celebrating its tenth anniversary under Jeremy Paxman. Past winners have been asked to take part in a one-off special show. Ruth has been invited.
Outcome: See Harry Pearce's note below.
Note from Harry Pearce: I'm sorry, but I'm going to have to say no. We can't risk someone recognising Ruth on television. And there are bound to be awkward questions and speculation as to what she is doing now.

Section X exists to keep tabs on members of the security services. We monitor private internet usage, spending habits and extra-mural activities. Our remit is to reduce the risk of blackmail and act as an early-warning system for renegade officers. These notes are retained on file which are "No Eyes" as far as the subject is concerned.

[Harry Pearce]

Private and Confidential

Name: Harry Pearce
Position: Head, Section D
D.O.B: 1.11.1953
Hair: Brown
Eyes: Brown
Height: 5'10
Marital status: Divorced
Dependants: Catherine (25.04.80); Graham (18.06.83)
Blood type: AB, Rh negative

Harry Pearce joined MI5 after a short-term commission in the army. His first posting was in Northern Ireland, followed by a brief secondment to MI6 in West Germany.

Harry returned to London in 1980 where he specialised in anti-terrorism. His successes led to rapid promotions until he was appointed Head of Section D within MI5 in 1993.

Harry has played a major role in all subsequent operations.

Jesus College
Oxford University
OX1 3DW

Matthew Davidson Esq.

15th October 1974

Dear Matthew,

I hope you're well.

It's October again and there is one excellent student for you among this year's finalists. His name is Harry Pearce and he's studying Philosophy, Politics and Economics. He's not the most dedicated of academics, but he has a fearsome intellect when he chooses to apply it.

Shall I investigate further?

Best wishes,

E McManus

Professor Emily McManus
SENIOR TUTOR   JESUS COLLEGE   OXFORD UNIVERSITY

Jesus College
Oxford University
OX1 3DW

Matthew Davidson Esq.

19th November1974

Dear Matthew,

Thank you for your letter of 5th November. I was interested to hear that Harry Pearce has already come across your radar. I am glad that you share our enthusiasm.

Tragically, though, his mother passed away at the end of last month. He is understandably very upset and unwilling to commit himself to any career path at the moment.

He has, however, made noises about following his grandfather into a military career. If he does so you might like to contact his future commanding officer to see if he'd reconsider your offer after a short-term commission. He is an excellent young man in many ways and would be an even better prospect, no doubt, after a stint of army discipline.

Best wishes,

E McManus

Professor Emily McManus
SENIOR TUTOR   JESUS COLLEGE   OXFORD UNIVERSITY

MI5 Application Form

Surname

Pearce

Forenames

Harry (Henry) James

Date of Birth

1.11.1953

Place of birth

Reading, Berkshire

Nationality at birth

British

Permanent Address

Windlesham Barracks
Cambridgeshire

Current occupation

Nearing end of Short-Term
Commission in army
Second Lieutenant

Date of availability for employment

Immediate

Medical

Do you have any conditions – either physical or psychological – which might affect your employment?

No

Father's name, address and occupation

James Henry Pearce OBE – Banker
Barn House
Tingleford
Sevenoaks
Kent

Mother's name, maiden name, address and occupation

Fiona Emily Pearce (nee Monro) – Died 1974

Brothers / Sisters (with names and D.O.B.)

Younger brother – Ben (5.6.1956)

Secondary Schools / Colleges
Dates : Names : Town

1964-1971 : Sevenoaks School : Sevenoaks

O Levels

O Levels: 13 As (English Language, English Literature, French, Latin, Greek, German, Maths, History, Geography, Religious Education, Biology, Physics and Chemistry)

A levels

Politics – A
Economics – A
History – A
English - A

Gap Year

How did you spend any break during your education?

I worked on a Kibbutz in Israel for 8 months and travelled in the Middle-East

University or Further Education

Jesus College Oxford – 1972-1975

MA (Hons) Philosophy, Politics and Economics
(PPE) – 2:1

EMPLOYMENT

Dates	Employer	Position
1975–	Short Service Commission	Second Lieutenant
1971–1972	Kibbutz in Northern Galilee	General labourer

FOREIGN LANGUAGES

Please indicate level of competence

French – fluent   Spanish - competent

German – fluent   Arabic – smattering

Hebrew – competent

OTHER INTERESTS

Literature, Wine, Theatre

TRAVEL

Give details of all foreign travel undertaken in the last 10 years, including reason for travel

Belize, Northern Ireland – army

Israel, Syria, Jordan, Egypt – gap year

Europe - tourism

REFEREES

Please give details of three referees. One of these should be a contemporary who knows you well

1. Colonel Sam Collins, Commanding Officer, Light Blue Dragoons
2. Professor Emily McManus, Senior Tutor, Jesus College, Oxford
3. Bill Crombie, childhood friend

Signature

Harry Pearce

Date

3rd January 1977

LIGHT BLUE DRAGOONS
LONDON HEADQUARTERS
780 NEW KING'S STREET
LONDON

REFERENCE: HARRY PEARCE

TO WHOM IT MAY CONCERN

I am delighted to recommend Harry Pearce for a job within the security services. He has been a popular and successful officer under my command for almost two years now. His men are fiercely loyal to him and he has shown great courage under fire as well.

My only regret is that he won't stay with us any longer. However, I can see that his cultured tastes, along with his intellectual curiosity, are perhaps more suitable for a civilian career. He has also recently met a delightful lady who is unlikely to want to put up with the demands of being an army wife.

[signature]

COLONEL SAM COLLINS

COMMANDING OFFICER
LIGHT BLUE DRAGOONS

SECURITY CLEARANCE & BACKGROUND CHECKS

Harry Pearce

I was tasked with carrying out routine background checks into Harry Pearce's family and friends, as well as standard fact-checking of his CV details. Although he has already undergone security checks pre-Sandhurst, here is my additional analysis.

Harry's childhood was fairly idyllic. He went to boarding school in Sevenoaks where he was popular, outgoing and a particularly fearsome rugby tackler at scrum half. He took part in most aspects of school life – from sport to music to the Combined Cadet Force. He also acted a little.

Although his father worked very hard (he was awarded the OBE for services to banking in 1971) he was a loving and steadying influence on Harry's early life. Harry's younger brother, Ben, followed him to Oxford and looks likely to join his father in the city. Harry's mother was a fairly typical middle-class housewife who helped out with church fetes and charity lunches. She came to watch many of his matches.

Harry spent a gap year in a Kibbutz in Northern Galilee where he mediated successfully between irate Swedish chicken workers (who didn't like getting up so early) and the canteen labourers (who worked half the amount of time for the same pay). By the end of his eight-month stint, he'd soothed over a lot of international tensions. He also travelled widely in the Middle East, smuggling himself into the Gaza strip when tensions were at their height.

Harry grew his hair long at Oxford. Further inquiries reveal that his rebellion went a little deeper than this. He rarely attended lectures in his first two years, and his membership of the infamous Bullingdon Dining Club (read Drinking Club) landed him in hot water with the authorities – both university and civil – on more than one occasion. He was very lucky not to get thrown out before he'd finished his degree.

However, his mother's death in his penultimate year was a watershed moment in his young life. He was always very close to her, and her father was a highly decorated First World War soldier. Harry could easily have achieved a First in PPE had he worked from the beginning. In the end he pulled his finger out in the last year and secured a high 2:1. His decision to go into the army was motivated by a sense of duty to his mother's memory.

Sandhurst initially came as something of a shock to the long-haired 21-year-old. In the first fortnight, he was one of their worst new recruits – continually performing slops and extra drills on the parade ground until he got it right. In the end, however, it turned out to be the making of him. I'm told that he prepared twice as hard as everyone else. If they were meant to be on the parade ground at 6am, he'd be there at 5.30am. If they had a ten-mile run coming up, he'd train at fifteen miles. At the end of the year, he was presented with the sword of honour for the best officer cadet.

Harry was popular in his regiment and Colonel Collins's reference is an accurate appraisal of the affection in which he was held by his fellow men. He was particularly effective in Northern Ireland. If successful during the rest of his application process, an initial posting to A Section should definitely be considered. As Colonel Collins hints, he should thrive within the more civil atmosphere of the security services. In the long-term the rigidity of the army's corporate structure was unlikely to appeal to him.

While on leave last year, Harry re-met, and fell in love with, an Oxford friend, Jane Womack. She is now working as an English teacher in the Cambridgeshire area and all security checks on her have been carried out successfully. The couple are currently engaged and look likely to marry later this year. They appear well-suited for each other, although some friends have expressed concern that they might be marrying a little young.

[signature]

APPROVED

George Burchill
HR Security, 2nd February 1977

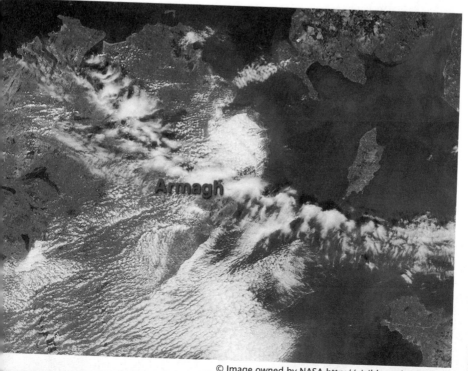

Armagh

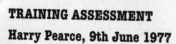

TRAINING ASSESSMENT
Harry Pearce, 9th June 1977

SCORES

Practical	
Surveillance	4.8
Counter-surveillance	4.8
Physical endurance	4.9
Shooting	4.7
Driving	3
Technical	2
Average	4.03

Intellectual	
Linguistic	4.1
Decision-making	4.9
Research	4.9
Average	4.63

Other core competencies	
Calm under pressure	4.9
Leadership	4.9
Team work	4.9
Communication	4.9
General attitude	5
Average	4.92

Overall average   **4.48**

*On a sliding scale of 1 to 5 where
1 is poor, 5 is outstanding and 2.5 is
average for a new recruit*

These excellent scores speak for themselves. Harry's high showing in the core competencies, in particular, show the advantage of taking mature recruits who have had other experiences beyond university. He is the first person to score a 5 in general attitude for some years.

Harry's driving was a little haphazard but I imagine it won't be long until he has someone to do his driving for him. He also displayed a surprisingly premature fogeydom when it came to new technical gadgets. These small quibbles aside, he is an excellent young officer who will be an asset to whichever department gets their hands on him first. I can imagine something of a scramble.

S Bishop

Susie Bishop, Head of recruit training, MI5

9th August 1978

Recorded disciplinary hearing with Harry Pearce following torture and death of MI5 operative Bill Crombie in Belfast

TRANSCRIPTS WITH APPROVED ANNOTATIONS FROM OBSERVING INDEPENDENT PSYCHOLOGIST	**SC** – Simon Cooper, Head of A Section, Northern Ireland **HP** – Harry Pearce

SC I'm sorry we have to do it like this, Harry. I know it's hard for you.

HP That's all right. I understand. Bill would have understood, too.

SC It's just that . . . Well, there have been murmurings . . . You know . . .

HP You don't have to pussyfoot around on this one, Simon. I'm not stupid. I don't think my job title of intelligence officer is meant entirely ironically.

SC laughs, nervously.

HP (*cont.*) So, yes, I know what people are saying. I'm aware of their "murmurings". I know that some people blame me for Bill Crombie's death. And do you think I don't blame myself? Of course I do. Every night. Every day. And most lunchtimes, too. But was I criminally negligent? No. Did I act unprofessionally? No. Do I deserve to lose my job over this? Again no.

SC It's okay, Harry. I'm on your side here, remember. I'm not one of the people murmuring. But we have to get this straightened out. The whole thing. From the beginning. Are you okay with that?

HP I'm okay with that.

SC What were you doing in Belfast in 1978?

HP Working for you. You know that.

SC For the tape, please, Harry. What were you doing in Belfast in 1978?

HP I was in Belfast in 1978 because I was working for the security services. I used to enjoy working for the security services until the IRA kidnapped my best friend and blow-torched his genitals . . .

SC Harry!

HP I'm sorry.

SC This is pointless if we don't do it properly. I hate this as much as you do.

HP Oh, I very much doubt that.

SC We're not in a competition here over who can feel the most grief.

HP I know, I know. Let's start again.

SC What were you doing in Belfast earlier this year?

HP I'd been there for a couple of years. Working in A Section – the one that used to be called Section A – and before that Section F and Section L. In plain English, I was working in the anti-terrorism department dealing with Northern Irish affairs.

SC And did you enjoy this work?

HP Yes, it was exciting. Northern Ireland is obviously our primary focus at the moment. I like being at the forefront of the action.

SC And what was your role in the last few years? Did you go undercover much?

HP No. As you know, I was mainly agent-running. I had one of the largest agent networks of any MI5 officer.

SC I remember. You were bloody good at it.

HP I enjoyed it. Agent-running can be a dirty business. You're asking people to put themselves at great risk. Sometimes you're asking them to do things they don't really want to do. But not in Northern Ireland. I had more volunteers than I had time or space for. I had huge budgets . . .

SC . . . don't talk to me about your budgets. I spent half my waking hours trying to convince Thames House you were worth it.

HP And in all modesty, I think I was worth it. I looked after my agents very well. I paid well. I respected them. I was like an older brother to some of them. And in return, they gave me excellent high-grade intelligence. Our work saved a lot of lives.

SC But not Bill's life.

HP No. Not Bill's. Not the one life I cared about.

There is a short silence.

SC What was the name of the operation, Harry?

HP Operation?

SC Yes, the one in which Bill died.

HP It was called Operation Leapfrog.

SC Leapfrog?

HP Yes.

SC Any particular reason?

HP No.

SC And what was the nature of this operation?

HP Basically, we'd been recruiting publicans as informers. As you know, the Irish are a garrulous, bibulous bunch, and they're especially talkative after a few gallons of Guinness in the local ale house.

SC And landlords are trusty pillars of the community?

HP That was the idea, yes. They overhear three-quarters of what goes on in their pub. Sometimes they're taken into the confidence of a useful drunk who needs a shoulder to cry on. "Tales of a barman" – that would make quite a story, wouldn't it? They see and hear everything, those guys.

SC   And you were overseeing this op?

HP   Ultimately, yes, but it was run more directly by Bill Crombie. He reported to me on this one.

SC   I don't follow. I thought the two of you were the same rank.

HP   We are . . . we were. But Bill hated being stuck behind a desk even more than I did. He was a field operative. That was his thing. You'll never see a more brilliant actor than Bill. He could have been huge on the stage, if he'd wanted to be. Olivier. Gielgud. He was as good as any of them.

SC   I remember reading that in his file.

HP   Oh, he was a man of many parts, all right. There was nothing he enjoyed more than dressing up and assuming a role. He liked to check up on how his publicans were getting on in Operation Leapfrog by playing the part of a drunk. He'd take three to four hours to get into his disguise. He could make himself look fifty years older, getting every little detail right – from the smell of his clothes to the dirty hair. But he was never a method actor, despite all that preparation. One click of his fingers and he was in character.

SC   How did he put up with the drink?

HP   Bill's always had a huge capacity. Ever since we were at school together. And he's also capable of acting drunk when he's not, and vice versa. That's another thing he picked up at school. Got him out of all sorts of trouble.

SC   I can only imagine the sort of trouble the two of you must have got into at school.

HP   On this op, he'd occasionally warn the landlords that he would be showing up. Just to keep them on their toes. But they never recognised him. There were enough anonymous drunks going among the Belfast bars that he could slip in unnoticed anywhere.

SC Except this time.

HP Yes. But it was a bit more complicated than that.

SC Go on.

HP This landlord was a double agent for the IRA. It turned out he'd
Bill followed back to his house. The Republicans therefore cloc
him coming into the pub.

SC And Bill never noticed?

HP He never noticed. He was a bloody good officer, but he could be careless at times with his counter-surveillance. Very careless. He was starting to become a little flamboyant. He was starting to believe his own reputation. I think he thought he was invincible. And the moment you think that, you're at your most vulnerable.

SC You noticed this at the time?

HP No, I notice it now, looking back. Hindsight is a horrible thing.

SC I don't think you could have been expected to notice that at the time. Such developments always start small. It's only when something happens later that we put two and two together to make five and conclude that all roads inevitably and inextricably led to this irrefutably logical end.

HP Exactly. That's how I see it too.

SC So what do you blame yourself for? Bill slipped up. He showed an error of judgement. He trusted a landlord too much. None of that is your fault.

HP I was there that night.

SC What?

HP That night. In Rosie O'Grady's. I was there, too. At the same time as they stormed in and yanked Bill out.

SC Rosie O'Grady's? Jesus, Harry. What were you thinking? That place is a vipers' nest of Republicans. They'd sooner torture you to death than serve you a pint.

HP Well, that's a sensitive point, Simon, considering what happened to Bill.

SC Shut up, Harry. What were you doing in a place like that?

HP I was recruiting.

SC More agents?

HP Yes.

SC In a pub?

HP What better place to do it without arousing suspicion? This just any old informer, Simon. The guy I was meeting there top-level. If well tapped, he had enough information to bring every single terrorist network in Ulster.

SC And you met him in a pub?

HP What else was I meant to do? He would only agree to the meeting on his terms. I'd been working on him for months through backroom channels. And I had sufficient dirt on his family that he knew exactly what would happen if any harm came to me. I was in no personal danger.

SC Unlike Bill.

HP Bill was playing silly games. He didn't need to be there. It was a low-level op. I was about to pull off one of the biggest intelligence coups this decade.

SC I thought Bill was the fantasist and you were the one blaming yourself for his death.

HP *(shouting)* That's unfair, Simon. Dammit, that's unfair. You're twisting my words.

SC I'm sorry. Tell me in your own words, then, what happened in the pub that night.

HP I was sitting with my contact in the corner. I'd probably been there twenty minutes or so when I caught sight of this old drunk by the bar.

SC   Who you recognised as Bill?

HP   Yes, there was something instantly familiar about him. I've known Bill for almost twenty years. Even when he was at his very best on stage, I rarely forgot that it was my best friend I was looking at, and not whichever character he was playing. There was always something – a glint in the eye, a twitch of the lip, a wave of the hand, whatever mannerism it was – that I recognised as Bill's. It would be undetectable to anyone else, I'm sure. But to me, it was unmistakable.

SC   So what did you do?

HP   Bill knew I didn't approve of these little jaunts. I thought if I bought another round he'd catch sight of me and quietly leave. But I was just standing up when two men burst in the door, grabbed him by the hair and said, "This man is a British spy." They started to drag him out towards the door.

SC   And what did you do then?

HP   Nothing.

SC   Nothing?

HP   I had to stop myself from reacting instinctively as I suddenly realised the ridiculous situation I was in. If I reacted, it would confirm that Bill was who they claimed he was. It would also jeopardise my new drinking partner as well as the four other people I'd clocked in the pub as part-time informers. It would probably have put the landlord in danger as well. And it would have completely compromised all my work in Belfast.

SC   That's the first thing you thought about, was it? Your work?

HP   No, it was the last thing I thought about, but these things aren't mutually exclusive – as you know. If my cover collapsed, everything around it collapsed, too. It was like a chain of dominoes, already teetering, waiting for the first one to fall so they could all fall down next. That's responsibility for you, Simon. That's when I felt grown-up for the first time in my life. When I made the decision to curb my instincts, act like a suitably enraged Republican and watch my best friend be led away.

SC So you just let them walk out of the door with Bill?

HP Yes.

SC Even though you had a gun?

HP Yes. What did you want me to do? Shoot the entire pub to bits?

There is a long silence.

SC You know you made the right judgement call, Harry. That's why you're so good at this job. You always make the right call.

HP I tried to follow them, of course, as soon as I could get out of the pub. But they were professionals. They got away. They had getaway cars and decoy cars. It was impossible for one officer to follow them.

SC Of course it was.

HP I recognised one of the kidnappers. Patrick McCann. He was a butcher of a man. Both parents killed by the British. Tortured for his own sadistic enjoyment. We shook every cage trying to find him. We brought in every known informer. Every grass, every sleeper, every errand boy, every fucking lollipop lady. We shook all their cages. But not a squeak. I spent two weeks driving around Ulster trying to find Bill. I knocked on thousands of doors. I barely slept. By the end I wasn't an intelligence officer conducting an investigation. I was a desperate man searching for his brother.

There is a short silence.

SC It's okay, Harry. Really, it's okay.

HP No, it's bloody not okay. At the end of those two weeks Bill's body was dumped outside his house in the early hours. It's pretty hard to identify a body when most of it has been burned away by a blow-torch. But I could. Because it was Bill. I could recognise him when he was disguised as an old, drunken tramp. And I could recognise him when he was tortured by barbaric Papists.

SC You know it's not as simple as that.

HP I'm sorry. But I hope you'll forgive me if I remain a little emotional about Irish matters.

SC Forgive you? Yes. But can you forgive yourself? That's the main question.

HP For the tape?

SC No, for yourself.

HP For cowardice? No, never.

SC I don't call what you did cowardice. I think what you did was incredibly brave. It's what we trained you to do. It's what Bill would have done, too.

There is a long silence.

HP Have you ever read E.M. Forster, Simon?

SC No.

HP There was one thing he said that always stuck with me. "If I had choose between betraying my country and betraying my friend, I hope I should have the guts to betray my country."

SC And you believe that, do you?

HP Yes. I think so. Maybe.

SC Then you're a silly fool. Do you know which other fool quoted those words? Guy Burgess, that's who. And along with his little Cambridge chums he betrayed us all to the Soviets. Don't be naïv Harry. Choice – that's what this job is about. If you want to serve your country, work here. If you want to put your friends first, go back and work on a Kibbutz instead. This is no place for idealists. Patriots, yes. Fantasists, no.

HP What are you saying?

SC I'm saying that you're an excellent intelligence officer already. An you'll make an even better one if you learn to trust your training a your instincts.

HP What you're really saying is that stuff happens. Isn't that it? Bad things happen to good people. Life is shitty. Then you die. Get ove it. Stuff happens.

SC Well, if you want to put it like that. I know it's not much of a creed to live by. I can't offer you Liberté, Egalité, Fraternité. But it's all we've got, Harry. Stuff happens. Most of the time we stop bad stuff from happening. Sometimes it happens anyway. First we look after the country. Then we look after our own.

HP He was a good man, Simon. Bill Crombie was a very good man.

SC I know. I recruited him, didn't I? Just like I recruited you. I've neve had a better team.

HP laughs gently.

HP You know why he didn't continue his acting career?

SC No, he never really talked much about that with me.

HP He was too modest, that's why. He gave it up because he wanted to matter. Matter in a deeper, longer-lasting way than signed programme notes and matinee flowers. He wanted to do something worthwhile. He wanted to give something back. He was every cliché in the book. But he chose something worthy over something he was very good at. He believed in this stuff.

SC And that's why the two of you were such good friends. The difference with you, Harry, is that the worthy profession you've chosen is also something you're very good at. Very good at indeed, in fact.

HP Really?

SC Really. But you have to choose to carry on with this. To put this behind you. To draw strength from your lowest moments. Is that something you can do?

HP To be honest, Simon, I'm not sure I have any choice in the matter.

****End of interview****

Note from Simon Cooper

I'm satisfied that those murmurings of misconduct were precisely that: murmurings. Harry Pearce has risen very fast through the ranks here and it is inevitable that this would cause some jealous resentment along the way.

I have no hesitation in clearing him of all disciplinary procedures and returning him to active duty. I do, however, recommend that he leave A Section straight-away. He currently remains far too emotional to continue working in Northern Irish affairs. Perhaps a secondment to MI6 somewhere in Europe would be in order.

KOLNER ALLGEMEINE ZEITUNG

BRITISH INTELLIGENCE SUSPECTED INVOLVEMENT IN COLOGNE BOMBINGS

TRANSLATED 7TH NOVEMBER 1979

As the city of Cologne returned to normal today after yesterday's chaotic scenes, the widow of the Minister for the Interior, Thomas Bergen, told this newspaper that she had found extracts in her husband's diary expressing fears that he might become the victim of a staged bombing campaign by British Intelligence.

Herr Bergen was widely criticised for his soft stance on communism. It is the view of his widow – as well as a number of senior members of the German police – that the current spate of left-wing extremist attacks are not all that they appear.

Until a year ago, left-wing organisations in West Germany were fairly thin on the ground.

The ones that did exist were relatively harmless. And while they organised occasional marches in sympathy with left-wing causes, their activities were far from radicalised.

At the end of 1978, however, the activities of these organisations became more and more violent. Marches turned into riots. Petitions became hard communism. This year socialism became a prolonged bombing campaign against government and corporate targets.

However, the police are suspicious about the apparent coordinated professionalism of these attacks. Some of the pamphlets have been written in such formulaic German that language

experts expect foreign involvement. Similarly, the bombing campaigns have all used the same explosives and devices, even when deployed by supposedly different left-wing organisations.

A former German intelligence officer, who asked not to be named, said today that these recent activities have all the signs of a trademark British "black op" – a low-level, deniable and ultimately illegal campaign. "My suspicion is that they're looking for justification for a crackdown on communism," he said. "They hope to push us so far that we'll have to perform this crackdown ourselves."

"We do not comment on security matters," said a spokesman for the British Foreign O...

ölner Allgemeine Zeitung

Accompanying note from Harry Pearce

As the MI6 desk officer in Cologne, I have been asked to pass comment on the enclosed newspaper cutting.

Needless to say, it is palpable nonsense. Yes, Herr Bergen was worryingly soft on Communism. This would probably explain why the more extremist groups had a number of successes in the last twelve months. Yes, the groups often used the same explosives and detonators, but that's because they used the same supplier in the DDR. And as for the formulaic German, I have yet to read any Communist treatise that doesn't sound somewhat stilted.

There have been rumours of a MI5/MI6 sanctioned operation, codenamed Omega. I am happy to report that this is nothing more than the delusional accusations of retired German intelligence officers, grieving widows and ill-informed journalists.

Should you wish for further details in this matter, Juliet Shaw will be only too happy to oblige.

Harry Pearce

12th November 1979

TRAVELLERS CLUB   PALL MALL LONDON SW11

Letter of recommendation for club membership for Harry Pearce

Proposer: Oliver Mace   7th November 1993

Dear Committee,

I would very much like to recommend Harry Pearce for membership of the Travellers Club.

He is just the sort we need more of in here: intelligent, successful and well connected. He also knows a large number of existing members: Sir Richard Bowman (the banker), Hugo Weatherby from Whitehall and Jools Siviter from the Foreign Office.

He is a decent sort who will pay his bill on time, dress appropriately and bring in the right sort of guests. I also think he needs a male sanctuary – somewhere quiet and conservative – away from the various hen-pecking women in his life. I am sure the Travellers is just the right sort of place.

I do hope you will be able to fast-track him up the waiting-list slightly. He is a colleague as well as a friend and has just been appointed to a position commensurate with membership of one of the gentlemen's clubs. Besides, we often require somewhere discreet where we can do business.

Yours aye,

Mace

3rd June 2004

FIRST-ROUND INTERVIEW FOR POSITION OF DIRECTOR GENERAL OF MI5

CANDIDATE: HARRY PEARCE

TRANSCRIPT APPROVED AND ANNOTATED BY INDEPENDENT OBSERVER	**HP** – Harry Pearce **IN1–6** – Interviewers 1–6

IN1 Thank you for applying for this job, Harry.

HP Well, I didn't exactly ask to apply.

IN1 I'm sorry?

HP I was invited to apply. I see that rather differently. When you're "invited" to do something that normally means something else in this building.

IN4 That's very honest of you.

HP I'm an honest man. Perhaps that's a disadvantage in this building, too.

IN1 Are you saying you don't want this job?

HP I'm not saying that at all. I'm merely pointing out the error in your line of questioning.

IN1 Thank you for that, Harry.

There is a brief silence.

IN1 Perhaps we should start again. What do you see as your strengths?

HP I like to tell things as they are.

IN1 We can see that. What else?

HP I believe I'm good at leading a team. I like to lead from the front. I like to lead by example, and I also like to muck in wherever possible. I have an excellent team down in Section D. I respect them, and I like to think they repay my loyalty. My door is always open to any of them.

IN6 You've listed your personal strengths. What about your strengths as an administrator?

HP I think it's a fallacy to distinguish between the two. Good administration stems from good inter-personal skills. And vi versa. I'm not too scared to delegate tasks. I give my young staff a lot of personal responsibility.

IN4 Have you ever given someone under you too much responsibility?

HP Not that I can recall, no. Officers have to learn to make mistakes.

IN3 What about your own mistakes Mr Pearce? What are your weaknesses?

HP (*laughing*) Oh, there are many of those. Ask my ex-wife. I have a particularly violent temper when things aren't going right. I'm a fuddy-duddy when it comes to modern slang and contemporary morality. I bend the rules, sometimes to breaking point. And I'm not that keen on politicians.

IN2 Politicians?

HP Yes. They interfere.

IN2 They interfere?

HP They interfere in matters they do not understand. They sti• their noses in where they are not welcome. And yet they remain rather useless at doing the job they've actually be• elected to do.

IN2 You are not aware, perhaps, that I am a politician.

HP On the contrary. I am fully aware of that.

There is a sound of spluttering from IN5. It is unclear from the tape whether this is suppressed laughter or indignation.

HP (*cont.*) Although what possible role you're playing on the DG's selection board, I have no idea.

IN1 coughs.

HP (*cont.*) Do you understand quantum mechanics, how there are six parallel, interlinked universes? No, neither do I. And I don't understand politics either.

IN1 I'm not sure this is getting us anywhere. Perhaps we should look at this from another angle. What role does politics play in the intelligence community? And what role should politics play?

HP I am glad you differentiate between the two. It is my firm belief that politics is currently far too involved in the intelligence community. No doubt you know of Oliver Mace, the head of the JIC. For the last year I have spent as much time second-guessing his moves as I have those of subversive terrorist elements. This is clearly a ridiculous state of affairs.

IN1 Could you be more specific?

HP I'd rather not be. What I'm saying is that intelligence must not be allowed to become politicised. If it does, it loses any independent value. Intelligence is intelligence. It cannot be produced on demand to justify pre-existing policies. If the politicians don't like what we give them, so be it. And if we can't find them the smoking gun, maybe they should ask themselves – is there actually a smoking gun? We should not be hunting down information like a pharmacist responding to a doctor's prescription. If the organisation is working correctly, information will find us, as much as the other way round. Our job is to know what to do with it.

IN2 So, you're saying that the security services and the world of politics should become completely separate, then? Is that it? Never the twain shall meet? You'd like to undo all our work over the last seven years and return to the dark ages of old school ties and a secretive state police force. You don't want to be accountable to anyone, least of all the great mass of unwashed public whom you profess to protect.

HP I'm sorry if I've upset you. But I couldn't disagree more. A secretive state police force is the one thing we're trying to avoid. Of course, we need political accountability. I've served under some excellent Home Secretaries in my time, and some bloody rotten ones, too. And I'll tell you the difference. The good ones oversee; the bad ones overrule. Leave us to do our job – that's all I ask. We'll wheedle out our own bad eggs much faster than any outsider can.

IN3 Let's move on to the Americans. Do you enjoy good working practices with our closest ally?

HP chuckles slightly, as if sharing a private joke.

HP If there's one thing I do enjoy it's good bluster with the Americans.

IN3 Bluster? What do you mean by that?

HP I like to keep them on their toes. I like to remind them of their mistakes.

IN3 Mistakes?

HP Yes, mistakes. Like missing a couple of Al Qaeda operatives learning to fly and sunning themselves on a beach in Florida.

IN3 That doesn't sound particularly diplomatic to me.

HP There's a time and a place for diplomacy. We should be diplomatic with our enemies. With our allies, on the other hand, we have to be more brutal. Brutally honest, at least. Especially in the current political climate.

IN6 Let's talk about the current political climate. Does it put anything off limits? Or does the end always justify the means?

HP The end can never justify the means entirely. Otherwise, what are we defending? What are we fighting for? But on a day-to-day basis, we deal with people who will stop at nothing to get their own way. So it's difficult to set your own limits. To resist behaving like they do. It's not always easy.

IN3 You mean you won't stoop to their levels?

HP I like to think one of my strengths is that I hold on to things that are good. If we don't have a certain ethical dimension in our work, then what are we? We won't defeat terrorism by destroying democracy.

IN1 That's an interesting way of putting it. Can you elaborate?

IP By democracy I mean the rights of the individual. Their rights to free speech, to freedom of movement. And so on. When a terrorist atrocity occurs, it is often our knee-jerk reaction to limit these freedoms. Stop them speaking. Prevent dissident voices from being heard. Lock up people we don't agree with. When we do this we're not stopping terrorism; we're fuelling it. We're not protecting democracy; we're undermining it.

IN1 So moral absolutes do exist in intelligence. No grey areas?

HP On the contrary. It is full of grey areas. Whenever I get a piece of intelligence, I think to myself, What is the worse thing I could do with this piece of information? I'll give you an example. Last week we were holding a mercenary for questioning. He had vital information concerning a guided missile in central London. We, on the other hand, had information concerning his ill daughter. We ended up using that against him.

IN4 (*shouting*) You animal!

HP I'm sorry?

IN4 All those high-blown words about protecting democracy and then you admit that you used a young girl to blackmail someone.

HP And prevent the deaths of thousands of innocent citizens.

IN4 I thought you said the end never justified the means.

HP I said it never justified the means *entirely*. You have to examine each individual case in turn. We didn't harm this girl.

She had no idea what was going on. But we used the threat of harm to manipulate her father.

IN4 That's stooping pretty low.

HP Perhaps sometimes you have to stoop low to conquer. And let's be realistic here. This man was a mercenary. He was prepared to let innocent people die. We were running out of time.

IN4 I still don't like it.

HP Well, maybe you should start liking it. You sanction this kind of thing, after all.

IN4 I do no such thing.

HP Oh yes, you do. Whether justified or not, you sit near the top of this little tree. Do you remember those "Not in our name" banners that appeared during the Iraq war protests? Well, this goes on in your name. All of this. When was the last time you left your desk?

IN1 Harry.

HP No, this is important. What was the last decision you made that wasn't to do with budgets or political skulduggery? What was the last operational decision you made? When did you last have people's lives in your hands? Answer me that.

There is an embarrassed silence.

HP (*cont.*) God, you are so far removed up here on the seventh floor, gentlemen.

IN4 And ladies. Do you have a problem with female authority, Mr Pearce?

HP No, I do not. But I do have a problem with Lord High Executioners who have become removed from everything they once lived for.

IN1 Then why let yourself be considered for this job?

HP Because if something's wrong, if there's something I believe I can do to right that wrong, then I believe it's my duty to step up to the plate. Even if I'd miss working with my team at ground level.

IN1 Thank you, Harry. We'll be in touch about the next round.

****Interview ends****

Assessment from IN1

Harry Pearce put in a combative performance during this interview and his long career in MI5 speaks for itself. He was invited back to a second round and shortlisted down to the last two candidates.

In the final analysis, however, we believed it prudent to give the job of Director General to someone at greater ease in Whitehall and Westminster. Although Harry is a shrewd political operator, he ultimately lacks the cunning and moral flexibility to fight our turf wars successfully. His almost total lack of respect for politicians would be likely to land us in constant hot water and his antagonism towards the Americans could make all our lives a little difficult.

There is another dimension to this decision. Harry Pearce has been one of our best section heads in decades. Section D has never flourished as it does now. Many people owe their lives to his ongoing good work, even if they remain unaware of the debt they owe.

I always suspected Harry was reluctant to apply for the job of DG. His interviews appear to confirm this hunch. In addition, the effect on his team of his removal is almost too catastrophic to imagine. He himself articulated his enjoyment of "mucking in" at ground level. As such, I do not see this rejection as a failure. It is rather a question of returning an excellent man to where he belongs. For once in this organisation, it is good to see a round peg in a round hole.

28th June 2004

OPERATION UNCLE SAM

FIELD REPORT
TITLE: SUSPENSION AND REINSTATEMENT OF HARRY PEARCE
FILED BY: JULIET SHAW
DATE: 5TH MAY 2005

Introduction

Just under a month ago Harry Pearce made an operational decision which left me with no choice but to suspend him. Over the course of the last four weeks Harry has continually broken the terms of his suspension, running a merry dance around the surveillance men tasked to keep an eye on him. He has also been aided and abetted by the loyalty of his former team, continuing to work on projects to which he was supposed to have no access.

However, I now find myself with no choice but to reinstate Harry Pearce to his former position. This field report details the facts and the decisions behind that choice.

CIA extraditions

Since 9/11 the CIA have been carrying out regular extraditions of British suspects from British soil. Although the majority of these have been conducted through official channels – or with our tacit approval – the situation has got out of hand in the last three months. In April, the CIA attempted to extradite three British citizens without our knowledge. All of these were bound for Guantanamo Bay.

NASA http://visibleearth.nasa.gov/

This was putting a great deal of strain on Section D, especially as American demands for additional paperwork and surveillance continued to escalate. Harry Pearce was under particular pressure and I began to worry about his mental stability at this time. His temper – which is never slow to appear – began to fray more regularly. On one occasion, I remember him sweeping an entire pile of files to the floor in frustration.

When an anonymous tip-off came through that another British citizen was about to be snatched without our knowledge, I was therefore happy to sanction attempts to stop it. On 29th April, Alex Roscoe – the CIA liaison man in London – was intercepted at the Isle of Dogs just as he tried to bundle a British citizen of Iranian origin called Louis Khurvin into a helicopter.

Louis Khurvin

Louis Khurvin had an Irish mother (hence Louis) and an Iranian father. While I was happy with Harry's interception of the deportation attempt – this was a matter of principle, after all, and a point had to be made to the Americans – I was decidedly unhappy with the way he handled Khurvin from then on.

Khurvin was released almost immediately and placed under low-grade category four surveillance. He shot both MI5 surveillance officers on the second day of their operation. One of them had three-year-old twins.

While Harry was devastated by this outcome, it was unquestionably his faulty judgement which had caused it. Like a failed politician, he wanted to stay on to sort out the mess he had made, but I had no choice in the matter. Someone had to be held responsible. You can't ride roughshod over White House policy and not expect repercussions when things go wrong. This outcome gave almost limitless ammunition to Alex Roscoe.

Suspension & surveillance

Pending the outcome of a full disciplinary hearing, I suspended Harry until further notice. He was placed under close surveillance at his house – much closer surveillance, incidentally, than he'd chosen to place Khurvin under.

To my dismay, however, this surveillance team turned out to be almost as useless as the ones who had been shot. It was like sending donkeys to guard a lion. Harry continually outwitted them at every stage.

I was also disappointed by the way in which Harry's colleagues on Section D continued to make contact during his suspension, despite official protocol and my explicit instructions to the contrary.

Section D loyalty

Managing the Grid without Harry proved to be an almost impossible task. Zafar Younis and Ruth Evershed were openly hostile. I was also disappointed by Adam Carter's inability to make the necessary step up from middle-management. Only Jo Portman was open to the possibility that Harry might have done something wrong.

This loyalty went beyond simple stubbornness to manifesting itself in outright disobedience. To some extent this took place in minor – even slightly touching – ways. Ruth was so worried about Harry living off crisps that she sent him daily food parcels. Even Zafar was thoughtful enough to send over a couple of videos in case he got bored.

But their mutiny became more serious when they started keeping Harry in touch with the ongoing operation. Harry managed to slip a note to the corner shop man asking him to tell Adam to meet at Wimbledon dog track. Although under surveillance at the time, they managed a muffled conversation next to the barking kennels. When I confronted Adam about this later, with photographic evidence, he seemed remarkably unperturbed by his protocol breach.

Similarly, it later came to light that Ruth met Harry on a night bus home and passed him a complete electronic file on David Pollard — a debt collector under suspicion of working as a CIA deniable.

CIA deniables

It was at this point, however, that Harry Pearce was able to redeem himself. His close attention to Pollard's smuggled file threw him onto the track of another CIA deniable, Michael Gorman. Eluding his surveillance teams again, he met with Gorman and confirmed his suspicion that Pollard was indeed working as a CIA deniable. His role in London was to stir up Iranians into committing a terrorist outrage on British soil, thereby justifying a coalition counter-attack on Tehran. It was Pollard who had tipped us off when we stopped Louis Khurvin from being extradited.

Pollard led us to Khurvin and we were able to neutralise him before he fired a missile into a passenger plane landing at Heathrow. Pollard was apprehended and retained in British custody – much to the chagrin of Alex Roscoe.

Conclusions

There are a number of conclusions to be drawn from this happy outcome.

The first concerns the nature of special relationships – both inter-personal and inter-governmental. Whatever the background details, Harry Pearce had clearly made a significant error of judgement in releasing Khurvin when he did. All the subsequent mitigating factors in the world do not make up for two dead MI5 surveillance officers.

Despite this, however, his colleagues showed a level of trust and affection tha
I have rarely encountered in twenty years of intelligence work. In the end, his input to
this case turned out to justify this loyalty. It is perhaps worth remembering, then, the
power of friendship in this job. We talk about team work all the time, but how often
do we honestly appreciate what it means?

The "special relationship" with the US, on the other hand, has turned rather sour o
late. I am not advocating a *Love Actually* moment, but it would be nice if they would
put their own house in order before messing around in ours again. We should exploit
this moral upper-hand for as long as possible. After all, we must deserve some return
on all our support by now.

It just remains for me to reinstate Harry Pearce without prejudice to his former
position. His work – however clandestine – on this operation is a thumping tribute to
wisdom and experience. Perhaps he should get out and about in the field more often.

J. SHAW

National Security Co-ordinator

MI5

ANNUAL MEDICAL REPORT

Name:	Harry Pearce
Date:	1st May 2006

Height:	5'10"	Weight:	12st 7lb	BMI:	25.15

Units of alcohol per week:	30
Cigarettes per week:	None. Occasional cigar.

Blood pressure:	160/100
Resting pulse:	96
Urine:	normal
Chest x-ray:	normal
Exercise ECG:	normal

I am a little bit concerned by Harry's health. His diet is poor, his blood pressure is raised and he's drinking too much. This is a shame for a man who used to be in excellent physical shape.

I have recommended that he looks after himself better. He could start by cutting down on whisky.

Dr Sally Chapman

SECTION X

EYES ONLY FOR LEVEL 1 AND ABOVE

LOG FOR HARRY PEARCE

Date: 12.05.2006
Subject: Dog. We suspect that Harry's dog might have died. Should we look at getting
          him another one?
Outcome: See Juliet Shaw's note.

Note from Juliet Shaw: Thanks for flagging this up. Harry has lent the dog to Adam's son
Wes for the week. No cause for alarm.

Date: 14.02.2005
Subject: Catherine Pearce. Harry has been emailing his daughter regularly. Catherine is
          currently making a documentary with a suspicious Palestinian group in the West
          Bank.
Outcome: See Juliet Shaw's note.

Note from Juliet Shaw: Don't be stupid. He's allowed to email his daughter.

Date: 19.03.1999
Subject: Blackmail. Harry is being blackmailed by a woman he dated who has started
          following him to work. She is threatening to go to the press with his identity if he
          doesn't pay her regularly.
Outcome: See note from Oliver Mace.

Note from Oliver Mace: Thanks, I'll reprimand Harry. Scare the hell out of the girl. And then
pay her to shut up.

Date: 7.06.1995
Subject: Speeding tickets. Harry currently has 9 points on his licence and has just been
          flashed by a speed camera on the Edgware road.
Outcome: Points erased from licence.

(CONTINUED)

Section X exists to keep tabs on members of the security services. We monitor private internet
usage, spending habits and extra-mural activities. Our remit is to reduce the risk of blackmail
and act as an early-warning system for renegade officers. These notes are retained on file
which are "No Eyes" as far as the subject is concerned.

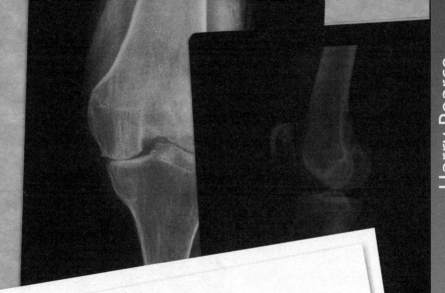

SECTION X

EYES ONLY FOR LEVEL 1 AND ABOVE

LOG FOR HARRY PEARCE cont.

Date: 30.08.1992
Subject: Health. A number of officers have mentioned that Harry is not in the shape he once was in the field. His left knee, in particular, is giving problems.

Outcome: Harry is to be shortlisted for any suitable desk jobs that arise.

Date: 9.10.1986
Subject: Mrs Pearce. Harry's wife was seen leaving the flat of another man. Should Harry be made aware of this?

Outcome: See note from head of Section D.

Note from head of Section D: Thank you for flagging this up but no, it is not our job to tell Harry about this. We should all, however, be ready to offer emotional support, if needed.

Date: 5.4.1981
Subject: Office affair. Harry has been conducting an affair with Juliet Shaw. Both are married.

Outcome: Juliet and Harry attended a joint disciplinary hearing. They have been told to stop.

[Zafar Younis]

Private and Confidential

Name: Zafar Younis
Position: Junior Field Officer
D.O.B: 02.02.77
Hair: Black
Eyes: Brown
Height: 6'0
Marital status: Single
Dependants: None
Blood type: B, Rh negative

Zafar Younis joined MI5 in May 2005 after almost three years on the North African desk at MI6. He's quick-witted and confident, working particularly well together with Adam Carter.

Major operations include:

- Inventive "proof" of Diana's murder
- Talking down of Algerian Nazim Malik
- Staged bandit raid on immigrant truck
- Dirty tricks campaign on The British Way
- Neutralisation of threat posed by Shining Dawn

MI5
Application Form

Surname

Younis

Forenames

Zafar (Zaf) David

Date of Birth

02.02.77

Place of birth

Croydon, London

Nationality at birth

British

Permanent Address

14 Selhurst Road,
Croydon, London

Current occupation

Unemployed

Date of availability for employment

Immediately

Do you hold a full, clean driving licence?

Yes

Medical
Do you have any conditions – either physical or psychological – which might affect your employment?

No

Father's name, address and occupation

Mahmud Younis. Lawyer (Solicitor)
14 Selhurst Road, Croydon, London

Mother's name, maiden name, address and occupation

Sarah Younis (nee Wilson)
Housewife
14 Selhurst Road, Croydon, London

Brothers / Sisters (with names and D.O.B.)

Robert – 09.08.1970
Fatima – 22.02.1973
Yasser – 12.06.1975
Clare – 09.12.1980
Lucy – 05.07.1983
Layla – 27.04.1986

Secondary Schools / Colleges (Dates : Names : Town)

1988–1995 : Dulwich College : London

O Levels or equivalent

GCSEs: 1 A – Geography; 4 Bs –
English Language, English
Literature, History, Religious
Education; 4 Ds – Chemistry,
Physics, French, Biology

A levels and AS levels or equivalents

Geography – A
Religious Education A
English - B

Gap Year
How did you spend any break during your education?

I had two gap years between school and university as I didn't get into my first choice university. I worked for an entire year in London earning money in temporary jobs. In the second year, I bought a round-the-world ticket and travelled.

University or Further Education

Manchester University - 1997-2001
BA (Hons) Geography - 2:1
Masters - International Relations

Awards
Please give details of any other awards (e.g. music)

N/A

EMPLOYMENT

Dates	Employer	Position
University term-time 1997-2001	Student union bar	Barman
1995-7	Various	Temp

Have you served in HM Forces (including Reserves)?

No

Do you have applications pending for other jobs?

No

PERSONAL QUALITIES AND SKILLS

SUMMARY
Provide a pen-portrait of your life to date

My elder brothers made life very easy for me at school and I had a very happy time there.

When I was about sixteen, however, I got involved with a strict muslim group which alienated me from some of my old friends. I spent a lot of the time in the mosque while they were growing up as more normal teenagers.

I've now put that period of life behind me and I had a pretty normal student experience at Manchester. I'm confident, ambitious and outgoing. I'm now looking for my next challenge.

MOTIVATION

Why do you think you would be suited to a career in MI5?

Leaving university last June put me in a bit of a quandary. I was ambitious, but I didn't want to do a graduate trainee scheme like the rest of my friends. I really wanted to get a job which would interest me, but I wasn't sure what this job might be.

But then the terrorist attacks in New York helped make my mind up: I wanted to work for MI5. I've always had a few problems with my identity. British or Asian? Asian or British? The 9/11 bombings helped put that crisis into perspective. I want to protect this country from people like that.

Also, I am yet to encounter a situation which I cannot talk my way out of. I am an excellent driver, good with gadgets and capable of flirting my way into most people's affections. I hope some of these skills will stand me in good stead.

POLITICAL CURIOSITY

Give three political topics (historical or current) which interest you

- Al-Qaeda
- PLO
- Kashmir

ADAPTABILITY

Give an example of a time when you had to adapt to unexpected circumstances.

One night after I'd been working at the student union bar I caught a bus back to my house with a girl I'd met that evening. Unfortunately, we missed our stop (for reasons I won't go into) and had to get out at the end of the line in Moss Side, a particularly dangerous part of Manchester.

We were just about to make our way back when a group of about nine teenagers confronted us. The girl I was with was really scared. I think I could have dealt with five of them. But the other four? What would they have done with her?

So I had to use my brain. I'd remembered reading in the Manchester Evening News about a number of different gangs operating in the area. The main two were the Sharks and the Hoods. I tried to scan their arms for signs of tattoos, but there was no time. I had to take a shot in the dark.

Summoning up as much courage as possible I said to the ringleader, "You don't want to get in the way of me escorting this girl."

"And why's that?" he asked. "Maybe she'd like to be <u>escorted</u> by me and my friends instead."

"Because this is Johnny's new girl," I said. "She's had a bit too much to drink and he asked me to check she gets home safe. Now you wouldn't want Johnny having a word to Gary about you, would you?"

I'd plucked the names straight out of the article in the local paper. Johnny was the Sharks' ringleader. Gary was his main enforcer. Luckily, I'd chosen the right gang. They left us in peace, and we caught a taxi home.

RESPONSIBILITY

What positions of responsibility have you held – at school, university or otherwise?

None

FOREIGN LANGUAGES

Please indicate level of competence

Urdu – fluent

OTHER INTERESTS

Socialising

Cars

Gadgets

TRAVEL

Give details of all foreign travel undertaken in the last 10 years, including reason for travel

Pakistan – to visit family

Europe – tourism

EQUAL OPPORTUNITIES

This information is not used as part of our selection procedures

Gender	Ethnic origin	Disabilities
(Male) Female	British Asian	None

REFEREES

Please give details of three referees. One of these should be a contemporary who knows you well

1. Dave Oliver - Bar Manager, Manchester University Student Union
2. Dr Peter Young - Lecturer in Geography
3. Simon Langdale - Headmaster, Dulwich College

Signature

Zafar Younis

Date

14 November 2001

PROCEED TO INTERVIEW

Manchester University Student Union Bar
145 Rag Street
Manchester

REFERENCE: Zaf Younis

To Whom It May Concern:

When I first met Zaf, I must admit that I didn't think much of him. He was older than many of the other students and very arrogant.

When he applied for a job here in his second week I almost threw his application straight in the bin, but a bit of me was intrigued. I decided to invite him for interview and found him extremely genuine and kind in a one-on-one situation. He is also an excellent cocktail maker and has a natural ability to strike up a rapport with any customer. I gave him the job on probation.

Over the next three years I grew to know and respect a very likeable young man. Of course, the girls all adored him. Soon he was their favourite barman and they would fight over who got to buy the next round. But there is also honour behind his surface charms. He is a sound bloke – a man's man as much as a ladies' man.

I'm not sure many people have got to see the real Zaf. He's too clever, too charming, too good-looking to give much of himself away. But I feel I've scratched a little bit beneath the surface. I've seen the guy who'll stay late unpaid to help clear away the glasses. I've seen the bloke who'll put his arm around a mate when he's having a bad time. And I've seen the fighter who'll always stick up for the underdog.

On one memorable occasion he took on an entire rugby team who were being unnecessarily lecherous towards some first year girls. He was beaten to a pulp, of course. But it was the way he didn't think twice about attempting to right a wrong which impressed me.

I have no hesitation in recommending him for employment, whatever this is he's applying for.

Dave Oliver
Bar Manager, Manchester University Student Union

ADDITIONAL SECURITY INTERVIEW INVESTIGATING MUSLIM BACKGROUND OF ZAFAR YOUNIS

2 February 2002

ZY – Zafar Younis
AH – Amy Hindle, Security interviewer, MI5

AH You understand why we have to do this, don't you, Zafar?

ZY Please, just call me Zaf, Amy.

AH Okay, Zaf. You can call me Ms Hindle, though.

There is a brief pause.

ZY I'm sorry, Ms Hindle. Distracted for a moment. What was it you were asking again?

AH I was asking whether you knew why we had to have this recorded interview today.

ZY Of course. It's just part of your standard vetting procedures, isn't it? You can't let any old Tom, Dick or Harry into MI5, can you?

AH Well, partly. But I'm afraid there's a little more to it than that. Of course, we vet all potential employees, but this interview is a little extra. It's a new thing post 9/11. We have to perform extra security checks on everyone from a Muslim background, and this interview forms part of that.

ZY Ah, I see. So you can't let any old Tom, Dick, Harry or Mohammed into MI5? That's what you're really saying, isn't it?

AH On the contrary. We want as many Muslims in the security services as possible, but they must be Muslims who are loyal to the crown. That's why we have to carry out these additional interviews.

ZY The crown?

AH Well, the country, at least. You don't have to be a budding royalist to work here.

ZY That's fortunate.

AH What I'm trying to say is that we need to talk a little bit more about your religion, your background and so on. Do you have any objection to that?

ZY No objection at all. I've got nothing to hide.

AH I saw you were very open in your application about a brief flirtation with radical Islam in your past. Can you go into that a little bit more?

ZY Yes, of course. It was when I was about sixteen or seventeen. I'd been turned down by a couple of white girls because of the colour of my skin, and I'd had some difficulty getting served in pubs. I suppose I started to think seriously about my upbringing. My father was something of a part-time Muslim, you see. He'd give some of his wages to charity, like we're supposed to, but then he'd happily drink beer as well. I began to resent that. I began to resent him. I thought he'd betrayed his roots.

AH Which are where?

ZY Pakistan.

AH So what did you do?

ZY I fell in with a bad group at the local mosque for a bit. I wouldn't call them extremists, but they were quite radical.

AH How do you mean?

ZY I mean they didn't believe in Jihad and killing infidels, or any of that stuff, but they were incredibly strict with themselves. Their main concern was among second-generation Asian youths. They felt we had strayed, gone soft in the West. They told us we'd never fit in properly here, that we had to stick together, stick to what we knew. They became quite violent when talking to our own. It was exciting for a while. I felt like I belonged. Change the world or burn it? It was an intoxicating thought for a while.

AH But only for a while?

ZY Yes, I realised I'd fallen into it out of weakness. Like a crutch, if you see what I mean.

AH I see.

ZY And then I started going out with a white girl. I started going out with a lot of girls, in fact. I discovered beer again. And whisky. And wine. And Snakebite. And I went to university and had the time of my life. It was a brief flirtation. Nothing more. My own little spell of teenage angst, I suppose.

AH You don't have to play it down, you know, Zaf. We have plenty of practising Muslims at MI5.

ZY Plenty? Really?

AH What I'm saying is that we're not trying to weed people out on religious grounds. We just can't have subversive elements within our ranks, that's all. Nothing can take precedence over loyalty to the country and to the service.

ZY Well, I'm not religious at all any more.

AH At all?

ZY Well, I still like to think of myself as a Muslim. Probably in the same way as many people in this country think of themselves as Christian. But I don't really go to the Mosque any more, and I don't like following its strict rules. University put paid to most of that. I just enjoyed myself too much.

AH And that's all it was. Beer versus God? Women versus self-control? The first one wins every time.

ZY Maybe. And I don't think there's anything wrong with that, to be honest.

AH That's very honest of you.

ZY It's what I think. That's all. But there's something else as well. I don't like what religious extremism does to people. Christian or Muslim. I hate it, in fact. With the very core of my being. It dehumanises. It alienates. It delineates along false grounds. British Asian? Asian British? Muslim British Asian? Which am I? None of them, I'd say. I'm just Zaf, and I love this country.

AH And how did you feel when the planes flew into the twin towers?

ZY I felt sick.

AH You weren't radicalised like other young Muslims?

ZY I've told you: I don't think of myself simply as a young Musli
My father is an agnostic first generation Pakistani. My mother
an agnostic white eighty-ninth generation Brit. Those planes
September last year inspired me to apply to MI5. It might n
sound like the most complex moral code in the world but I believ
there are good people and there are bad people. Bad people k
indiscriminately because of things they profess to believe in. Goo
people stop the bad people from doing that.

AH And you'd like to be one of the good people.

ZY Exactly.

AH I hope you didn't mind me asking all those questions, Zaf.

ZY It's fine. I was in New York in October last year, in fact. I wanted
to see the destruction for myself. I wanted to see if there was
anything I could do to help. And then I arrived at JFK and I was
held for twelve hours by immigration officials. When I eventually
got to walk around the city a few people spat in my face. I went
to Ground Zero and someone came up and shouted, "Admiring
your handiwork, are you?" Everyone stared at me.

AH And how did that make you feel?

ZY Angry, of course. I'm not particularly good at taking insults lying down. But it made me more sad, really. I knew the guy didn't really mean it. I knew there were underlying reasons. There always are. Fear, grief. The bits that make up a person which we can never really understand. But I knew there and then that I had to do something about this.

AH I'm glad to see idealism isn't dead among the young.

ZY (*laughing*) Are you patronising me, Ms Hindle?

AH Would I, Mr Younis?

ZY Have I passed this little test, then?

AH We'll see.

ZY And if I've passed, can I take you to supper?

AH laughs.

AH Thank you, Zaf. That will be all. We'll be in touch.

****End of interview****

SECURITY CLEARANCE & BACKGROUND CHECKS

Zafar Younis

I was tasked with carrying out routine background checks int
Zafar Younis's family and friends, as well as standard fact-
checking of his application details.

I must admit that my first reaction on reading Zafar's
application was one of dismay. We see this type of
application a lot: feckless, bored young men who think that
MI5 will offer a glamorous alternative to a normal career.

There was also a worryingly immature element to his
application. Why do so many people applying here think that
their ability to talk themselves out of a fight will impress
us? We have enough fantasists as it is in the intelligence
services without adding any more.

As I dug deeper, however, I found the truth to be a little
more interesting. Zafar's father is a successful first-
generation Pakistani lawyer. His mother is an upper-class
former model. They gave the children a mixture of Moslem and
British first names (hence the somewhat strange-sounding
"Zafar David Younis").

Zafar's siblings form a mainstream, tight-knit family. Robert
and Yasser are both successful lawyers like their father.
Fatima is a doctor. Clare, Lucy and Layla all dote on Zafar.

Clearly, I was very worried by Zafar's acknowledged
flirtation with radical Islam in his past. However, I
commissioned an additional interview on this which satisfied
many of my queries. Intensive research on the ground also
backs up his evidence. It appears that his elder brothers
(who are a very strong influence on him) soon pulled him
through this phase. His father is also highly westernised.
The phrase "more British than the British" comes to mind.

Zafar is naturally bright but performed poorly in some of
his GCSEs — which we can mainly put down to laziness. His
subsequent political views are fairly mainstream (although he
was a member of the Palestinian society at Manchester). His
behaviour with women stretches the limits of our tolerance
but still falls within acceptable parameters. He has no
history of gambling or bad debts.

Ultimately, Zafar's ability to pass undercover as an Arab or
North African Moslem makes him such a valuable asset to the
service that I'm happy to pass him on to training. With this
in mind, however, he may be thought a better candidate for
MI6 than MI5.

Rebecca Moore

Rebecca Moore, HR Security
17th February 2002

APPROVED

TRAINING ASSESSMENT

Zafar Younis, 7th May 2002

SCORES

Practical		Other core competencies	
Surveillance	4.2	Calm under pressure	4.7
Counter-surveillance	4.2	Leadership	3.2
Physical endurance	3.8	Team work	4.7
Shooting	2.8	Communication	4.1
Driving	5	General attitude	1.8
Technical	3.3	Average	3.7
Average	3.88		

Intellectual		
Linguistic	4	**Overall average** **3.62**
Decision-making	3.8	*On a sliding scale of 1 to 5 where 1 is poor, 5 is outstanding and 2.5 is average for a new recruit*
Research	1.1	
Average	2.97	

Zafar's driving was quite exceptional, which might be explained by the expensive convertible he turned up to work in every day. He was competent in most other areas although his research skills were particularly sloppy. This partly reflects his general attitude which could be worryingly insubordinate at times.

I would recommend, therefore, that Zafar starts in MI6 (if they're willing to have him) in the hope that this will knock some of the corners off. His Asian appearance will also be particularly useful over the river although a number of his fellow recruits will be sorry to lose him. He was very popular here.

R Ferguson

Robin Ferguson
Head of recruit training, MI5

[FIELD REPORT]

OPERATION LAWRENCE

Introduction

Eighteen months ago I was posted as a cultural attaché to Rabat, Morocco. It was meant to be a fairly straightforward first posting to ease me into the job gently. I attended embassy receptions, cultural events and kept my ear to the ground for any developments which I could relay back to London.

But then in February it came to our attention that a group of aid workers in southern Morocco were operating under false pretences. We were used to kidnappings in that area. We knew that desert routes were being used to traffic drugs and weapons, and we were aware that UN aid to the area rarely reached its intended destination. What we hadn't realised was that aid workers themselves – a mixture of Western and Moroccan – were aiding these criminal activities. We needed to find out how and why.

"Faraaz Owen"

A back-story was worked out for me: I was the idealistic younger son of a doctor. I'd spent a gap year building toilets in Peru. At university (Cambridge) I was part of the Free Tibet society – including one arrest in the Mall for throwing eggs at the car of a visiting Chinese dignitary. I'd gone on to take a masters at SOAS in international development, then worked for one year on a fast stream civil service placement with DFID before leaving to work on the ground. Since then, I'd spent one year in Sudan coordinating relief efforts on behalf of the UN in Lokichoggio.

Using the legend of Faraaz Owen I was set up with a job with the UN in southern Morocco.

Moroccan Aid

You can usually spot a bogus organisation. They either call themselves something overly complex – such as "The North London charitable appeal for charity towards Iraqi orphans requiring charity". Or something extremely simple – such as "Moroccan Aid". They think both extremes will fool the intelligence services.

Within a week at the UN, my suspicions about Moroccan Aid were confirmed. Many of the staffers there were former SAS men with little interest in aid work. UN food and medical supplies were being traded with Sahrawi tribes in exchange for protection as they smuggled guns and drugs into neighbouring Algeria. There were few ideological motives behind their activities – simply huge sums of money.

To find out more about what was going on I had to try and join the Sahrawi themselves.

Sahrawi tribes

Along with my section head in Rabat we discussed the various ways of infiltrating the tribe. Although my language skills were good, they were not sufficiently proficient to pass as a native in a close-knit community. Attempting to infiltrate Moroccan Aid themselves as a way into the tribe was seen as too risky. So we settled on the boldest, least obvious means of approach: I would assume a new legend, this time as an eccentric British explorer.

The approach worked perfectly. I learned to ride a camel. I memorised desert maps. I grew to recognise the warning signs of quicksand and sand storms that would materialise from nowhere. And I managed to effect a meeting with the Sahrawi near one of their main watering holes.

They were extremely hostile at first, as might be expected. For a moment I thought I might be shot on sight, but the part of the bumbling Brit in love with the desert seemed to capture their imagination. Their natural desert hospitality took hold. I was invited to eat with them that evening. I stayed the night. And when I mentioned the next day that I should be getting on, they asked if I'd like to travel with them for a week. It was, of course, exactly what I wanted.

Everything went well for the first three days. I pretended to understand much less than I did, so I picked up many vital pieces of information on their activities as they talked unguarded. I learned the names of the people in Moroccan Aid who were running the arms routes. I had a pretty good idea of the routes themselves. More alarmingly, I found out who the eventual purchasers were in Algeria: a well-funded group of Al-Qaeda sympathisers who were planning on acting against British and American interests in the region. It had suddenly become a priority to act as soon as possible.

On the fourth day, however, I was suddenly told that they had a very important meeting and I should now continue on my own way – ideally in the opposite direction. I could see jeeps in the distance and it was obvious that they were about to meet their Moroccan Aid contacts.

After saying goodbye, I was able to conceal myself behind a sand dune amid the chaos, dust and confusion as the two jeeps approached. It was an impossible situation. I had no back-up. I couldn't confront the men from Moroccan Aid in case they recognised me from my previous legend. And the stakes were very high now that I knew the final destination of the arms shipment.

As the two jeeps came closer I could see that only one carried weapons (it had two occupants, one armed). The other appeared to be full of supplies and only had one driver. My best chance was to take out both cars before they stopped. I was carrying a disassembled marksman's rifle which would give me time for one shot – two at the most. Using my camel's body for cover I shot the lead vehicle's front tyre just as it turned sharply in front of the convoy of Sahrawi. The vehicle flipped and landed on top of the other one, killing the sole driver instantly.

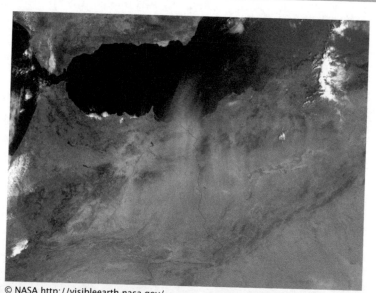

© NASA http://visibleearth.nasa.gov/

The armed passenger of the other car started shooting wildly from his suspended position, upside down on top of the still-sliding jeep. Reloading, I took aim and shot him dead.

Conclusions

If these developments surprised the Sahrawi, they didn't seem to show it. As I emerged again from behind the sand dune they looked at me as if this sort of thing happened all the time. They were a phlegmatic bunch. Their old paymasters were dead; I was their new one.

When I offered them all the financial aid they needed, they agreed to work as MI6 scouts in the area, monitoring trade routes for any signs of suspicious behaviour. Unfortunately, I was unable to stop them lynching the third member of Moroccan Aid. Desert justice lay outside our remit.

Five of Moroccan Aid's other workers were arrested. Two were turned and started to work for us. The rest disbanded and joined other jobs.

In retrospect, Operation Lawrence was a definite success. Arms were prevented from getting into the hands of our enemies. Former SAS soldiers were again shown that they will not be allowed to operate unlawfully without consequences. And we achieved a number of other successful raids.

Although it has now been wound down, its structural foundations remain should we wish to reconsider our interests in the area at a future date.

RE: Zafar Younis

Email transcripts between Harry Pearce and Giles Connelly (Zafar Younis's former section head in MI6, North African Desk).

-----External mail [medium risk]-----
-----Secure intranet-----
From: Harry Pearce
To: Giles Connelly
Date: 3 May 2005 14.39

Hello Giles. Long time, no see. We've got one of your bright young sparks from the North African Desk helping us out over here. Zafar Younis. Personable, confident, slightly cocky. Uses the word "cool" altogether too much for my liking. Ring any bells?

-----External mail [medium risk]-----
-----Intra-department communication system-----
From: Giles Connelly
To: Harry Pearce
Date: 3 May 2005 15.21

Hello Harry. Very nice to hear from you. I haven't seen you in the club for ages.

Of course I know Zaf. He was one of our best recruits. What's he doing for you over there?

-----External mail [medium risk]-----
-----Intra-department communication system-----
From: Harry Pearce
To: Giles Connelly
Date: 3 May 2005 15.22

He's helping us out with a little local difficulty. A few of our agents got into hot water and we needed someone with North African expertise to bail us out.

Tell me more about his work for you.

-----External mail [medium risk]-----
-----Intra-department communication system-----
From: Giles Connelly
To: Harry Pearce
Date: 3 May 2005 15.23

You want a reference?

-----External mail [medium risk]-----
-----Intra-department communication system-----

From: Harry Pearce
  To: Giles Connelly
Date: 3 May 2005 15.24

Nothing too formal. Email's fine. I'm just intrigued as to what he got up to over the water.

-----External mail [medium risk]-----
-----Intra-department communication system-----

From: Giles Connelly
  To: Harry Pearce
Date: 3 May 2005 15.39

As I said, he's one of our very best. He was fast-tracked out of Vauxhall in record time and spent 18 months in Morocco. Found his feet as a cultural attaché in Rabat before going undercover in the desert south of Marrakesh. Like a Lawrence of Arabia without the weird sexual tastes. They took to him - offered him wives, camels etc. He discovered an aid company trafficking arms to Algeria. He killed 3 of them, arrested 5 and turned the remaining 2. It was one of our most successful operations in the region.

-----External mail [medium risk]-----
-----Intra-department communication system-----

From: Harry Pearce
  To: Giles Connelly
Date: 3 May 2005 16.00

3:5:2? I've never been keen on MI6's ratios.

-----External mail [medium risk]-----
-----Intra-department communication system-----

From: Giles Connelly
   To: Harry Pearce
Date: 3 May 2005 16.01

And I've never been keen on MI5, full stop.

What's this all about anyway?

-----External mail [medium risk]-----
-----Intra-department communication system-----

From: Harry Pearce
   To: Giles Connelly
Date: 3 May 2005 16.03

Giles - sharp as a button, as always.

I was rather hoping you might extend the loan period for young Zaf. We're quite keen on him over here.

-----External mail [medium risk]-----
-----Intra-department communication system-----

From: Giles Connelly
   To: Harry Pearce
Date: 3 May 2005 16.04

Not a chance. You've already taken Adam Carter. Why don't you start recruiting your own officers?

-----External mail [medium risk]-----
-----Intra-department communication system-----

From: Harry Pearce
   To: Giles Connelly
Date: 3 May 2005 16.10

Well, that's partly it. Zaf and Adam work very well together. Zaf really looks up to him.

-----External mail [medium risk]-----
-----Intra-department communication system-----

From: Giles Connelly
   To: Harry Pearce
Date: 3 May 2005 16.30

I'm not bloody surprised! Adam trained him. MI6 trained him. You're not having him, Harry. I'm sorry. It's as simple as that.

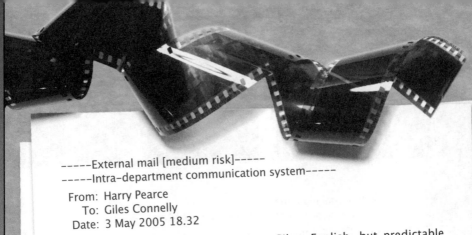

-----External mail [medium risk]-----
-----Intra-department communication system-----

From: Harry Pearce
    To: Giles Connelly
Date: 3 May 2005 18.32

Now, I thought you might say that, Giles. Foolish, but predictable nonetheless. Which is why I took the precaution of compiling a little file on you. Some very interesting things in your past. Maybe a few things Mrs Connelly wouldn't like to hear about. Or the headmaster of the school where you're a governor, for that matter.

-----External mail [medium risk]-----
-----Intra-department communication system-----

From: Giles Connelly
    To: Harry Pearce
Date: 3 May 2005 18.59

You're a bastard, Harry Pearce.

-----External mail [medium risk]-----
-----Intra-department communication system-----

From: Harry Pearce
    To: Giles Connelly
Date: 3 May 2005 19.10

Oh, I wouldn't go that far. Just looking after the best interests of my team.

-----External mail [medium risk]-----
-----Intra-department communication system-----

From: Giles Connelly
    To: Harry Pearce
Date: 3 May 2005 19.20

Nope, you're a bastard. You're also working very late for someone at Thames House. I thought you chaps all went home at 17.30.

-----External mail [medium risk]-----
-----Intra-department communication system-----

From: Harry Pearce
    To: Giles Connelly
Date: 3 May 2005 19.21

Spying on us, Giles?

ADD TO FILE

-----External mail [medium risk]-----
-----Intra-department communication system-----
From: Giles Connelly
  To: Harry Pearce
Date: 3 May 2005 19.23

Oh do shut up. I just wondered whether you'd like to go for a drink at the club to chat this over a little further. I'm sure we can come to some arrangement.

-----External mail [medium risk]-----
-----Intra-department communication system-----
From: Harry Pearce
  To: Giles Connelly
Date: 3 May 2005 19.23

I think we've already come to an arrangement, Giles. Anyway, I have to go home and let the dog out. Have a good evening.

-----External mail [medium risk]-----
-----Intra-department communication system-----
From: Giles Connelly
  To: Harry Pearce
Date: 3 May 2005 19.24

You too (bastard).

****End of transcript****

Note from Harry Pearce

Please insert this into Zafar Younis's file. I approve his transfer to MI5 following the statutory probation period.

7 September 2005

Dirty tricks training for new recruits

Presentation by Zafar Younis

Speaking notes

Introduction by AN Other Officer

Today we have one of our youngest officers – Zafar Younis – to talk to you about some of the dirty tricks you might have to deploy in this job. He has one of the most deviant imaginations of any in our team so I hope you enjoy what he has to say. Over to you, Zafar.

ZY's introduction

Thank you. But please, everyone, call me Zaf.

Perhaps I should start off by saying that we use dirty tricks very rarely. Despite popular belief, we do not make a habit of setting-up, framing and destroying innocent lives. Indeed, we do this sort of thing fairly seldom with guilty people.

There are, however, certain circumstances where it is believed advantageous to national security to tamper with someone's life. This might be the simple matter of deterring them from continuing with whichever activity has displeased us. In these circumstances we use a dirty tricks campaign as a warning shot across their bows. The subliminal message is this: "We're aware of what you're up to. You know what we can do. Continue with this and things will get a lot worse for you." This is an excellent way of neutralising and diluting threats without the need for full-blown operations, arrests and court cases.

In more extreme circumstances dirty tricks will involve the destruction of someone's reputation. We have the power to close off all avenues of employment, turn neighbour against neighbour, brother against brother. If needs must, we can make someone's life pretty unpleasant, even unbearable.

And who are the unfortunate targets of these operations? Well, at the lowest level we use them on nuisance groups who threaten the status quo – animal rights protestors, militant anti-abortionists and so on. It warns them that they've come across our radar. And it often persuades them to scale down their activities. At the highest level it can involve anyone we can't get at through the normal channels – dangerously fascist politicians, renegade ambassadors with diplomatic immunity, media barons with powerful friends and so on.

Here, then, are some of the tricks we deploy – starting from the most minor and working upwards.

Minor irritations

1. We can make the minor irritations of everyday life a whole lot worse. Recently, we had to deal with a renegade MP who was trying to set up a fascist party – The British Way. We disconnected the water pipes outside his house so he couldn't wash for a week. We painted his door blue and then posed as council workers fining him for "aesthetic anarchy". We set off his car alarm at 4am. And we tampered with his online shopping so he was delivered lobster instead of washing powder.

Get 1 month's free broadband, order online

Special online broadba...

2 This is where your devious imaginations come into play. Think about what annoys you on a day-to-day basis and then apply it to your target. Cancel his oyster card: he'll be late for every meeting. Divert his phone so that every call he makes ends up in a holding system playing *Eine Kleine Nachtmusik*. Make sure his rubbish is never collected from outside his door. Send him email viruses. Leak his email address to spam sites. Clamp his car. Steal his bicycle, leaving only the back wheel. Tamper with his credit ratings. Break a key inside his front door lock. Give cold callers his home telephone number. Put charity muggers onto him. Send Jehovah Witnesses around to his house every 45 minutes. They say bad things come in threes. You can make them come in hundreds.

3   If you observe someone on the verge of a stress-related breakdown you'll notice that it's these minor things that push them over the edge. Most people are surprisingly good at coping with the big events – the death of a parent, the loss of a job etc. They psych themselves up to face it head-on. It's only when they break a glass washing-up or stub their toe on a doorframe that all the repressed emotion comes flooding out. And so it is with low-level sabotage. Keep this up for long enough and you'll drive your target so mad with paranoia that they'll do anything to stop it.

Damage their career

1   With higher-level targets there are any number of things you can do to make their working lives very uncomfortable. If they are a well-known personality the rumour mill can be exploited to great

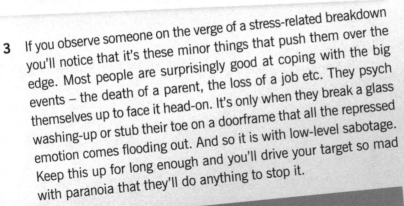

effect. Place stories with friendly gossip journalists on the diaries. Set up anonymous blogs which make disparaging references to their activities. Encourage speculation in as many forums as you can. MI5 has dossiers on most people of any importance. This is the time to use them.

2   Powerful people also have powerful enemies and you should play on these rivalries for your own ends. Leak selective pieces of information to people who can damage the target, and exploit rivalries within their own organisations as well.

3   Let's consider a few specific examples. You could damage the career of a politician with faked pamphlets purporting to come from them. A journalist could be destroyed with allegations of plagiarism or fabrication. An anti-abortionist with revelations about their own past terminations. Dangerous foreign diplomats framed as "going native". Find that killer fact, and then find the "evidence" to fit it.

4   This is also an area where MI5 can call upon its large network of sleeper agents. Wake them up and get them to do your dirty work for you.

Reputation damage

1   This leads on from the previous point. Once you've destroyed someone's livelihood, it doesn't take long to get to them as well. Most people care a lot about what others think of them.

2   Again, the list is as long as your imagination is wide. Think about the worst way you could portray them in the eyes of their friends, family and community. Paedophilia? Religious extremism? Socialism? Perhaps you could arrange for the police to make a very public visit to their house to "help them with enquiries".

3   And then you can set the rumour mill in motion again.

Dirty tricks training for new recruits

Conclusion

These are only a few ideas to get you thinking along the right lines. The best thing about dirty trick campaigns is that each one is as individual as the person you're targeting. Your job is to use your imagination – and your knowledge of that person – to hit them where it will hurt the most.

Is this moral, you might ask. Let me answer that another way: it's not immoral. Dirty trick campaigns are never an end in their own right. They're a preventative measure to stop anything worse from happening, and we only use them under particular circumstances. Intelligence services in less enlightened countries would simply shoot or torture their suspects. I know which methods I prefer.

MI5

ANNUAL MEDICAL REPORT

Name: Zafar Younis

Date: 1st May 2006

BMI: 22.82

Height: 6'0

Weight: 12st

Units of alcohol per week: o

Cigarettes per week: none

Blood pressure:	110/60
Resting pulse:	55
Urine:	normal
Chest x-ray:	normal
Exercise ECG:	normal

Zaf is in excellent physical shape although
I suspect he may be lying about his weekly
alcohol intake.

PASSED

Dr Sally Chapman

SECTION X

EYES ONLY FOR LEVEL 1 AND ABOVE

LOG FOR ZAFAR YOUNIS

Date: 19.04.2006

Subject: Pool cars. Zaf has been signing out pool cars on spurious business reasons while using them to pick up his dates.

Outcome: Zaf has been issued with a final warning regarding his behaviour in this area.

Date: 12.02.2006

Subject: Valentine cards. Zaf has been using the office franking machine to send out a number of Valentine cards. Government couriers have also been used instead of florists.

Outcome: Reprimand issued.

Date: 7.08.2005

Subject: S24 dating forms. Zaf has given us ten S24 forms to check up on within the space of a fortnight. Our resources and manpower are tight — there is no way we can check up on this many women.

Outcome: Referred to Harry. See note below.

Note from Harry: Don't worry about following up any of his S24s for the time-being. I'm afraid none of these is likely to last long. If someone becomes serious, I will ask him to fill out a form properly.

Date: 22.06.2005

Subject: Zakah. Zaf is continuing the Muslim practice of Zakah which involves giving a proportion of his wages to charity. We investigated the charities — they include Guide Dogs for the Blind and the NSPCC.

Outcome: Leave, but continue to monitor, just in case.

Section
usage,
and a

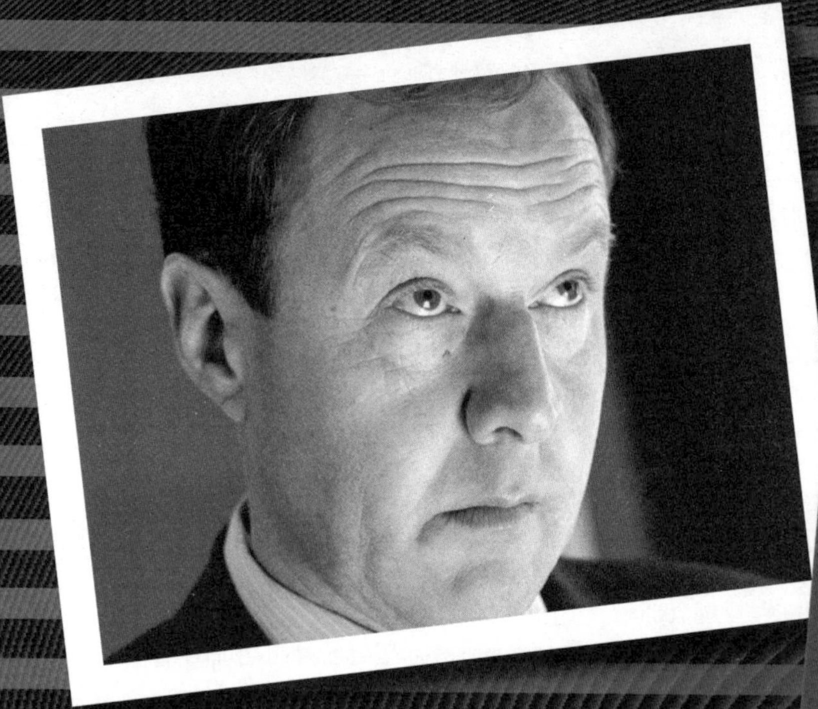

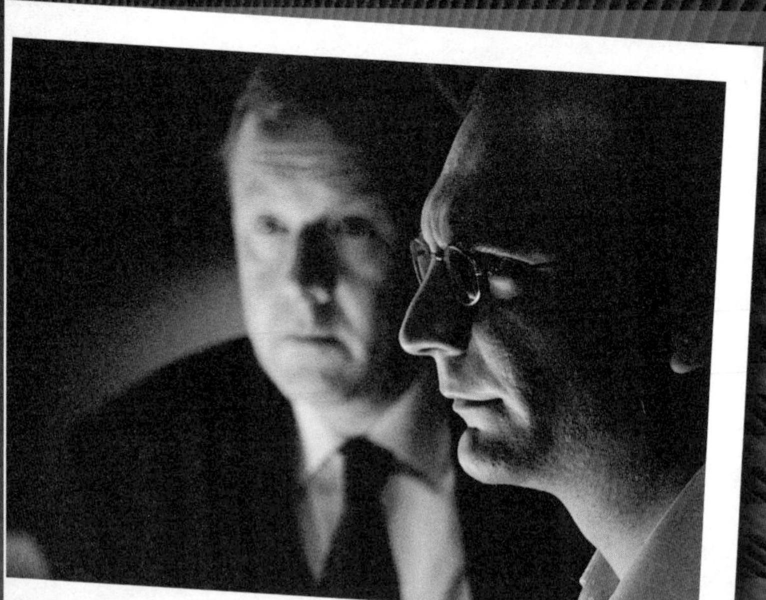

Private and Confidential

Name: Malcolm Wynn-Jones
Position: Senior Technical Officer
D.O.B: 29.12.1958
Hair: Brown
Eyes: Blue / grey
Height: 6'0
Marital status: Single
Dependants: None
Blood type: AB, Rh positive

Malcolm Wynn-Jones joined MI5 in 1990 after an early career in the Home Office and a 5-year stint in the private sector. He heads up the technical section, providing valuable background support on all major operations.

MI5
Application Form

Medical

Do you have any conditions – either physical or psychological – which might affect your employment?

Asthma

Father's name, address and occupation

Rev. David Wynn-Jones, local vicar (died 1986)

Mother's name, maiden name, address and occupation

Amelia Wynn-Jones. Housewife

The Old Vicarage, Dunvant, Nr Swansea

Brothers / Sisters (with names and D.O.B.)

None

Secondary Schools / Colleges

Dates : Names : Town

1969-1976 : Dunvant School for boys : Dunvant, Swansea

O Levels or equivalent

O Levels: 10 As (English Language, English Literature, French, Latin, Greek, Maths, History, Chemistry, Religious Education, Physics)

A levels and AS levels or equivalents

Chemistry – A

Physics – A

Maths – A

Latin – A

Greek - A

Surname

Wynn-Jones

Forenames

Malcolm Peregrine Geoffrey St. John

Date of Birth

29.12.1958

Place of birth

Dunvant, Wales

Nationality at birth

British

Permanent Address

12 Camden Hill Mews, London W8

Current occupation

Business – IT

Date of availability for employment

Immediately

Do you hold a full, clean driving licence?

Yes

MAF|05.fa|vii.

Gap Year
How did you spend any break during your education?

After school I spent a year in Italy in museums and working on various archaeological digs.

University or Further Education

St. John's College, Cambridge - 1977-1980

MA (Hons) Natural Sciences - First

Awards
Please give details of any other awards (e.g. music)

Grade 8 singing

National Schools Chemistry medal - 1975/6

National Schools Physics medal - 1976

Cambridge Francis Crick prize for Chemistry - 1979

EMPLOYMENT

Dates	Employer	Position
1985-1990	Whizzfizz Media	IT Director
1980-1985	Home Office	Fast Stream

Have you served in HM Forces (including Reserves)?

No

Do you have applications pending for other jobs?

No

PERSONAL QUALITIES AND SKILLS

SUMMARY
Provide a pen-portrait of your life to date

I was born in a small village near Swansea where my father was the local vicar. This never made life particularly easy at school where I struggled to fit in.

Cambridge was therefore something of a revelation for me when I went up in 1977. I enjoyed letting my hair down for a few years.

After graduating I followed my father's wish to go into the civil service. I always had a desire to work in the FCO but it was the Home Office instead who employed me. I spent a rather dreary five years there before a family friend set up a business and asked me to come on board. It was a new media enterprise which floated an initial public offering. My share holding at that time was 30 per cent.

MOTIVATION

Why do you think you would be suited to a career in MI5?

I made a rather tidy sum when Whizzfizz Media floated on the stock exchange. Aged 30 I found myself in the somewhat strange situation of never having to work again. From my experience of civil service salaries this would appear to be a useful state of affairs. I think it highly unlikely that Russian subversives will attempt to compromise me with a couple of roubles in a grubby envelope.

On the other hand, I really didn't enjoy the private sector, particularly its naked, arriviste greed. And I hated the way it continually flouted the rules. Rules have always been something by which I abide. The Home Office, on the other hand, was rather mundane.

I hope, therefore, that MI5 will offer a happy medium between these two extremes. I would very much like to return to public service and I still feel I would have a lot to bring to the role. In particular, I believe my temperament to be well suited to such an environment. I am conservative (with both small and large 'cs'), discreet and dedicated. Also, there are few things that I can't do with computers.

POLITICAL CURIOSITY

Give three political topics (historical or current) which interest you

* The Great Reform Act, 1832
* The miners' strikes
* The Exchange Rate Mechanism

ADAPTABILITY

Give an example of a time when you had to adapt to unexpected circumstances

I wouldn't describe myself as the most adaptable person in the world. "Defend the status quo." Isn't that the motto of the security services? I've spent most of my life trying to preserve my own status quo.

On the other hand I don't want to sound as if I'm entirely stuck-in-the-mud and immune to change. It was quite a brave decision for me to leave the security of the Home Office for the unpredictability of a media start-up. Having taken the plunge, I made a big success of the role.

RESPONSIBILITY

What positions of responsibility have you held – at school, university or otherwise?

Church Warden, All Soul's, Kensington

FOREIGN LANGUAGES

Please indicate level of competence

```
Russian - fluent (self-taught)
Arabic - fluent (self-taught)
Chinese - fluent (self-taught)
German - fluent
```

OTHER INTERESTS

```
Music, particularly church music
```

TRAVEL

Give details of all foreign travel undertaken in the last 10 years, including reason for travel

```
Italy - architecture
Greece - archaeology
Russia - music
```

EQUAL OPPORTUNITIES

This information is not used as part of our selection procedures

Gender	Ethnic origin	Disabilities
(Male) Female	White British	None

REFEREES

Please give details of three referees. One of these should be a contemporary who knows you well

1. Dr Terrence Howard, Senior Tutor, St. John's College, Cambridge

2. Simon Muir, CEO Whizzfizz Media

3. Geoffrey Campbell, Church Warden, All Soul's, Kensington

Signature

Date

7 January 1990

Whizz*fizz* Media
176 Camden High Street, London

REFERENCE: Malcolm Wynn-Jones

To Whom It May Concern:

Malcolm was something of an anomaly at Whizzfizz Media where the average age is 19. I know that he is not quite as old as he looks, acts and sounds, but it did take him rather a long time to fit in here.

On day one we all turned up to work in jeans and a t-shirt. Malcolm came in a three-piece pinstripe suit. It took him three years to lose the waistcoat; another two to take his jacket off occasionally while he worked.

That said, I don't want to make cheap jokes at Malcolm's expense (don't ask him to make any jokes, by the way; he has a stash of appalling knock-knock jokes). He is one of the loveliest people I have ever met. He really cares about people and he has an unimpeachable sense of moral integrity (which occasionally caused us to cross swords in this job).

He is also far and away the most intelligent person I've ever met. You have the feeling that he's going to burst into Latin at any moment. Or ancient Greek. I have yet to find a problem which he doesn't have a solution for.

He made me (and himself) very rich and I will always be grateful for his work here. I am sorry to see him go, but I know he feels he should give something back to society. This sense of duty might not be one I share, but I certainly find it admirable.

Simon Muir
CEO, Whizzfizz Media

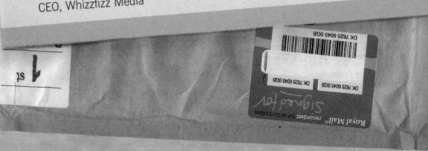

From the Headmaster of Dunvant School for Boys
E.L. Hall B.A. (Hons) PGCE
Dunvant
Nr Swansea

5th September 1973

Dear David and Amelia Wynn-Jones,

I know we've voiced shared concerns about Malcolm in the past – his inability to fit in with other children, the constant bullying – but this time, I fear, we really have to take some affirmative action.

Let me explain. Last Friday, as is our wont, we held our traditional pre-term staff meeting. We discuss many things on these occasions – lesson timetables, exam performances, staffing issues, departmental budgets etc. It is an opportunity for the common room to get together and let off some steam before we're inundated with the day-to-day rush of a new term. It is not supposed to be an opportunity for a 14-year-old boy to bug the meeting and play the recording to the entire school during morning assembly.

This, I'm afraid to report, is exactly what Malcolm did. As you know, I encourage boys in his year to take the lead in morning assemblies in the Autumn term. Malcolm chose "What I did during the school holidays." I thought it would be good for his confidence.

Unfortunately, it seems that Malcolm spent the latter half of his school holidays secreting tiny recording devices throughout the common room. His contemporaries now think he is some kind of hero. You'll understand that the staff think otherwise.

Perhaps you would like to come in and talk to me about this some time. I'm aware that we have something of an eccentric genius on our hands. However, we need to nip this sort of behaviour in the bud before it goes off the rails. If channelled in the right direction, Malcolm's undoubted technical wizardry could make him a very successful man. If not, goodness only knows what will become of him.

Yours sincerely,

Ted Hall

Ted Hall

SECURITY CLEARANCE & BACKGROUND CHECKS

Malcolm Wynn-Jones

I was tasked with carrying out routine background checks into Malcolm Wynn-Jones's family and friends, as well as standard fact-checking of his application details.

As befits someone with so many forenames, Malcolm comes from a rather aristocratic background. His father was the youngest son of a baronet and followed the family tradition of going into the church. The small parish of Dunvant was run on almost feudal lines until his death (from bowel cancer four years ago).

The Reverend Wynn-Jones was a strong influence on young Malcolm, forcing him to wake up early and recite Latin verbs before breakfast. The family had fallen on hard times recently so Malcolm was sent to the local school where he had a miserable time. I have tracked down a letter from his headmaster which shows a brief streak of non-conformism in an otherwise conservative upbringing.

Malcolm makes no secret of his own conservatism. School contemporaries described him as middle-aged before he reached his teenage years. His idea of "letting his hair down" (his words) at Cambridge was to skip chapel on Mondays. He has also inherited a distinct snobbery from his mother. Her next door neighbour described her as a "ghastly old bag" — a verdict I, having met her, find myself unable to disagree with.

Despite these caveats, however, I believe Malcolm's conservatism to be more social than political. There are certainly no signs of borderline fascism which have plagued some of our recent applicants.

Malcolm performed in the top ten percentile during his time at the Home Office but he found the work rather mundane. Whizzfizz Media was an interesting interlude in his life — a start-up company founded by his father's godson, Simon Muir. Wynn-Jones Senior disapproved somewhat of his son leaving the Civil Service but was glad that he could help out a family friend. If anything, Malcolm's report of his ensuing wealth is rather modest. Our estimates put his current assets at around £5 million.

It is Malcolm's work at this somewhat unlikely company which makes him such an attractive current prospect to MI5. During his time there he revolutionised their computer systems, rolling out media databases and search facilities that were more successful than any to date. This work formed the lynchpin of Whizzfizz's success.

Malcolm has never entirely overcome his natural awkwardness with members of the opposite sex. There were rumours at university that he might be homosexual but I can find no evidence for this. There certainly appear to be no obvious opportunities for blackmail. He seems to have devoted himself entirely to any job he's undertaken, and his social life outside work is very quiet indeed.

Malcolm's complete ease with all gadgetry allied to his formidable natural intelligence make him an excellent candidate for the service.

James Carle

APPROVED

James Carter, HR Security
17th March 1990

TRAINING ASSESSMENT
Malcolm Wynn-Jones, 9th June 1990

SCORES

Practical		Other core competencies	
Surveillance	4.8	Calm under pressure	0.6
Counter-surveillance	0.3	Leadership	1.5
Physical endurance	0.1	Team work	3.8
Shooting	5	Communication	2.5
Driving	2	General attitude	4.1
Technical	5	Average	2.98
Average	2.86		

Intellectual		Overall average	3.1
Linguistic	4.9	*On a sliding scale of 1 to 5 where*	
Decision-making	3	*1 is poor, 5 is outstanding and 2.5 is*	
Research	4.1	*average for a new recruit*	
Average	4		

Malcolm was never going to be anything other than a technical operative (where he scored very highly indeed). It was interesting, however, to see him score well in a number of other disciplines. His shooting, in particular, was excellent. I understand this derives in part from many long weekends on Scottish grouse moors. He is also an excellent linguist.

Malcolm's asthma means that his physical endurance is very low. I was also slightly concerned by his tendency to panic whilst under pressure. I'm sure this will improve with time, however.

He will make an excellent technical operative.

Sarah Hilliard
Head of recruit training, MI5

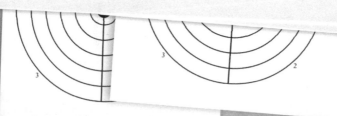

Technical training for new recruits

Presentation by Malcolm Wynn-Jones

Speaking notes

Introduction by AN Other Officer

In our final session before lunch today, we're going to listen to a brief talk from Malcolm Wynn-Jones. Malcolm heads up the technical team in Section D – our very own egg-headed Q. Over to you, Malcolm.

MWJ's introduction

Thank you. This is actually the first year I've given one of these talks. Traditionally, it was thought best to keep the technical and operation sides separate. We were the geeks toiling away in darkened rooms on elaborate gadgets and cryptic pieces of linguistics.

Recently, however, it was decided that it would be sensible for all new recruits to learn a little bit more about what we do. After all, we often work very closely alongside one another – both in the office and in the field. And even if you're never going to grasp the nitty-gritty details of our work, you should at least have a handle on the overall picture.

Perhaps you're a complete technophobe who can't even program a video recorder. Or maybe you have absolutely no intention of working in a technical capacity at MI5. Nonetheless, it still makes sense for you to have some idea of what we get up to.

I work closely with my deputy, Colin Wells. These are some of the things we get up to while the rest of you are out there driving fast cars and saving the world.

Hacking

1   Nearly everything of any value – either monetary, social or political – is controlled by computers these days. It is often our role to hack into these computer systems, either as a research tool to find out what is really going on, or as an active operational decision to close something down.

2   We can whisk funds out of most people's accounts in a matter of seconds. We can break into companies' websites and find out who they're really selling their products to. We can read the emails and internet history of nearly anyone we choose. A poorly guarded rogue website can be closed down with the press of a button.

3   For years, we've had an inter-departmental rivalry with GCHQ over who can hack into the other's systems the most successfully. There is an annual trophy for the best effort on either side.

4   Our American allies are less keen to indulge in such horse-play. When one of our brightest and youngest recruits successfully hacked into the Pentagon, he was threatened with a couple of months in Guantanamo, special relationship or no special relationship.

5   Clearly, some of our work in this area is also defensive. There is a large community of hackers around the globe and entry to a security service's system is considered the ultimate coup. We have the most state-of-the-art firewalls imaginable. Particularly good hackers on computing forums are often contacted and invited to join the service. If you can't beat them, recruit them. That's our motto.

© NASA http://visibleearth.nasa.gov/

Bugging and surveillance

1   I believe you've already listened to training lectures on surveillance techniques. The technical team is obviously intimately involved in all these operations.

2   Often, our first job is to lay bugs in premises. This requires an undisturbed window of opportunity to access the room, which is why we try to use a hotel room if at all possible. Anti-bugging technology is becoming more and more sophisticated so we have to be incredibly careful where we hide our devices. If we're expecting professionals we try to avoid all the obvious places such as picture frames and flower pots. The most successful bugs are often the most ingenious – hidden in toothpaste or a CD cover. We can go through walls, if necessary.

3   Once the bugging operation is in place technical officers remain involved throughout the surveillance stage. It is our job to monitor the screens and switch between different cameras and microphones. This is often done from a mobile surveillance van outside the premises or from a neighbouring property. When the going gets heavy we recommend sending in the field officers. However, that is their decision and not ours.

4   Sound and picture quality are vital. Currently, the law doesn't take into account evidence obtained through secret recordings. Yet they remain an integral part of our intelligence-gathering. No one is more unguarded than when they think no one is listening.

Gadgetry

1 I don't want you to get carried away with Bond-esque gadgetry ideas. We don't make invisible cars with rocket grenades, neither do we manufacture watches with a shoot-out lasso that can hold two people's weight.

2 We do, however, have access to some of the finest and most inventive minds in science. We can – and we have – designed microphones that can be swallowed, substitute-cocaine with no harmful side-effects and diamonds with poisonous coatings. The list is as long as the imagination is wide.

3 Boys with toys, you might think, but many of these toys have saved people's lives.

Back-up dogsbodies

1 Another less glamorous aspect of our work is to act as general creative dogsbodies behind the scenes. It is thought that our scientific, engineering based approach to problem-solving adds an angle which would otherwise be left uncovered.

2 Let me give you a few examples. On one occasion during a training exercise we found ourselves cocooned inside the Grid with no means of communicating with the outside world. Colin and I manufactured a small satellite dish using the wheels from the photocopying machine. On another, we used the knife from the cutting-arm of the guillotine to attempt to slice through the walls.

3 Once, someone spilled an entire pot of tea into a case of documents we'd "liberated" from the American Embassy. Whose job was it to clean them up? Ours, of course. I am also something of a dab hand at sticking shredded papers back together. "The Leonardo of the Dustbins", that's what my boss used to call me.

4 In some ways, I suppose, we are the *Blue Peter* minds of MI5: give us a couple of hours and we'll come up with a solution we made earlier.

IT support

1 Our final role – and by far the most tedious – is to double-up a IT support in the office. If your log-in doesn't work, or your ema attachments won't open, then we're the men to fix it.

2 Hardly sexy, I know, but I distrust sexy. It's a vital job we do a I hope some of you, at least, will be interested in working in r team. Come and talk to me about it any time.

Technical training for new recruits

TEMPEST

FIELD REPORT
TITLE: Tempest Technology in Operation Nightingale
FILED BY: Malcolm Wynn-Jones
DATE: 11 March 1998

Introduction

Over the years technology has improved rapidly from bulky, cumbersome phone taps to bugs which are almost invisible to the naked eye. Yet as surveillance technology improves, so do counter-surveillance devices to match and block their progress.

In the last fifteen years, in particular, surveillance operations have focused more and more on information technology. Much of people's working lives are spent at their computers. Much of their personal life is on there too – their emails, their contacts, their bank details, their internet history. Imagine how much you could learn if you could look over their shoulder while they type.

It was with this in mind that we recently invented Transient Electronic Magnetic Pulse Emanation Surveillance Technology, or TEMPEST for short.

Any computer monitor gives off radiation from the screen. TEMPEST technology recognises and organises that radiation into an exact replica. It allows us to see exactly what they're seeing.

Operation Nightingale

It was decided to road-test this new equipment in a non-critical situation so that we could tell how trustworthy it would be on a proper operation. We decided the best place was Kensington Palace Gardens in West London – or Embassy Row as we sometimes refer to it. Many of the foreign delegations have offices there. And we didn't want to get caught trying out unwieldy new equipment on members of the public.

TEMPEST is run through a large computer which just fits inside the back of one of our surveillance vans. For the purpose of this experiment it was disguised as a plumber's van (there is currently a lot of building work in Kensington Palace Gardens). We encountered some initial difficulties with the targeting device – an awkward piece of equipment which looks a little bit like a speed camera. Pointing this without arousing suspicions was never going to be easy and we had to move on from the Russian Embassy when security guards started looking in our direction.

We had more luck outside the Nepalese embassy where we were able to pick up exact copies of four different computers in the front offices. We were also successful outside the Lebanese embassy (even if the pictures on the second consul's laptop were rather alarming). The offices in the Slovak embassy were on the other side of the building and out of range of TEMPEST, and the Czech embassy had very dark windows which made reading the monitors difficult. The Romanian and Philippine embassies had no computers switched on at the time.

Our real obstacle, however, came with the Israeli embassy at the end of the road nearest to Kensington High Street. They appeared to be using some kind of counter-surveillance device (which we now know to be called E-Bing). This disguises the screen with a cloud of radiation – much like a plane firing out chaff to deter a missile.

The Israelis seem to be one step ahead of the rest of us.

Conclusions

TEMPEST should become a valuable intelligence device over the next decade, especially in accessing computers which are not connected to the internet. We are pleased with our success on its first trial run.

Going forward, our first priority is to modify the targeting device to make it less obvious. We also need to look at widening its range and adding filters if light conditions are not at optimum levels.

The Israeli's possession of E-Bing suggests that we are not the first to develop this kind of technology. As a matter of urgency, we need to look at protecting our own systems with a similar device. We are also currently investigating ways of overcoming E-Bing through a modified version of TEMPEST which can counteract E-Bing distorting chaff. Trials to date, however, have been unsuccessful.

Note from Harry Pearce:

Malcolm's Magnum Opus made for some fascinating reading. However, I think the 179 pages are probably superfluous to convey a message which boils down to one sentence: "Please remember to use your call signs."

The executive summary can be retained in his file for future reference.

THE USE OF CALL SIGNS ON OPERATIONS

SYSTEMIC REPORT

TITLE: *Systemic Report*

FILED BY: *Malcolm Wynn-Jones*

DATE: *3 August 2003*

Executive Overview

Espionage demands secrecy to work effectively. Officers in the field are referred to by their aliases. Operations themselves are given untraceable codenames. Messages are encoded; communication lines are secure. If we lose this, we lose everything.

Recently, however, it has come to my attention that officers have grown slack over using their call signs on operations, namely the individual codewords – e.g. Foxtrot Romeo 7 – by which they confirm and conceal their identity.

Communications with mobile surveillance units are beginning to resemble conversations in a southern Indian call centre. Officers are giving their real names over insecure lines. Surveillance operators are chatting about what they're having for lunch. It's thoroughly unprofessional. And, what is more, it's dangerous.

I have compiled a report into this breach of protocol.

Psychologist's sessions
with Malcolm Wynn-Jones
following panic attack in Pegasus (royal protection) bunker

Case ID: M15/92
Date: 09/05/200

TRANSCRIPTS WITH APPROVED ANNOTATIONS FROM OBSERVING INDEPENDENT PSYCHOLOGIST	**MWJ** – Malcolm Wynn-Jones **DJ** – Diane Jewell, Head of Psychology, MI5 rehabilitation centre, Tring

MWJ (*laughing*) God, I never thought it would come to this.

DJ What do you mean by that?

MWJ I mean this: you, me, psychology, microphones. Tring. This is where they send the brave people. The agents who've been tortured in far-flung places. The officers who've suffered long-term stress fallout after years in the field. This is not a place for me.

DJ Where is your place, then, Malcolm?

MWJ Oh, you know. The back-office boy. The quiet egg-headed geek in the background, bugging hotel rooms, filling in the *Telegraph* crossword and sitting around in surveillance vans.

DJ laughs.

MWJ (*cont.*) I piece together discarded shreddings, I translate snippets of ancient Aramaic, I make obscure links between the wordings of terrorist demands and extracts of the *Iliad*. But this . . . this I don't do.

DJ But you chose to come here? Because of something you did.

MWJ Yes, but I'm beginning to regret it now.

DJ Tell me what happened, Malcolm.

MWJ I was in Pegasus – that's the royal protection bunker.

DJ I know what Pegasus is.

Case ID: M15/921
Date: 09/05/2006

MWJ Really? I thought only a handful of people were aware of its existence.

DJ I'm part of that handful. You'd be amazed how much I hear about down here.

MWJ Okay. I was in Pegasus and trying to defuse a bomb. Angela – our renegade ex-MI5 officer – had coated the wires herself and replaced the casings. It must have taken her months to do. The entire building was rigged up to explode.

DJ Why didn't you call the bomb squad?

MWJ No time. The counter was down to the last 50 seconds by the time we discovered it. We had to do something there and then.

DJ We?

MWJ Yes, Adam was there, too.

DJ Yes, I know Adam.

Case ID: M15/92
Date: 09/05/20C

MWJ Well, I'm not his greatest fan. He can be sloppy and slapdash, but I've got a new respect for him after what he did for me that day.

DJ Go on. Tell me.

MWJ It was impossible to know for certain which wire to cut. So I froze. I don't know why. I just went completely still and quiet. I could hear Adam's breath behind me – increasingly ragged. And then he just took the tool out of my hand and cut all the wires in one go. There were 2.16 seconds left on the clock.

DJ Wasn't that incredibly dangerous of him?

MWJ Yes, it was suicidally risky. But it worked. And, as he said, less dangerous than waiting for the counter to hit zero.

DJ Why do you think you froze?

MWJ I suppose it had been a pretty horrendous day. I'd known Angela for years. Respected her. Liked her as a friend. And then she went and almost blew us all up because of some mad Princess Diana conspiracy theory.

DJ So, it was stress-related then?

MWJ Yes, I suppose it was. I'm good behind the scenes. Very good, even. I don't panic when I have other people's lives in my hands. I give officers clear instructions in their headphones. I've even talked people through dismantling a bomb.

DJ But this time it was different?

MWJ Yes, I suppose it was. This time it was me. That was the difference. I get very close to operations. I'm in the surveillance van just outside. Or I'm giving technical support down a secure line. But I've never been this close before.

DJ I think we can forgive you for that, Malcolm.

MWJ But that wasn't the worst thing. The worst thing was the way in which Adam covered for me. He phoned in a field report. He told them that I'd defused the bomb. They gave me a hero's welcome when I walked back onto the Grid.

DJ Colleagues cover for one another all the time, Malcolm. That's what keeps you together in this job.

MWJ Maybe. I prefer to get things out in the open.

DJ Is that why you told Harry?

MWJ Yes. After I told Ruth first. He was very good about it, too.

DJ laughs.

Case ID: M15/921
Date: 09/05/2006

DJ   And so he should have been. That man has done far worse himself.

MWJ   Call me a silly old fool but there are certain inalienable truths I like to hold on to. I believe in accountability. I believe in taking responsibility for your own actions, for your own mistakes. Most of the time I'm happiest sitting quietly in the corner. But if the time comes to stand up and be counted, I'm not going to shirk it.

DJ   You're a good man, Malcolm Wynn-Jones.

MWJ   How can a coward be a good man?

© NASA http://visibleearth.nasa.gov/

DJ Bravery manifests itself in many different ways. It is not the absence of fear – some of the bravest people are also the most scared. Bravery is the courage to face up to things. There's moral bravery as well as physical bravery.

MWJ Bravery is a thing I dread, Diane.

DJ And that's why you do the job you do so well. You're not an adrenaline junkie looking for adventure. You're a highly-trained professional supporting your fellow officers.

MWJ You might think you're looking at a mature man in his fifth age of life, in fair round belly with good capon lin'd. You might think that, Diane. But at heart, I'm still that little boy who's scared of the monsters under his bed and sleeps with the light on.

There is a long silence.

DJ You've stood up and been counted, Malcolm. You can sit back down with your crosswords now. The others need you, you know. More than you'll ever realise.

MWJ Thank you.

****Transcript ends****

> Note
>
> I approve Malcolm Wynn-Jones's return to work.
>
> Diane Jewell.

MI5

ANNUAL MEDICAL REPORT

Name:	Malcolm Wynn-Jones
Date:	1st May 2006

Height:	6'0	Weight:	12st 6lb	BMI:	23.77

Units of alcohol per week:	8
Cigarettes per week:	None

Blood pressure:	160/100
Resting pulse:	80
Urine:	normal
Chest x-ray:	normal
Exercise ECG:	normal

Apart from his asthma, Malcolm is in good shape for a man of his age - especially for someone who is not required to work actively in the field. He drinks one glass of red wine at home every night - and two on Saturdays.

Dr Sally Chapman

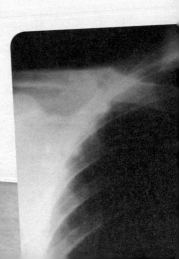

SECTION X

EYES ONLY FOR LEVEL 1 AND ABOVE

LOG FOR MALCOLM WYNN-JONES

Date: 10.06.2006
Subject: Mensa. Malcolm entered an online Mensa competition during work hours.
Outcome: See enclosed note from Harry Pearce.

Note from Harry Pearce: Malcolm is to be congratulated for winning the competition.

Date: 19.04.2005
Subject: Office canteen. Malcolm continues to take more than 90 per cent of his evening
           meals in the office canteen. This is a far higher proportion than any other officer.
Outcome: See enclosed note from Harry Pearce.

Note from Harry Pearce: Malcolm lives alone and is barely capable of making a cup of
coffee for himself. His kitchen, as far as I'm aware, is entirely devoid of sustenance. Our
canteen is there for a reason. Please don't pass any more notes of this sort my way.

Date: 05.11.1997
Subject: Office canteen. Malcolm used the office canteen for his evening meal on all 31
           nights of last month. This was referred to Harry Pearce.
Outcome: Harry confirmed that Malcolm has been working hard on an extra project and has
           not been able to return home to eat.

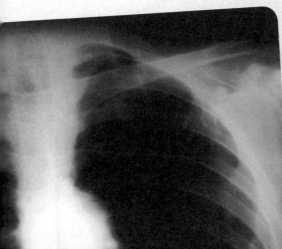

...rvices. We monitor private internet
...it is to reduce the risk of blackmail
...These notes are retained on file
...ct is concerned.

M E M O R A N D U M

To: ▮▮▮▮▮▮▮▮▮▮▮▮▮▮▮▮
From: ▮▮▮▮▮▮▮▮▮▮▮▮▮▮▮▮
Date: ▮▮▮▮▮▮▮▮▮▮▮
Subject: Spooks: The Personnel Files
Postscript

Terrorist organisations come and go. New threats materialise, mutate and vanish. Intelligence work used to focus on entire armies. Today, it is more likely to concern a small group of extremists in an anonymous urban flat.

There are many good people in this country: decent, honest citizens who wish to live long and peaceful lives. They work hard, contribute to their communities and provide for their families.

But where there is society, there will always be outcasts. And where there are people, there will always be evil.

At any given moment, there is a handful of extremists on these shores planning an atrocity. Someone, somewhere, intends that you will not be there to pick up your child from school; that you won't live long enough to celebrate your wedding anniversary; that another short life will be pointlessly cut even shorter.

As you have seen, MI5 officers are our unsung heroes. These are the people who make sure we sleep at night and wake up safely the next day.

For some, the service asked the ultimate question, and they did not shirk their responsibility. Danny Hunter and Fiona Carter gave their lives. Zoe Reynolds gave up her past. Tom Quinn almost sacrificed his sanity.

We mourn, but we must also move on. Atrocity leaves no time for grief.

MI5's Counter Terrorism Department, Section D, is in capable hands. Harry Pearce continues to lead an excellent team. New recruit Ros Myers joins Adam Carter, Zafar Younis, Ruth Evershed, Malcolm Wynn-Jones, Jo Portman and Colin Wells to honour their colleagues' memories.

It's a fine line between safety and terror, and they're working around the clock to patrol it.

MI5, not nine to five.